ANALYTICAL PHILOSOPHY OF
KNOWLEDGE

SOCRATES. Let us begin again and ask, in the first place, whether it is or is not possible for a person to know that he knows what he knows and that he does not know what he does not know, and in the second place whether, if perfectly possible, such knowledge is of any use.

CRITIAS. That is what we have to consider.

PLATO, *Charmides*, 167b. Trans. Benjamin Jowett

Thou canst not know what is not.

PARMENIDES, *Nature*. Trans. J. Burnet

ANALYTICAL PHILOSOPHY OF KNOWLEDGE

BY

ARTHUR C. DANTO

Professor of Philosophy
Columbia University

CAMBRIDGE
AT THE UNIVERSITY PRESS
1968

Published by the Syndics of the Cambridge University Press
Bentley House, 200 Euston Road, London, N.W.I
American Branch: 32 East 57th Street, New York, N.Y.10022

Library of Congress Catalogue Card Number: 68–30951
Standard Book Number: 521 07266 2

Printed in Great Britain
at the University Printing House, Cambridge
(Brooke Crutchley, University Printer)

FOR MY DAUGHTER
ELIZABETH

CONTENTS

PREFACE

It is difficult not to sound darkly portentous in proclaiming that men exist at once within and without the world, but in fact both relationships, as well as their simultaneous satisfaction, are altogether banal. I shall underscore this banality by suggesting an analogy. A *sentence* may be said to exist at once within and without the world. It is within the world as a physical event and a linguistic one, a fragment of the domains of such sciences as acoustics and linguistics. It is without the world only in the sense that it is the world which renders it true or false. As bits of the world, sentences stand in various relationships, typically causal, with other bits of the world, sentential and otherwise. As *truths*, sentences stand to the world in a relationship of a wholly different order. Men, as complex bits of the world, stand in various relationships, typically causal, with other of the world's bits, human and otherwise. They are *without* the world only in the respect that there exist between men and the world relations of a wholly different order, relations of a kind comparable to that which holds between a sentence and the world when the sentence is *true*. There is, in brief, between men and the world, as between language and the world, a space of an extra-worldly sort. It is not a natural space, not a space *within* the world, but a space between the world and what, for every other purpose, must be counted amongst the world's bits.

It is an argument of this book that men exist without the world when what they know is the world. And I should like to suppose that, other than the world, there is nothing to know with the sole exception of that class of relationships which, though their *terms* are bits of the world, are not intra-worldly relationships. But since this must still sound portentous and dark, a few more prefatory remarks may not be amiss.

As bits of the world, in predominantly causal relationships with other bits of the world (including one another), men are in every metaphysically crucial respect objects for scientific description. And I should suppose the world to be wholly open to science, its only dark spots being shadows cast by momentary ignorance. Science itself may be regarded as a conglomerate bit of the world, a causal force amongst causal forces, changing the face of nature. As a bit of the world, science itself is open to science. Whatever questions may be settled by examining the world are scientific questions, including those asked about science, when science is reckoned a bit of the world. The task of science is to answer all scientific questions, and so to provide a complete description of the world. Let us imagine a description which is complete in that whatever is to be said truly about the world is said in it. But in saying that all that is to be said about the world is said in this description, we are not saying something *further* about the world. For then our statement would have been false, there after all having been something about the world not said in the description we have imagined. No: we are rather saying something about a relationship which is satisfied by this description and by the world together. And this relationship, which connects a description with the world, traverses an extra-worldly space. And the latter is the locus of philosophical investigation. Philosophy is concerned with science, as it is concerned with language or with men, primarily as these are regarded as external to the world, and hence with the relations between these and the world. Science, language, and men are bits of the world. But not all relations between bits of the world are further bits of the world.

Let *s* be a sentence which is about the world. Any such sentence I shall call *descriptive*. If *s* is descriptive, and about the world, what shall we say of the sentence '*s* is true'? The latter, unlike *s*, is about *s*. But it is not wholly about *s*, the way, for example, '*s* is a sentence' is about *s*. Rather, it is about *s* and the world together. And it tells us something which *s* does not. It does not tell us anything about the *world* beyond what *s* alone tells us. It only tells us that what *s* says about the world is so. Sentences which are about the relations between the world and sentences, I shall speak of as *semantical*. Relations within the world find verbal expression in descriptive sentences. Relations between the world and descriptions of the world find verbal expression in *semantical* sentences. The distinction is absolute and irreducible, quite as the relation between language and the world is not reducible to just another intra-worldly relation. The world is an *external* world only in the respect that semantical relations are not intra-worldly. Bad philosophy is always generated by trying to flatten semantical relationships into further bits of the world, and allowing the distinctions we have been drawing to collapse.

One main way in which men exist without the world is as knowers of the world. To say that *m* knows that *s* is, to be sure, to say something about *m*. But it is not wholly about *m*, the way in which '*m* is a man' is about *m*. Rather, it is about *m* and the world together. The sentence *s* is a bit of knowledge which *m* has, and we may suppose it to be descriptive of the world. But just as *s* and the world are external to one another when we speak of *s* as true, the world and *m* are external to one another when we say that *m* knows that *s*. Here the world is external only in the respect that knowledge is not an intra-worldly relation. This has been deeply misunderstood in the history of philosophy, and the response to the externality of the world, when not skeptical anguish, has typically consisted in attempting to make knowledge of the world *part* of the world, to collapse the distinction between intra-worldly relations and the sort of relation which is knowledge. This is the program of Naturalism.

Naturalists believe the world to be everywhere open to science, and that whatever is, is in the world. For Naturalists, the classical problems of epistemology were corruptions: the task of philosophy, as they saw it, is not to determine whether we have or *can* have knowledge, but to describe the knowledge we plainly have, i.e., in science. Knowledge is attained through the methods of science, and philosophers concerned with knowledge should be concerned with these methods. There is a certain robustness in these attitudes, and even the shadow of an argument, as when, by striding across a field, a man purports to show that since space *is* crossed, it *can* be crossed, Zeno be damned. So the problem is not to determine whether motion is possible, but to describe the mechanics of spatial translation. One admires the hearty common sense of such attitudes (and much of contemporary philosophy is but a flourish of common sense), and certainly it permits the philosopher to engage in fascinating and almost empirical investigations of how science achieves truths. Yet there remains the grinning skeleton of unmet arguments in the closet of one's background assumptions, and so a haunting sense that something deeply disturbing has merely been repressed. We will not surrender the world, however compelling the argument which tells us that we must. Yet why do such arguments continually arise?

I believe the Naturalistic intuition regarding knowledge is sound, and that the classical problems of epistemology *are* corruptions. In the latter part of this book I endeavor to establish this. Yet the intuition is only negatively sound. For the space which the classical theorists of knowledge despaired of traversing—the space between themselves and the external world—is a space the Naturalists have no way to account for, and indeed they have forgotten its existence. It is a traversable space. Across it, on the other side, lies the world. But for just that reason, it is not a space *in* the world. The problems which arise in its domain have been treated with characteristic brusqueness by Naturalists, as though they were problems concerning only the world. So Naturalists tend to give irrelevant, i.e., scientific answers to questions which are philosophical: *irreducibly* and *autonomously* philosophical. And I should like to suggest another failing. In collapsing the relation between language and the world into some sort of intra-worldly relation, and hence in collapsing the ultimate differences between philosophical and scientific questions, Naturalists arrived at a picture of what men are which was all right so far as it went, but which lacked a crucial dimension. For men, in so far as they are distinctively men, do not exist only within the world. Never ceasing for a moment to be (complex) bits of the world, they also exist without the world, entering it, so to speak, from across an extra-worldly space. If this still sounds portentous and dark, there is no remedy save to work through the volume to which this means, after all, only to be the preface.

Darkness in a preface may not inspire confidence in the translucidity of the book to follow, so I ought perhaps to say that the voice of the preface is not the sole voice of the book. It is a voice I permit myself to speak with only at certain critical points, to alert the philosophical reader to the deeper issues which foreground logical fiddling may lead us to forget. I am too aware of the inartistries of the book, and of the unredeemed aridity of too many protracted stretches, to be able to pretend that I have composed a work of sustained polyphony. But I feel the central theses of this book to be of sufficient urgency for the advance of philosophical thinking on a variety of matters, that I am willing to violate conscience by permitting to appear a work which I know could be better shaped. I need draw little attention here to flaws which will be conspicuous to the reader, but I have at least made no cosmetic attempt to use this preface's gnomic voice to conceal them. *That* voice has been used deliberately, and solely for the rhetorical purposes I mention here.

An article compounded of fragments from chapters 1, 4, and 6 appeared as 'On Knowing that We Know', in Avrum Stroll (ed.), *Epistemology: New Essays in the Theory of Knowledge* (New York; Harper and Row, 1967). The material on sentential states in chapter 5 was originally presented in a paper read at the State University of New York at Brockport, as part of the International Philosophical Year, in the symposium on the philosophy of belief. A modified version will appear in the proceedings of those meetings. Chapter 10 and portions of chapter 11 grew out of my 'Reflections on Randall's Theory of Language', in John P. Anton (ed.), *Naturalism and Historical Understanding* (Albany; State University of New York Press, 1967)—a *Festschrift* devoted to my esteemed colleague and teacher, John Herman Randall, Jr. The brief polemic against Austin repeats some points made in 'Seven Objections against Austin's Analysis of "I Know"', which appeared originally in the journal, *Philosophical Studies*. All of this material is two-thirds *aufgehoben*—preserved and transcended, but not negated—in the present writing, but I am grateful to the editors of these respective works for permission to quarry my earlier papers. Application of certain of the theories developed here to the more traditional contests in the theory of knowledge may be found in my book *What Philosophy Is* (New York; Harper and Row, 1968), especially chapter III.

I am grateful to the Columbia Council for Research in the Humanities for summer grants, enabling me to work at the writing of this book, and to Robert W. Adamson, Patricia Skinner and David Winsor, of Cambridge University Press, for unstinted help and encouragement at various points in the preparation of the manuscript. Bernard Rollin was singularly generous in helping me with the proofs and in suggesting improvements. My friend and colleague, Leigh Cauman, read portions of an earlier draft, and her stubborn resistance to browbeating saved me from a ghastly philosophical error. My deepest debt is to those from whom I have learned most, the sharp tribe of philosophical writers and critics, that company of contenders and clarifiers, speculators and logical iconoclasts, upon whose mercies the present work must now be cast, and for whose benefit it was hopefully conceived.

A.C.D.

New York 1967

1

KNOWLEDGE CLAIMS

I shall begin by pretending that the theory of knowledge is best appreciated as the philosophical explanation of claims to knowledge; of the things we may justifiably claim to know; and of the manner in which these claims may be justified. Ultimately I shall cast this pretence away. But it offers a good orientation in the conceptual maze we are to run, and it has some initial advantages which are considerably in its favor.

First of all, the verb 'knows' in such sentences as 'm knows such and such', is unclear at least to the extent that we are not immediately prepared to explain what the verb refers to. It is not like saying, for example, that m *eats* such and such, where we can easily show what we mean. I am not suggesting that we have difficulties either in using or in understanding such sentences, nor even in determining whether they are true or false, but only that we should have to think hard to say what corresponds to the verb 'to know'. There is no comparable difficulty with *claiming* to know, for *claiming* is plainly an action of some sort. But no one would want, without further argument, to declare or to deny that *knowing* is an action.

Again, although it certainly is permitted to say that m's knowing such and such is justified—or that m is justified in knowing such and such— our meaning in saying this would be quite different, and far less philo-sophically crucial, from our meaning were we to say that m's claiming to know such and such was justified—or that m was justified in claiming to know such and such. The best we might make of the first sort of state-ment is that m is entitled to the piece of knowledge he is said to have, e.g., because his military position requires it; or that it would be wrong if m did not know, e.g., of his son's illness. But for the latter sort no special context has to be eked out, for no *special* facts about m are relevant. Rather, the considerations are perfectly general and would have application to anyone who made such a claim. It is at any rate more natural to think of actions as justified or not, than to think so of anything else; and 'to know' is not, as I have said, spontaneously taken as a verb of action. If it were so taken, we should still have to admit that we could produce no easy criterion for identifying a cognitive act. But no comparable difficulty goes with identifications of knowledge *claims*. This is so in part because the very words 'I know' are used for making knowledge claims with. There are, of course, other forms of words with which to do this; there are tones with which other words are used; there are gestures which amount to much the same thing. Our problem is not so much to work these out as to indicate that we could do so if we wished, and even if there were some difficulty in exhaustively specifying every way in which we urge knowledge claims, the fact remains that we would be in a position to certify any proposed list, since it is our practice, after all, which would be described.

A further advantage perhaps is this. If we think of the actual use of the words 'I know' as paradigmatic for urging knowledge claims, then we will in some measure be able to conduct our inquiries upon a linguistic plane. We will be able to frame some of our problems in terms of the rules that govern the use of the words 'I know', that determine, e.g., with what other words these naturally go, or with what other words they must contrast. Thus, 'I know' is grammatically a complete sentence, but it is so much in the manner of a unit-sentence, e.g., 'Red'. In actual use a context must be presupposed. There must be something with respect to which a knowledge claim is being urged, even though this is not brought to the surface of language in the context, since presumably understood by the present or intended communicant. Certainly we do not use 'I know' to ascribe an unmodified condition to ourselves; when we say 'I know' we must be able to follow it up with mention of *what* we know, or claim to know, in case this is not already clear. There is no absolute state which merely is a state of knowing, without reference to anything known or claimed to be known. It is not like saying 'I hurt', which not only is grammatically complete but expresses a 'complete thought'. As the school-book phrase runs, 'I know' requires completion with a phrase, a word or a clause telling *what*. So 'I know', grammar notwithstanding, must be regarded as a fragment. The object of the verb—or more profoundly, the object of knowledge—must be put into language in order to complement the verb and produce a sentence which stands on its own. But the more we can bring to the surface of language, the better off we are.

I do not believe we can bring everything to the surface of language. This is not because the world is immeasurably richer than the capacity of our language to describe it with, for we can at our convenience enrich our language to any required capacity. What cannot be put in language is not part of the world. But that which centrally concerns us as philosophers belongs neither to the world nor to the descriptive part of language, but rather to the space between language and the world. A source of almost every philosophical confusion is that we in fact have words that apply to this interspace, provoking philosophers at the same time to treat them descriptively and to peer into the world for that which they describe, and even to pretend to find it. We dissolve such confusions by showing that these words belong to a different dimension. But just for this reason it is a philosophical obligation to bring to the surface of language as much as is logically possible. Whatever is rejected by the surface of language will be a philosophical discovery.

II

These advantages accrue, it might be objected, only providing we confine our attention primarily to the first person singular of the present indicative of the verb 'to know'. 'I know' may indeed be claimative. But what of saying that *m* knows such and such, where *m* is some other person? '*m* knows such and such' ascribes knowledge to *m* rather than claims knowledge on behalf of the speaker.

I do not think we can avoid concern with knowledge claims, however, even if we finally accept this objection. To begin with, '*m* knows such and such' is an assertion. And the assertive mode, except where otherwise specially qualified, is already the *form* of words with which knowledge claims are made, whether or not these are exactly prefaced with the operative fragment 'I know'. We have subjunctive moods for use when we do not wish to claim knowledge, or to commit ourselves to the consequences of such claims. We have conditional idioms,

3

and disavowing fragments like 'I believe', or concessive adverbs like 'perhaps' or 'possibly'. Indeed the very stiltedness of the phrase 'I know' indicates that it is rarely used explicitly, that is is overemphatic or pontifical, and apt to be employed in response to challenge rather than as something one says unprovoked and as a matter of course. We might think of it as something that accompanies all declarative utterance roughly in the way in which, according to Kant, the *cogito* accompanies all our judgments.[1] And just as *cogito* is not a judgment in its own right, so perhaps 'I know' is not an assertion in *its* own right. It converts whatever it accompanies into an assertion without making any further assertion of its own. This would bear out the grammatical observation that 'I know' is properly construed as an incomplete expression. Well, '*m* knows such and such' is an assertion *I* make, hence urges a claim to knowledge just in virtue of being an assertion, whatever its content. I could not sensibly say '*m* knows such and such and I *don't* know that *m* knows such and such'. So the *claim* to know whatever I assert is entailed by the fact that I assert it, in that the negation of that claim is ruled out by exactly the same fact. Thus we are returned to knowledge claims.

But this is only a delaying tactic, an objector would say. Granted that when I assert anything at all, I am urging a knowledge claim. Yet, when the *content* of the assertion is that *m* knows such and such, I am ascribing *something* to *m*. And surely the meaning of '*m* knows such and such' is radically different from '*m* claims to know such and such'. For the first can be false though the second is true, and the second can be false though the first is true. So they are distinct and independent things. And ought we not to be dealing with *knowledge*? Even if there

---

[1] Immanuel Kant, *Critique of Pure Reason*, B132; B405–6; A347–8. Kant's point is that the 'I think' gives form to judgments, e.g., making judgments *mine*, without contributing to their content. In this regard, his is very like a point attributed to Gottlob Frege: 'A thought may have just the same content whether you assent to its truth or not; a proposition may occur in discourse now asserted, now unasserted, and yet be recognizably the same.' Peter Geach, 'Assertion', *Philosophical Review*, LXXIV, no. 4 (1965), 449. Like the 'I think', the act of assertion does not enter into the content of what it operates upon. Geach insists, in fact, that there is 'no expression of ordinary language...carrying with it assertoric force'. *Ibid.*, p. 457. Hence the 'I know' would not be a pragmatic equivalent for Frege's specially invented '⊢' since there are non-assertoric uses of 'I know' while no use for '⊢' exists save what it was specially invented to discharge.

is no absolute condition of *m* which is described by '*m* knows', even if in the third person this fragment has to be completed, it does not follow that it is not a description of *something*. Even if neither the implicit 'I know' nor the implicit 'Cogito' express independent assertions or judgments, still, 'I know that *s*' or '*Cogito j*' might describe some fact in excess of what is described by *s* or by *j* alone. There must be *something* about *m* which makes the difference between the truth and falsity of '*m* knows such and such'. Where then do our advantages take us? They lead us off into interesting socio-linguistic irrelevancies. If a man might know without urging a knowledge claim, so might we know without urging one. What then am I saying about *m* or about myself when I say that *m* knows, or that *I* know such and such?

These are main questions, of course, but I do not wish just yet to forgo the benefits of our linguistic approach: and at any rate the issue has been joined in just those terms. For the legitimacy of the objection presupposes an affirmative answer to the question whether 'I know such and such' *is descriptive*, i.e., says something true or false and, hence, admits of truth-values in a clear, straightforward way. These days we have become circumspect in bestowing descriptive status to a sentence, and should it turn out that 'I know' is *not* descriptive, that it requires no truth-conditions in excess of those required for whatever it is one is claiming with these words to know, then the quest for these truth-conditions will be merely vain.[1] And in that event no sense could be given to the demand that we say what knowing *is*. But then, if it is not descriptive in the first person, neither need it be in the third person either. To say that *m* knows such and such might mean only that *m* would be justified in saying 'I know such and such'. And the analysis

---

[1] The important suggestion that 'I know' is not descriptive is of course due to J. L. Austin, and entered philosophical literature first in his paper 'Other Minds' which appeared in a 1946 Aristotelian Society symposium, reprinted in his *Philosophical Papers* (Oxford; Clarendon Press, 1961). That seemingly descriptive expressions are not so in fact has, naturally, a longer history. That this is the case with 'I promise'—on the analogy between which and 'I know' Austin made a great deal—was perhaps first pointed out by David Hume. See *A Treatise of Human Nature*, Book III, Part II, section 5. The most influential contemporary example is the Non-Cognitivist accounts of '*x* is good' which allegedly says nothing about *x* but only conveys an attitude on the part of him who says it. But descriptive accounts of seemingly descriptive terms abound in recent literature, e.g., in Toulmin's analysis of 'is probable' and Strawson's analysis of 'is true'.

of knowledge would dissolve into the analysis of the justification of knowledge claims. That one could know without urging a knowledge claim would be but another case of a man being entitled to perform an action he happens not to perform. At least in our own case it is far more evident that 'I know' is used to advance a knowledge claim than that it is used to describe any feature of ourselves. Think again of the rarity with which this expression comes up at all. It *may* be descriptive in addition. Then there will be a question of what is described. But let us not take for granted in the objection what must first be established, namely that these words are descriptive. Since that issue must be determined by our objector no less than ourselves, it clearly is prior to any investigation he enjoins upon us, and it might circumvent the need to undertake it. Let me clarify this in a slight digression.

Of a sentence *s*, or a term *t*, which happens to exercise the analytical energies of philosophy, the first question to be asked is whether it is descriptive; whether, if a sentence, it admits of truth-values or, if a term, of what we might call instantiation-values. When a sentence or term is not descriptive, its meaning is merely its use; and occasionally an advance is made in philosophy when it is successfully demonstrated that a sentence, heretofore thought to have truth-conditions, or a term, heretofore believed to have instantiation-conditions, is not, after all, descriptive, and the entire enterprise of looking for that in the world which it might describe has accordingly been a waste.

If an affirmative answer to the question of descriptivity is attained, then there are three main possibilities to consider in case the sentence should be true or the term instantiated. Either what is described is simple or it is composite; and, if composite, either it collapses into its components wholly and without remainder, or it resists such resolution, and only stands in a certain relationship to components that do not exhaust its essence. Let *t* be instantiated by *a*, so that *t* is a descriptive term. Then either (1) *a* is simple, in which case *t* is undefinable and *a* is primitive; (2) *a* is constituted wholly of some set of elements, in which case *t* is explicitly definable and eliminable, while *a* is non-primitive or secondary; or (3) *a* is not simple but is not wholly resoluble into any set of components, in which case *t* is reducible but non-eliminable and *a* is semi-primitive—a function of the components into which it is partially to be resolved. The constructive achievement of determining which of these alternatives is correct will be to help us to specify, linguistically, the least number of indefinable terms and, ontologically, the least number of primitive elements we are required to countenance in a philosophical reconstruction of the world as we are obliged to conceive of it.

A philosophically satisfactory choice amongst these alternatives is not always easily made, as may be seen perhaps most conspicuously, in meta-ethical investigation, where not even the question of descriptivity has been settled. There are, accordingly, partisans of all positions, with no immediate prospect of determining which are misguided. Thus there are (1) the Non-Cognitivist school, united only in refusing to accord descriptive status to ethical terms, but frequently divided on whether these terms are used to express attitudes and feelings, to persuade, or to commend; (2) the Intuitionist school, for which at least some ethical terms are indefinable but descriptive, either of entities (Plato) or of properties (Moore); (3) the Naturalistic school, for whom ethics is in principle a science and for whom ethical terms are definable totally by means of non-ethical ones, so that their designata, whether entities or properties, are wholly constituted out of more elementary components, not themselves ethical in character; and, finally, (4) the semi-Naturalistic, or semi-Intuitionist school, according to which certain natural properties (or entities) are 'good-making' (for example), enabling us to say when an ethical term applies without permitting us to define that ethical term explicitly and without remainder by their means. And, of course, a descriptivist of either of the three persuasions can allow that ethical terms, in addition to whatever descriptive status they may have, *may* be used to commend, or persuade, or express a feeling, or whatever.

There is much the same array of positions to be found in the theory of knowledge, which is a meta-cognitive investigation. Since the work of J. L. Austin, there have been those for whom 'I know' is not descriptive, for whom it does not admit of truth-values and its meaning is its use. When I use it, I perform an action, *viz.*, giving my word, but I do not report any fact. This we might somewhat archly describe as a Non-Cognitivist theory of knowledge. It was, I think, intended by

7

Austin that it unseat its descriptivist alternatives, of which, naturally, there are three. (1) Cognitive Intuitionism, as we might characterize it, is the theory that knowledge is a simple, primitive condition of an individual who knows something in virtue of enjoying this condition. Such a view would have been held by Prichard. (2) Cognitive Naturalism is a theory according to which 'knows' is explicitly definable or exhaustively analyzable, e.g., as justified true belief. Defenders of this position might agree with Austin that 'knows' is not descriptive of a simple condition, but hold nevertheless that it is descriptive but of a non-primitive condition. They are divided only on the correct definition or analysis of 'knows'. (3) Critical Cognitivism is the view that knowledge is semi-primitive, reducible but not explicitly definable. I am not certain that any philosopher is committed to such a view of knowledge, but it would perhaps amount to a theory that certain factors are signs of cognitive grace, as it were, making it reasonable to suppose we have knowledge without knowledge itself being analyzable into these marks. But this would be tantamount to Intuitionism at least to the extent that it is not definable *what* it is that these are marks *of*. But none of this need be faced if 'I know' is not descriptive.

III

Suppose 'I know' were descriptive, as the objector insists. Why should there be a problem at all in saying what it describes? He might say that he knows, for example, that water freezes at 32 degrees Fahrenheit. He can identify water easily, can identify its frozen state, and has mastered simple thermometry. Why should there be any further special problem in identifying *knowledge*? Why indeed should we require an investigation: let *him* say what knowledge is: *he* uses a word which has balked philosophical clarification for millennia! Perhaps it is a word that does not belong to the descriptive surface of language? So those philosophers were looking in the wrong place for clarification? It could be a *deep* solution to ascertain that our difficulties lie not in trying to describe something singularly elusive, but in treating as descriptive a word that has merely a use.

Consider a consequence of classing 'I know such and such' as descriptive, i.e., that it says something true or false in excess of whatever is said by 'such and such'. Recall that the bare assertion of a sentence, in virtue just of being an assertion, is a knowledge claim. Suppose then that *m* asserts the sentence *s*, thereby advancing a knowledge claim. If 'I know that *s*' is, in its turn, descriptive, describing something over and above what *s* alone describes, then to assert *it* is to make a larger claim than merely to assert *s*. When a man merely asserts something, that is one knowledge claim. When he makes it explicit that it *is* a knowledge claim, when he uses the words 'I know', then if 'I know' describes a *further* fact, he makes *another* knowledge claim, distinct from the first. Why not make this one explicit by using the words 'I know' again? Then they will describe yet another thing, and this will be a *third* knowledge claim which, if made explicit, constitutes a fourth, and on and on. Might it not be more plausible that 'I know that *s*' does not make a knowledge claim over and above what is made with *s* alone, but merely draws attention to the fact that it *is* a knowledge claim? So that the whole force of 'I know' is contained in making a knowledge claim forcefully, rather than describing any fact in excess of what is described with *s*?

If, moreover, 'I know that *s*' is a *double* knowledge claim—a claim with respect to *s* *and* a claim with respect to *knowing* that *s*—then to claim to know that *s* is also to claim to know that one knows that *s*; and our program requires us to explain under what conditions the latter is justified. It would be an awkward consequence if it could not be justified. If I am not justified in my claim to know that I know that *s*, I can hardly be justified in just claiming to know *s*. But if the bare assertion that I know commits me to the further claim that I *know* that I know, how can any knowledge claim be justified? For an infinite regression appears. If, on the other hand, 'I know that I know that *s*' does not describe any fact other than what is described with 'I know *s*', and does not arise as a fresh assertion, why should 'I know *s*' describe any fact other than what is described with just *s*? If it does describe a further fact, then parity suggests that there must be an infinity of further facts of knowing that one knows that one knows. If there is no end, no knowledge claim can be justified, but if there *is* an end, why should it not just have come at the beginning with the first occurrence of 'I know' which it was a mistake to regard as descriptive? To justify the claim 'I know *s*' might merely amount to justifying the assertion of *s*. So no further question of justifying the *claim* to know that one knows would arise.

This would be an important result. If 'I know that *s*' is not descriptive, no further thing is asserted by 'I know that *s*' than is asserted by *s* alone. The fragment 'I know' would not be part of the content, then, of what is asserted, but would merely emphasize the fact that what it is attached to is being asserted. Then there is no separate question of the justification of 'I know that *s*' beyond what is required for justifying the assertion of *s*. Then 'I know that I know that *s*' is easily taken care of. It cannot emphasize the fact that an assertion is being made, because 'I know that *s*' does not make a separate assertion over and above what is made with *s* alone. So 'I know that I know that *s*' reduces to 'I know that *s*' which reduces to *s*. And the awkward consequence alluded to in the preceding paragraph need never be faced. There *is* no separate problem of justifying 'I know that I know that *s*'. A moment ago, then, we faced a dilemma generated by the supposition that 'I know that *s*' is descriptive in its own behalf, conveying information, and taking truth-conditions in excess of those pertaining to *s* alone. But if 'I know' has only the force of asserting what it is attached to, its meaning is its *use*, and the descriptive theory of 'I know' was but an attempt to assimilate the *use* of a description to a further part of what is described. But of course 'I know that I know' would not be the use of a use. It would only perhaps bring further emphasis. To use the idiom of Frege, the extra '⊢' in '⊢⊢' is but a shadow of the other, bringing no extra substance of its own.

These tensions, which result from forcing 'I know' up to the descriptive surface of language, dissolve when we relinquish the attempt. So far, then, the descriptivist assumptions of our objector are more than merely controversial. Until more carefully formulated, they merely lead to dark troubles.

IV

Whether descriptive or not, it must be common ground that the words
'I know' are used to make knowledge claims. But unless they *are* descriptive, 'I know that I know' reduces to just 'I know', and an old
philosophical speculation whether, when we know we must know that
we do so, is not so much answered as foreclosed. The reduction can
be argued just at the level of knowledge claims, taken as performances.
Were a man to utter the sentence 'I know that *s*' we would all recognize
something as having gone weirdly wrong were he to add 'But I don't
know that I know that *s*'. The entire conjunction is *somehow* inconsistent, though not formally so. Well, in whatever way 'I know that
s but I don't know that I know that *s*' is inconsistent, 'I know that *s*
and I know that I know that *s*' is redundant. To determine the nature
of the redundancy, we need but explain the nature of the corresponding
inconsistency.

There is a considerable temptation to explain it in terms of certain
alleged facts pertaining to knowledge as such. There are, for example,
views in philosophy that to know is to be in a cognitive condition
such that, just by being in that condition it is transparently clear to
him who is in it that he is so: he cannot know without, in virtue of
this transparency, knowing that he does so. Hence it is inconsistent,
through the nature of knowledge itself, that one should know and not
know that one knows that *s*.

This could be a correct thesis concerning knowledge itself, but it
cannot explain the weirdness of the conjunction. For that weirdness
would come through to any ear tuned to correct English. But since
few who possess such ears have so much as heard of the Transparency
theory of cognitive states, and since fewer still believe it true, the weirdness cannot be accounted for in terms of the theory. It is at least as
important that no support may be derived from the noted weirdness
for the Transparency theory. I believe we can explain it at the level
of language as such.

Consider the scheme (1) '*p*, but I don't know that *p*'. Let *p* be the
sentence 'I know that *s*'. Upon substitution in (1) we derive (2) 'I
know that *s* but I don't know that I know that *s*'. Now (2) makes

reference to its speaker twice over, and it is doubtless this double reference to the speaker of the sentence (2) which might appear to lend some support to the Transparency theory. But we get something quite as weird no matter what sentence we put in place of *p* in the schema (1). Thus let *p* now be the sentence 'The Prussians are coming'. This yields (3) 'The Prussians are coming but I don't know that the Prussians are coming.' It is simple enough to see what is wrong with (3), and indeed with any sentence obtained by uniformly substituting in (1). The pronoun 'I' which is embedded in the schema works retro-actively upon the first substituend to make it an assertion on the part of him who utters the entire conjunction. Hence it is a claim to know. But then the fragment '...but I don't know that...' constitutes a dis-claimer, a refusal, as it were, to assert the second occurrence of the substituend. So (3)—and any sentence sharing parity of form with (3)—is at once an assertion and a withdrawal of assertion of the same sen-tence, the two pieces of behavior then neutralizing one another. It is like crossing one's fingers while promising. And since this leaves things exactly as they were—like administering simultaneously a poison and its antidote—it is in effect a self-defeating performance. It is the *per-formance* itself that is incoherent, and the Transparency theory of cognitive conditions is merely irrelevant to its explanation.

Consider now (4) '*p* and I know that *p*'. Once more, the embedded pronoun constitutes the sentence we put in place of the first occurrence of *p* an assertion. But 'I know that *p*' has exactly the force of asserting the sentence it prefixes. So (5) '*s* and I know that *s*' asserts *s* twice over. So it is a redundant performance, like crossing one's heart and saying 'I promise'. If you assert a sentence, then it is gratuitous to say 'I know'. Well, suppose a person *says* that he knows that *s*. Then it is gratuitous to say that he knows that he knows that *s*.

v

If the matter ended here, anti-descriptivism would have a triumph, and the theory of knowledge would peter out into socio-linguistic de-scriptions of the uses of 'I know'. But we have gone, perhaps, as far along these lines as we can.

Let us shift the explicit pronoun which occurs in schema (1) to the third person, making any grammatical changes now required to give us (1') '*p* but *m* does not know that *p*'. Making whichever substitution one wishes, this yields no inconsistent performance on the part of him who asserts it (since he is distinct from *m*), and it does not seem in general to involve any incoherencies. Or if it does so, (1') yields inconsistencies only on the untypical presupposition of omniscience on *m*'s part. We have plain uses for sentences built on the armature of (1'). And we have comparably plain uses for others built on the armature of (4') '*p* and *m* knows that *p*'. But these latter are curious enough to merit a closer look.

When I say '*s* and *m* knows that *s*' the force is different from what it would have been had I said '*m* knows that *s*, and *s*'. The first seems to add information not contained in nor entailed by *s* alone, but the second seems to give no information not already contained in or entailed by '*m* knows that *s*'. The reason is that *s* follows from '*m* knows that *s*' though the latter hardly follows from the former. And it follows in such a way that '*m* does not know that *s*' follows from not-*s*. Or, putting this semantically, the truth of *s* is entailed by the truth of '*m* knows that *s*' and the falsity of the latter is entailed by the falsity of *s*. But of course, these results follow only in case '*m* knows that *s*' is regarded as descriptive, even if, in addition, it is a knowledge claim on the part of whomever asserts it. Now I cannot, save in heavy irony, assert '*m* knows that *s* but *s* is false'. But here is no inconsistent *performance* of the sort we have been characterizing: I am rather making an inconsistent *statement*, a statement inconsistent through what we take to be a logical feature of the concept of knowledge. But of course there is no comparable inconsistency in asserting '*m* claims to know that *s* but *s* is false'. So we cannot establish an equivalence between '*m* knows that *s*' and '*m* claims to know that *s*'. *Perhaps* we could establish an equivalence between '*m* knows that *s*' and '*m* would be *justified* were *m* to claim to know that *s*'. But should we be able to say this of *m*, why not then use a similar locution to describe a similar fact regarding myself? If every time I in fact use the expression 'I know', I make a knowledge claim and not a description of a state or condition of knowing, it would not follow that I could not, by means of some other, less energized expression, describe in my own case the sort of fact which, in *m*'s case, I describe with '*m* knows . . .'. Thus I could easily follow my own paraphrastic recommendation and describe the fact that I knew something by saying 'I would be justified were I to make a claim to know'. So if '*m* knows' is descriptive, in admitting of truth-values, then 'I know' could be descriptive as well, once we have taken note of its performative dimensions: I could be at *once* making a knowledge claim and describing myself as justified in making it, the sentence bearing a not unmanageable overload of communication. And surely, to play the game we have been playing, I could not coherently say 'I know that *s* but I am not justified in claiming to know that *s*'. So the Descriptivist is able, like an oriental fighter, to use the thrust of our argument as an energy for an Anti-Descriptivist defeat.

That *s* should be entailed by but not entail '*m* knows that *s*' seems the common sense of the matter, and, as such, is found in Aristotle in whom common sense is enshrined: 'While we are men', wrote Cardinal Newman, 'we cannot help, to a great extent, being Aristotelians, for [he] does but analyse the thoughts, feelings, views, and opinions of human kind.'[1] Aristotle, in discussing relations, characterized knowledge and whatever it is knowledge of, as non-simultaneous correlatives, in contrast with simultaneous correlatives such as 'the double and the half'. Thus, *a* can be the double of *b* when, and only when, *b* is the half of *a*. But

While the object of knowledge, if it ceases to exist, cancels at the same time the knowledge which was its correlative, the converse of this is not true. It is true that if the object of knowledge does not exist, there can be no knowledge: for there will be no longer anything to know. Yet it is equally true that, if the knowledge of a certain object does not exist, the object may nevertheless quite well exist.[2]

Aristotle went on to say 'It is likewise the case with regard to perception', never envisioning the ingenious possibility that *esse est percipi*.

[1] John Henry, Cardinal Newman, *The Idea of a University* (London; Longmans Green, 1927), p. 109.
[2] Aristotle, *Categories*, 7b, 25–30; and *Metaphysics*, Book Delta, section 15. See Julius Weinberg, *Abstraction, Relation, and Induction* (Madison, Wisconsin; University of Wisconsin Press, 1965), part II.

But if there is the analogy between knowledge and perception which he himself insisted upon, there would be room for an analogous theory that to be the case is to be known, where knowledge and its objects are simultaneous correlatives. This would, I think, not be an exciting theory. Worked out on Berkeleian lines, it would in the end just require an omniscient God, and leave room for something to be an object of knowledge and *m* (who is not God) not know it. And worked out along lines analogous to phenomenalistic reconstructions of Berkeley, it would yield the merely optimistic credo that everything is knowable, which again leaves room for something to be the case without *m* or anyone *knowing* it to be so. So in the end we would retain the non-simultaneous correlativity which is presupposed by our allowing coherent substitutions for (1′).

But now let *p* be '*m* knows that *s*' and substitute this into (1′) to yield (2′) '*m* knows that *s* but *m* does not know that *s*'. I see no tension arising here of the sort we detected in (2). We could get (2′) to sound *false*, perhaps, but not weird. It might sound false, for example, were we to bring in the Transparency theory. That theory was brought in, gratuitously as we saw, to dissolve a tension that could readily be explained without recourse to it. It hardly seems responsible to invoke the theory now to *cause* a tension we would not feel without it. If it is plausible to suppose that knowledge and its object are non-simultaneous correlatives, why should not knowledge and knowledge of knowledge in turn be non-simultaneous correlatives? Perhaps they could not be. But since we cannot rule out their being so at the level of linguistic performance alone, we shall have to provide a theory if we believe them simultaneous correlatives. But even if we did so, we should be drawing—or at least we should leave room for drawing—a distinction between knowing that *s* and knowing that one knows that *s*. We don't suppose, after all, that the double of *a* collapses into the half of *a* simply because they are simultaneous correlatives!

If *m* could know something and not know that he knows it, conceivably that could be my state as well. I cannot exactly say of myself that I know that *s* but do not know that I know it. But this is because of the dissonances set up between the claimative and the descriptive functions of 'I know'. Yet if I can say of someone else what he cannot

say of himself, why should he not be able to say of me what I am prohibited by a feature of language from saying about myself? There are
other such cases. I shall never be in a position to say truly 'I am dead'.
Yet no one would base an argument for immortality on such a fact,
any more than one would complain of insomnia on the grounds that
one is logically incapable of saying truly one is asleep. But we are, in
fact, no longer entitled to appeal merely to the inconsistent performances of (2) and (3) to decide an issue which turns on a descriptive
use. We have allowed that it would be *sensible* to say '*m* knows that *s*
but *m* does not know that he knows that *s*'. But is it ever true? The
status of a sentence as descriptive does not exempt it from being *false*.
And if it is *false* in *m*'s case, it must be through whatever fact makes it
so that it is false in my own.

VI

It is a simple matter for anyone having the slightest acquaintance with
the history of philosophy to find a basis for supposing that a man might
know something and yet feel absolutely reticent to urge a knowledge
claim because he feels he is not entitled to advance one. And so we
would truly say of him that he knows that *s* while he would deny that
he knows it: he would say—falsely, if we are right in our ascription—
that he does not know that *s*. And might we not then say he knows that
s but plainly does not know that he knows it? The sort of case familiar
to philosophers will be that in which the man does not know, or has
an incorrect understanding of *what knowledge is*. He might hold, for
example, to a theory that requires *s* to meet impossible or irrelevant
standards before he would feel justified in claiming to know it. He
might hold, for instance, that unless the denial of *s* is self-contradictory,
or unless *s* contains in some fashion its own truth-conditions as satisfied,
then we are never justified in claiming to know that *s* at all. He might
none the less know that *s*, and to show him that he does, we need not
furnish him with any primary information he might lack, for he has
all the information required, but only point out the manner in which
his standards are inappropriate. Think of how many conflicting theories
of knowledge there are! They cannot all be right. So there have to
be disagreements about what knowledge is. So if *any* of them *is* right,

16

the upholders of the others would be wrong either in claiming or in refusing to claim themselves as knowing certain things.

Philosophy itself provides us with cases to make some exceedingly important points. First of all, we can finally dismiss the Transparency theory of the cognitive condition. For there must be any number of epistemologists who, if that theory is correct, must at least know one thing they don't *know* that they know: namely that they must know whatever they know. But secondly, and rather less sophistically, knowing that one knows that *s* is not in any regard essential to, or presupposed by just knowing that *s* as such, so that men might have a great deal of knowledge without knowing that they have it. Yet if they are to claim with any justifiability to have it, they must not only have and know that they have it: they must *know what knowledge is*. How, then, could men justifiably make any claims to knowledge without a correct theory of knowledge? Of course a man might have an incorrect theory of knowledge, might claim to know something, and be right in spite of that. But he could not know he was justified. He would be right, but for the wrong reasons: a blind man taking the right road by accident, to use an image of Plato's. And so he knew without knowing that he did: he merely *thought* he knew, happening to be right.

I believe we have a great deal of knowledge which, distracted by one or another incorrect philosophy of knowledge, we believe we do not have and so in honesty cannot justifiably claim. Caught in the spell of wrong philosophy, we might, as Bishop Berkeley beautifully expressed it, 'Sit down in a forlorn scepticism', having 'first raised a dust and then complain[ed] we cannot see'.[1] Correct philosophy would then not so much provide us with knowledge we had lacked, but restore us to the knowledge which was ours all along. We need, as Berkeley again said, 'only draw the curtain of words, to behold the fairest tree of knowledge, whose fruit is excellent and within reach of our hand'.[2] But what word has stood more opaquely between ourselves and the knowledge we might rightly claim than the word 'knowledge' itself, in its various cases and along with its various cognates?

Knowledge and the theory of knowledge—like any *x* and the theory

---

[1] George Berkeley, *A Treatise Concerning the Principle of Human Understanding*, Introduction, sections 2–3.   [1] *Ibid.*, section 24.

of *x*—are non-simultaneous correlatives. So men may know without having a theory of knowledge, and they even may claim to know, and be justified in so doing, whether they have a theory of knowledge or not. Yet they would never know whether their claims were justified, and hence would never truly know that they knew, without a correct theory of knowledge. This then is the connection between epistemology and knowledge claims which I began by remarking, only it is a connection we might now regard as analytical. For epistemology not only tells when knowledge claims are justified, but it is necessary for the establishment of these claims and without it we should not know when our claims were justified and could not then be secure in the knowledge we possessed: it is through epistemology that we establish our right, as it were, to claim our knowledge.

The claiming of knowledge is a linguistic performance, which does not require the use of any special word or set of words, but only that a certain performance be acknowledged as an assertion. Possession of knowledge perhaps does not require a language—animals may possess considerable amounts of knowledge—but lacking a language and a concept of assertion, they could not know that what they possessed was knowledge, or that they possessed knowledge at all. Assertion is a linguistic performance, and a social one, and it is this sort of factor we shall wish to invoke in explaining how we know that we know. As a social act, assertion could have no point for a solipsist. This, I believe, is part of what is implied in current discussions concerning the possibility of private languages.[1] The question of privacy does not bear either upon the content or the form of a language—for there might be private content and syntax—but rather upon the fact that we do not say anything unless we make an assertion, and there cannot be any private assertions. Asserting is not, of course, part of language, and so the questions which arise in connection with privacy do not appear

---

[1] Ludwig Wittgenstein, *Philosophical Investigations* (New York; Macmillan, 1953), especially sections 202 and 258–9. It is difficult to summarize the issues which Wittgenstein's suggestion of the impossibility of a private language was meant to dissolve. The literature is extensive and inconclusive. For helpful discussions, see Judith Jarvis-Thomson, 'Private Languages', *American Philosophical Quarterly*, I, lx (1964), 20–31; and Moreland Perkins, 'Two Arguments against a Private Language', *Journal of Philosophy*, LXII, 17 (1965), 443–59.

upon the surface of language.[1] A sentence cannot be used to express knowledge unless it is asserted, so if I am prohibited from asserting a sentence, I am prohibited from claiming knowledge. I neither make nor avoid mistakes unless I assert a sentence, but even if I make an assertion *internally*, assertion itself is (logically) a non-private action.

It would be a great convenience if, in specifying the conditions under which a man is justified in claiming to know that *s*, we also were specifying the conditions under which it would be true that he knew that *s*. This would mean that *m* would be justified in asserting *s* if, and only if, *m* knew that *s*. A man would then never be justified in claiming to know what he did not. But this then imposes a condition which might be regarded as intolerably severe. A man is held justified, for example, in claiming to have won an election long before it is certain that he won, and it is, thus, compatible with his being justified in claiming to have won, that he in fact has lost. Often, again, we are considered justified in performing an action in view of likely consequences, and we remain justified even in the event that the consequences in fact prove untoward. The question then is how permissive we are to be. It might be impossibly restrictive to making knowledge of *s* a condition necessary for justified assertion of *s*.

If we fail to impose this restriction, then we sacrifice, of course, the logical connection, admitted by Descriptivists and Anti-descriptivists alike, between '*m* knows that *s*' and *s*, at least to this extent: a man might *justifiably* claim to know that *s* and it would be all the while understood that he might be wrong; i.e., not know. So the falsity of *s* would be compatible with '*m* is justified in asserting (claiming to know) *s*' and incompatible with '*m* knows *s*'. But perhaps we may keep the connection tight, in case, for example, knowledge is far more prevalent than our cautionary observation suggests. It would of course be restrictive in insisting that *m* would be justified, or is in fact justified in asserting *s* if, and only if, *m* knows that *s*. But not *impossibly* restric-

---

[1] 'If I had to say what is the main mistake made by philosophers of the present generation, including Moore, I would say that it is that when language is looked at, what is looked at is a form of words and not the use made of the form of words.' Ludwig Wittgenstein, *Lectures and Conversations on Aesthetics, Psychology, and Religious Belief* (C. Barrett, ed.) (Berkeley and Los Angeles; University of California Press, 1966), p. 2.

2-2

tive unless knowledge were impossibly scarce. In *that* case, we should be recommending what in effect would be the abandonment of assertion, and demanding that people use language conditionally and subjunctively, never saying what *is* but only what *would* be *if*, what *might* be *in case*. Philosophers have not hesitated to propose criteria of knowledge which would entail, if adopted, such a socio-grammatical reform. But as I hope to show that they are ill advised in their philosophy, I shall suppose that in analyzing under what conditions we are justified in claiming to know, I will also in effect, be analyzing those conditions under which knowledge is possessed. There will be time to weaken or abandon this connection if we must, but so long as we maintain it, we shall be supposing that 'I know' is at once claimative and descriptive, at once *says* something which is either true or false, and *does* something which is either justified or not.

VII

It follows from this characterization that I shall be interested primarily in claims to know *that* something is the case, not in claims concerning one's skills and efficiencies: in 'knowing that', to use Ryle's distinction,[1] rather than 'knowing how'. The difference is sufficiently marked that we might consider ourselves to be dealing with distinct concepts rather than with merely different shades of meaning of the same concept of knowledge. Grammatically, 'knows that...' and 'knows how...' are distinguished through the feature that the first is commonly completed with a declarative sentence and the second by a verb in the infinitive (cf. *savoir que* + sentence, in contrast with *savoir* + verb in infinitive). There are of course exceptions. Thus we say 'Smith knows how the nightingale sings'. Grammar itself helps dissolve this exception, since there is a shift here from an adverbial to a conjunctive 'how', but grammatical solutions are of only limited help: 'that' is a conjunction, but 'Smith knows that the nightingale sings' obviously differs in meaning from 'Smith knows how the nightingale sings', being entailed by the latter, and rather weaker, since it could be true that Smith knows nightingales sing without knowing *how* they do it. To know *how* they

[1] Gilbert Ryle, *The Concept of Mind* (New York; Barnes and Noble, 1949), chapter II.

sing implies possession of some ability, e.g., to be able to identify their song, or some such thing.

Since Ryle introduced this distinction, philosophers have wondered whether the two forms are not mutually reducible.[1] We must, if only briefly, indicate the metaphysical aspects which make these intended assimilations of perhaps greater importance than the contestants have recognized. It is, to begin with, an absolute property of *m* that *m* knows how to do something, even if a dispositional property, since dispositions are absolute properties. It may be that neither *m* nor we will know with certainty that *m* knows how to do something until he exhibits this knowledge, namely by *doing* the thing. Yet even if his behavior remains our criterion (and his), 'knows how to do *a*' remains a predicate which is absolutely true of *m* if '*m* knows how to do *a*' is true. It is, however, by no means obvious that 'knows that *s*' is in this respect an absolute property of *m*, true of him if it is true that '*m* knows that *s*'. If it were, then in principle *m* could determine whether he knew that *s* merely through observing himself (including his behavior), as in the case of 'knows how'. But it is not typically the case that we find out whether we know something merely by observing ourselves. There may be some observation of ourselves involved, but typically also there must be observation of the world. And in general, as I shall hope later to demonstrate, knowledge involves a relation between us and the world, rather than any absolute trait of ourselves alone.

To be sure, when a man knows how to climb trees, say, he enters into various relations with the world when he exhibits this knowledge. But these relations, if I may put it so, are not so much relations *between* him and the world, but relations *within* the world, which includes him, as a climber of trees, as part of itself, exactly as it contains trees as parts of itself. And it is here that the issue becomes genuinely philosophical. In attempting to assimilate knowing-that to knowing-how, we convert the former into an absolute trait of whomever 'knows that *s*' (say) is true. But at the same time, and by virtue of the same logic, we collapse the relation *between* knowers and the world, by making knowers part

[1] See John Hartland-Swann, 'The Logical Status of "Knowing-That"', *Analysis*, XVI (1965), 111–15; and Jane Roland, 'On "Knowing How" and "Knowing That"', *Philosophical Review*, LXVII, 3 (1958), 379–88.

of the world, and by making such relations as they may enter into with other parts of the world, *intra-worldly* relations. This lies behind Ryle's move, though Ryle, of course, was only trying to deflate knowledge-that, not reconstruct it as a kind of skill. But Ryle was attacking a theory which supposed a space, and perhaps a cognitively intraversable space, between ourselves and the world. Should knowing-that be assimilated to knowing-how, then, since knowing-how locates us *in* the world, the space would have been obliterated. Then, by making knowing that we know-how to be a matter of observation of behavior, even in our own case, the space between ourselves and others would equally be collapsed, and we all should thus be tumbled into the world of purely public objects. It is too early in our discussion to evaluate these strategies, but it must be pointed out that there remains an un-resolved residue of knowing-that even here. For if knowledge *of* know-ledge is always knowledge of knowing-how, how is our knowledge of knowledge to be analyzed? Have we not opened up here precisely the sort of gap which reduction to knowing-how was to have elimi-nated? There is, as I shall argue, a difference between the knowledge which is *in* and a knowledge which is *of* the world, and confusion of these is always philosophically disastrous. So I am plainly opposed to the principle of the assimilations.

There is a third form of 'knows...' where the blank is filled by a proper name, a definite description, a noun or noun-phrase, e.g., as in 'Smith knows Jones'. It is not an exception to this grammatical criterion for distinguishing this form from 'knows that' to point to the paradigm 'Smith knows that man'. For here, 'that' goes with 'man' as a demon-strative adjective, leaving 'knows' standing alone and taking an accusative, as could be shown by merely identifying that man as Jones: 'Smith knows Jones' was our paradigm. This form goes with a concept rather closer to that connected with 'knows how' than with 'knows that'. For in asking Smith if he knows Jones, he might reply that he does, but *not very well*. And in asking Smith whether he knows how to play the cello, he might similarly reply that he does, but not very well. But nothing like this qualification goes with an affirmative answer to a question whether he knows that Dr Suzuki is dead. There are degrees and gradations of skill and of acquaintance but not of knowledge in the sense of knowledge *that*. Accusative knowledge was the traditional philosophical conception of knowledge, involving a relationship between a knower and an object, a relationship which could be intensified and improved in various ways, depending as a general rule on the complexity of the object. So there would be degrees of knowledge, stages of cognition. But none of this need concern us if our concern is with knowledge *that*, not even if we know that *s*, and *s* is about an object *a* which we know to some minimal degree. That our knowledge of *a* could be improved in no respect entails that our knowledge that *s* could be improved. We may come to know more and more about *a* and hence there may be more things *that* we know, but the increase in the number of things that we know does not affect, since it cannot be sensibly supposed to affect, the degree in which we know any of them.[1] In this specific respect, knowledge *that* is absolute.

Minimally, to say that *m* knows *n* is to say that *m* is acquainted with *n*. In order for this to be so, we might wish to say that he knows how to identify or can recognize *n*, and hence there are certain things, regarding *n*, that he knows to be the case. So acquaintance might involve knowledge that and knowledge how. And similarly, it may be that, for *m* to know that *s*, *s* must have to stand in some relationship to an object *a* with which *m* is acquainted,[2] and hence there must be certain things which *m* knows how to do, etc. This brings me to my own chief reason for making this trite reference to the different forms of words in which the same word 'knows' figures. It is that it may be a mistake to suppose there is a common element, marked by the common appearance in these various contexts of the word 'knows', when in

[1] See C. I. Lewis, *An Analysis of Knowledge and Valuation* (Lasalle, Illinois; Open Court, 1946), pp. 54–5. Idealism with its doctrine of degrees of truth and internal relations, is logically committed to the accusative theory of knowledge. Here, I think, the Idealist would insist that if a sentence *s* is about an object *o*, then if *m* knows that *s*, this presupposes, and hence entails, that for every sentence which is about *o*, *m* must know that sentence, and the number of such sentences approaches infinity. There are, in fact, echoes of such a view in Lewis himself.

[2] 'The fundamental epistemological principle in the analysis of propositions containing descriptions is this: Every proposition which we can understand must be composed wholly of constituents with which we are acquainted.' Bertrand Russell, 'Knowledge by Acquaintance and Knowledge by Description', in his *Myticism and Logic* (London; Allen and Unwin, 1917), p. 219.

fact we are dealing with different things altogether, dealing with concepts which may have some logical connection with one another, but which nevertheless have no common factor which it is the task of epistemology to analyze. Thus, it is quite possible that, in giving my analysis of 'knows that' I shall have to make use of the accusative sense of 'knows' and even of 'knows how'. This would be the case, for example, if *m* knows that *s* only if *m* knows how to use *s*, or only if *s* is related to *a* and *m* knows *a*, or some such thing. I should not wish my analysis to be criticized as circular through the fact that the *word* 'knows' appears in the definiens. For I am not trying to analyze 'knows' as such, but the *whole expression* 'knows that' as it comes up in such sentences as '*m* knows that *s*'. If we require that it, or some word having the same force as it, appear nowhere in our analysis, we should perhaps have to say in the end that the concept is unanalyzable. This strategy is not unfamiliar in philosophy. It is only beginners, for example, who find the famous Frege–Russell definition of the cardinal number of a set circular. That definition is that the cardinal number of a set M is the set of all sets having the same cardinal number as it. But it is not 'cardinal number' as such which is defined here, it is 'the cardinal number of a set M', taken as a whole. The definiens employs, again, not the bare expression 'cardinal number', but the expression 'having the same cardinal number as', again taken as a whole. And this would have been previously defined.

Thus, 'knows that', 'knows how', and then just 'knows' must be taken as wholes, and the latter need not figure in the former merely in virtue of the fact that the *word* happens to figure there: that word is not an isolable part of those expressions, which may be, for our purposes, regarded as atomic. The art of sectioning a sentence correctly, of finding those fissures where it falls into neatly distinguished but philosophically integral fragments, is a fine and difficult exercise of skill the *tao* of which is not easily mastered.[1] Ordinary grammatical

[1] 'When I first began to carve I fixed my gaze on the animal in front of me. After three years I no longer saw it as a whole bull, but as a thing already divided into parts. Nowadays I no longer see it with the eye; I merely apprehend it with the soul. My sense-organs are in abeyance, but my soul still works. Unerringly my knife follows the natural markings, slips into the natural cleavages, finds its way into the natural cavities. And so by conforming my work to the structure with which I am dealing, I have

distinctions are only sometimes helpful, for occasionally they cut across the distinctions which are philosophically relevant. *Philosophical* grammar is sufficiently an independent craft that mere appeal to usage can never finally arbitrate the issues it must resolve.

arrived at a point at which my knife never touches even the smallest ligament or tendon, let alone the main gristle.' This is the carver Ting speaking, one of the characteristic heros of the Taoist, Chuang Tzu. The translation is from Arthur Waley, *Three Ways of Thought in Ancient China* (New York; Anchor Books, 1956), p. 48.

2

DIRECT KNOWLEDGE

I

The members of a community are sources of information for one another, and a main office of speech consists in reporting facts for one another's benefit and at one another's request. Hence *asserting*, which is that act of speech whereby facts are reported, is essentially a social act, and is institutionalized to the extent that if *m* asserts *s*, then I feel justified in asserting *s* in my turn: justified assertion is transitive, but only because we take it that men do not assert unless they know, and if I know that *m* knows that *s*, then I know that *s*. Obviously, there must be a first member in any series in which later members derive their justification for asserting a sentence *s* from the fact that it was asserted for their benefit by an earlier member: at some point an original communication must be made, and whoever made it must have been justified in *his* assertion not because someone else asserted it, but for some other cause. My concern is with us as originators rather than transmitters of knowledge claims, and the question is when is *m* justified in asserting *s* as the originator in a possible sequence of assertions?

A natural suggestion is this: *m* is justified in asserting *s* only if *m* is in possession of evidence *e* for *s* where *e* satisfies a certain criterion of adequacy. It is a commonplace that evidence will differ in strength, that men in possession of evidence of differing strengths will have stronger and weaker grounds for believing that *s*, and this variation in evidential strengths might appear to license the view that a man is justified in asserting *s* when his evidence is of a certain strength. What must be the criterion of adequacy *e* must satisfy in order to justify *m*'s assertion of *s*, in view of our resolution to keep a logically tight connection between *m*'s knowing that *s* and *m*'s being justified in asserting *s*? This is a matter we must determine. But at the moment I am interested in a rather more general consideration, for I do not feel we can dissolve the concept of justified assertion into the two notions of possession of evidence and evidential adequacy. Sound as the suggestion is for an analysis, it at best provides a sufficient condition for *justified assertability*. It is demonstrably not a necessary condition.

We must now ask whether, in advancing *e* as adequate evidence for *s*, *m* is justified in asserting *e*. There would on the face of it be something absurd in claiming to know that *s*, offering *e* as (admittedly adequate) evidence for *s*, but not being able to claim knowledge that *e*. In such a case, adequacy of *e* for *s* notwithstanding, we should, I think, disallow the original claim to know that *s*. In general, I think, we will allow *m* as justified in claiming to know that *s* when *m* possesses *e* which satisfies a criterion of adequacy, only if *m* is justified in asserting *e*. This reflects a sound logical intuition: if it is a theorem that P implies Q, then it is a theorem that Q only if it is a theorem that P.

By the analysis we have offered, however, *m* is justified in asserting *e* only if he possesses evidence *f* for *e*, where *f* satisfies a criterion of adequacy. And while he may in this manner be justified, it is perfectly plain what the issue is before us: identically the same question may be raised at every point, and the analysis, if taken as expressing a necessary as well as a sufficient condition for the justified knowledge claim (and by our own resolve, for knowledge itself), generates an infinite regression. Since it does so, our claims to knowledge must always leave something naked and exposed to the mocking skeptical eye, and we can cover ourselves only at the price of baring another, no less humiliating patch. But humiliation is not the worst of it, for if we are anywhere uncovered we are everywhere exposed. For if we cannot justifiably claim to know that which expresses the evidence which was to have justified our claim to know originally, that latter claim loses its justification entirely.

It certainly would be but a delaying tactic to tamper with the notion of adequacy, e.g., by permitting *m* to claim justifiably to know that *e* providing he has any evidence at all for it, for apart from raising a question of why we should tolerate a weaker criterion of adequacy for this than for *e* in relationship to *s*, the regression merely reappears, requiring that, whatever we offer in however weak support of *e*, something in turn will have to be offered for it, and so forth to infinity—so the regression arises independently of the notion of adequacy. Accordingly, if we wish to retain our intuitions (a) that it is a sufficient condition for a justified knowledge claim that he who makes it be in possession of evidence and (b) that unless a man is justified in claiming to know that *e*, when *e* is offered in evidence for *s*, he is not justified in claiming to know that *s*, then we have only one choice before us. Either there are *no* justified knowledge claims (and hence no knowledge) or some claims to know are justified though he who makes them is in possession of *no evidence in their support*: however we are to say he is justified, it is not through possessing evidence *e* which stands to the asserted sentence in the relationship of evidential adequacy.

II

Whenever *m* is justified in asserting *s* but has, in the sense indicated, no evidence in adequate support of *s*, I shall say that *m* knows that *s* directly. Obviously it would be a caricature of my thesis to say that I know directly any sentence for which I have no evidence, and in fact I have expressed no such view. For only if I am first *justified* in asserting *s*, hence *know s*, do I know *s* directly when, as a further condition, I do not know that *s* because I possess evidence for it. It remains to be said in what justification for a claim to direct knowledge may or must consist. When I know that *s* in a direct way, though there is no sentence *e* which I also know and which is evidence adequate for *s*, I might still be able to justify my claim by saying how I know that *s*. It is only that in telling how I know, I am not always producing *evidence*.

I shall define a sentence *s* as *a basic sentence for m* if, and only if, *m* knows that *s* directly. I speak of these as basic because it is through them that we finally must express the evidence we have for any sentence we know but not directly, and which we must hence offer in justification of any sentence for which evidence is required. They are basic in that all our knowledge which is not direct is, in an obviously architectural sense, based upon them, and they support whatever *beliefs* we are justified in holding. For the present, I put no syntactical conditions upon basic sentences; I have required of them that they use no special class of predicates; I have placed no restriction on what they might be *about*. This is in part because I do not regard basicality to be an absolute property of any special class of sentences. A sentence derives its basicality through the manner in which an individual knows it, not through any features it may have as such. It is sometimes urged that it is not the office of any special kind of sentence to express evidence,[1] and in support of this it is argued that any sentence might be known on the basis of evidence, hence no sentence, as such, is basic. But this is perfectly compatible with my characterization of basicality. It does not follow from the fact that *s* is a basic sentence for *m* that *s* could not be known on the basis of evidence, but only that *m* does not know it on that basis. On the other hand, there may be sentences which never are basic, and such, accordingly, that if they are known at all, they at least are not directly known. That no sentence must always be evidential does not entail that *any* sentence *can* be evidential, i.e., basic for somebody. Some sentences are, as a type, non-basic, but to specify the intrinsic characteristics of the class of essentially non-basic sentences would be at once to define the limits of direct knowledge. And for the moment this is not a matter I wish to broach.

A second favorite argument used against the existence of basic sentences is that if *s* is considered basic, then circumstances can be conceived under which *m* could be mistaken in asserting *s*. There is, however, no class of sentence whatever in connection with which mistakes are not possible, no set of sentences the instances of which are touchstones of *incorrigibility*. Of course that *s* is a sentence in connection with which mistakes are possible does not entail that *m* is mistaken in asserting *s*. But it at any rate is no part of my characterization of basicality that a sentence, which happens to be basic, should as such be incorrigible. That *s* is basic for *m* means only that a certain *sort* of mistake is excluded. Since *no* sentence is, as such, incorrigible, it is trivially true that basic sentences are corrigible in virtue just of their sentencehood. I have introduced basic sentences not as stopping points in a quest for certainty, but as starting points in the justification of knowledge claims. Questions of corrigibility take us well ahead of our story.

[1] 'It is not the case that the formulation of evidence is the function of any special sort of sentence...[and] in general, *any* kind of statement could state evidence for *any* other kind, if the circumstances were appropriate.' J. L. Austin, *Sense and Sensibilia* (Oxford; Clarendon Press, 1962), p. 116.

III

Let *e* be asserted as evidence for *s*: what logical requirements must it satisfy in order to be said to express evidence for *s*? I wish to specify only the weakest condition for the moment: *e* must be distinct from *s*, which rules out only that *s* (or any sentence synonymous with *s*) expresses evidence for *s*. Let us introduce an analogy which will prove illuminating at various points of our investigation: a comparable minimal condition which a given event *a* must satisfy in order to stand in the relationship 'cause of' to an event *b* is that *a* and *b* be distinct events. This takes us admittedly a very short distance in understanding either the concept of causality or of evidence, but it is presumably non-controversial and presumably squares with practice. The repetition of a knowledge claim, for example, is never taken as evidence for the sentence it iterates, certainly not when repeated by the same person: there is a legal convention that *two* distinct *persons*, each making the same knowledge claim, constitute one another witnesses, but this requires only that we build into our notion of distinctness some reference to the individual who urges the knowledge claim. If *m* and *n* each know that *s*, there are two pieces of knowledge here, but if *m* knows that *s* and *m* knows that *s*, there is just the one piece: so when *m* and *n* each assert *s*, there are distinct knowledge claims while, if *m* asserts *s* twice over, there is only one knowledge claim, twice advanced.[1] Lewis Carroll, in *The Hunting of the Snark*, has the Butcher offer three repetitions of a sentence, considering the sentence thereby proven. 'Keep count I entreat! You will find I have told it you twice. / 'Tis the song of the JubJub! The proof is complete, / If only I've stated it thrice.'[2] As a matter of logical form, the proof is impeccable: the conjunction (P and P and P) materially implies P. But then P materially implies

[1] Since two assertions of *s* by distinct persons can constitute distinct knowledge claims, it might appear that we cannot define distinctness through non-synonymy. But this can hardly be taken as a serious objection. If *n* asserts *s*, then *m*'s assertion of *s* is a distinct knowledge claim only in case *m*'s justification for asserting *s* is not the fact that *n* asserted *s*: *m* must have arrived at *s* independently of *n*. But even so, *s* asserted by *n* is not *evidence* for *s*, asserted by *m*: the two independently arrived at assertions constitute one another as evidence. This leaves us altogether free to adopt non-synonymy as our criterion of distinctness, since not even in the disputed case is *s* evidence for *s*.

[2] Lewis Carroll, *The Hunting of the Snark*, Fit the Fifth. 'The Beaver's Tale.'

itself, so if this is the principle the Butcher's proof rests upon, it is (at least) inelegant. Requiring *three* iterations is perhaps the Butcher's way of recognizing that something more than mere *formal* adequacy is wanted for evidential adequacy. Hume held that a and b are causally connected if constantly conjoined: but what is more constantly conjoined with a than a? The analogue of the Butcher's proof in the theory of causation would be that if a happens to be seen three times over, a causes itself.

It would be wildly inapposite to reject the Butcher's argument on the grounds that one can never be sure one has kept correct count.[1] The madness of the objection consists in the fact that we accept a principle as valid which ought initially to have been rejected, and then within its own terms raise sly irrelevant doubts concerning its applicability. Many skeptical reservations have this form: philosophical hounds take enthusiastically off in pursuit of pointless skeptical hares, and the attempt to settle these doubts often merely obscures the total insufficiency of the principle originally called in question. Skeptical doubts, when genuine, are philosophically crucial, but this reservation is only misplaced slyness. I shall consider several instances in the course of this book of what I term The Fallacy of Misplaced Slyness, which is always just an unwitting lampoon of philosophical circumspection.

The minimal condition on evidential status must be urged because it can conceivably arise that a man is justified in asserting s when all that could be counted as evidence would have to be expressed with s itself, or a synonym. But this is to know s directly, by our criterion, and not on the basis of evidence if s is not to be taken as expressing evidence for s. In such a case the man might not need to say that he *simply* knows that s in reply to a question as to how he knows. He might merely point out that s, for example, is the sort of sentence which could be basic and is basic in his case. And this is so not through any special feature of s but through the circumstances which typically govern such cases. He would justify his claim to know that s by specifying, for example, the context or the manner in which he knows it, but the

---

[1] *Ibid.* 'It felt that in spite of all possible pains, / It had somehow contrived to lose count, / And the only thing now was to rack its poor brains, / By reckoning up the amount.'

contextual factors are not evidential, and may rule it out that there should be evidence when *m* is in that context and happens to know that *s*.[1] I believe that a great many of the assertions we make about *ourselves* are of this sort: we do not know them in our own case because we have evidence, or at least we could express evidence only by exactly that sentence which expresses what we claim to know. And this is ruled out as evidential by our minimal condition.

IV

At the risk of starting irrelevancies, I should like to descend to some examples which have had some peculiar importance in recent philosophical discussion. These are first-person reports, assertions a man makes about himself which he is peculiarly situated to make with a certain authority. The danger in using these as illustrations of basic sentences is that I may be taken as implying that the class of first-person reports exhausts the class of basic statements, or that the only things we know directly are expressed in sentences which are first-person reports. There are theories of knowledge which in fact require this, but I would consider it a failure in mine were I forced back to a point which required it. But the turn in recent philosophy which makes first-person reports of singular interest is not concerned with whether they are the *only* basic sentences, but whether they are basic sentences at all. For rather than constituting a sort of knowledge which the man who asserts them is either best or uniquely qualified to claim—since they refer to states of himself which he is best or uniquely qualified to know—the recent view is that there is no speaking of knowledge here at all. There is not because the concept of knowledge is disqualified from application precisely by those conditions which traditionally were

---

[1] 'The situation in which I would properly be said to have *evidence* for the statement that some animal is a pig is that, for example, in which the beast itself is not actually on view, but I can see plenty of pig-like marks on the ground outside its retreat...But if the animal then emerges and stands there plainly in view, there is no longer any question of collecting evidence; its coming into view does not provide me with *more* *evidence* that it's a pig, I can now just *see* that it is, the question is settled.' J. L. Austin, *Sense and Sensibilia* (Oxford; Clarendon Press, 1962), p. 215. Much the same insight is to be found anticipated in J. L. Wisdom. *Other Minds* (Oxford; Blackwell, 1952), Part III, especially p. 61.

32

taken as assuring the man in question a certain cognitive privilege: it cannot, under those conditions, *be* knowledge. And not only this. The sentence with which the pretended knowledge was to have been claimed cannot in fact be asserted, and hence is disqualified for use in claiming knowledge. I shall consider here the shopworn example 'I am in pain'.

It is customary to think of pain as one of a philosophically crucial class of exceptions to Aristotle's thesis that knowledge and its objects are non-simultaneous correlatives: at least for him whose pain it is, the pain and the knowledge of the pain are simultaneously correlative, so that in this one case (at least) *esse est percipi*. Indeed, Berkeley used pain as the pivot upon which his argument in favor of *esse est percipi* turned. To be sure, on just the grounds that one accepted Aristotle's dictum as a criterion, one might rule pains out as objects of knowledge altogether. If it is of the essence of objects of knowledge that they might be known or not, everything else remaining equal, then pain might through its essence be excluded as an object of knowledge. But whatever view one takes, even if it is *not* an object of knowledge, it implies the strangest sort of self-alienation to suggest that were it not for a bit of evidence, I should not have known I was in pain. A stoic might resolve to pay no attention to his pain, but the rest of us don't know that we are in pain when we are so because we happen to have been paying attention. Pains are insistent, and not to pay attention to them cannot mean what it means in other cases: it means that I am to act as though I did not have a pain, which requires (a) that I have the pain and (b) that I pretend I do not. But I cannot 'put it out of my mind'. I have no *choice*, no freedom not to notice: knowledge here seems inevitable and unmistakable. It is this which makes pain a favorite of the epistemologist in quest of certainty.

Of course we are here thinking of evidence for *s* as something correlated with whatever it is that *s* describes. Certainly, there are things correlated with pains. I might thus have a recurring headache at four o'clock regularly, so that its coming tells me with chronometrical accuracy that it is that hour. A habit of expectation arises which I ought, if Hume were right, to convert into a causal law, so unvaryingly constant is the conjunction. Be this as it may, we could appreciate the fact that after a period of time, a man would no longer feel constrained to consult his timepiece when his headache appears: it always is four o'clock. It might be strange that there should be this correlation, but we would have to allow it as an interesting fact. What we would not allow on its basis, however, is this: that the man should look at his watch, find it is four o'clock, and infer that he must have a headache. So that, after a period of time, he need not consult his *head*. It would betray the misplaced slyness of the amateur skeptic to suggest that, since clocks sometimes run slow, he might not have a headache? I don't have to check my head to see whether I have a headache, and note with satisfaction that I do. I have, as I have said, no choice. The concept of pain, it might be objected, is not so completely clear as to rule out unfelt pains. People speak of sleeping off a pain, or of failing to do so, waking with the same pain they had when they went to sleep. By a sick-bed, I am certain I should say of the sleeping patient who moans in his sleep that he must be in pain. A man who *dreams* he is in pain *is* in pain though he is not in a position to know it. Psycho-analytical theory has taught us to speak of thoughts so painful that we displace them in favor of substitute but tolerable agonies at the level of consciousness. So there may appear logical room to insert the possibility of unconscious or unfelt pains, and hence room for he whose pain it is to infer that he has it. Yet when we seek to find claims to this effect, we would certainly not honor them. I may infer, since one who has his abdomen sliced feels great pain, that I have great pain when the surgeon slices mine, though fortunately it rages the other side of an anesthetic curtain. But the best we would allow, I think, is that the man who says this *would* be in pain did he not have an anesthetic, not that there *is* a pain he is now protected from by courtesy of the deadener. And this would be our general strategy: we say the thought *would* be painful, if it were conscious, not that it is painful but fortunately unconscious; we say that the patient would feel pain if he *were* awake, or that, if he moans, he is not in deep sleep, and so forth. In general, when I might in fact justify the claim that I am in pain by the indication of evidence, what I indicate may serve in support of my claim for some other person, but not for me: for it is not on the basis of it that I know I am in pain. I know I am because I feel the pain and the feeling is not dis-

34

tinct from the pain in the manner required for it to be evidence that I am in pain. Such is our concept.

On the other hand, there are circumstances in which for a man to *say* that he is in pain is almost to belie himself, roughly in the manner in which, were a man to cast ten-foot letters in Gothic shape, and put them together to spell 'I am ecstatic' he would belie himself through a kind of operatic falseness: for 'I am ecstatic' is, in its typical occurrence, not something we say, much less cast in bronze, but something rather which we do: it is a manifestation rather than a description of the emotional state it is connected with, a symptom of transport. A scream again, is not something we say, but something we do, a response to terror rather than a description of a state of terror. There are words, in extension of these examples, which ring true only when they are expressions rather than the descriptions of the state they might naively be taken to report. So 'I am in pain' might be one of these. It is a verbal grimace, not a report. To be sure we can *say* it. But so might a woman have the positive abnormal characteristic of voluntary lacrimation. She could simulate sorrow. But only genuine tears go with true sorrow, and tears, surely, are responses: they tell others that we feel sorrow, they do not say but *show* that we grieve. Some such analysis of this was offered by Wittgenstein, according to whom the words 'I am in pain' are wrongly classified if taken as an ordinary description. They belong, rather, to what he terms *pain-behavior*, they *evince* rather than describe the state of pain.[1] Let us elaborate this suggestion. *If* descriptive, then they are false, given that the conditions under which they could be said are incompatible with a true ascription to him who says it that *he* is in pain. But if merely a symptom, then they are neither true nor false. We assimilate these words to such non-controversial cases of pain-behavior as, say, crying 'Ouch'. But 'I know that ouch' fails to make syntactical sense. So 'I know that I am in pain', though syntactically unexceptionable, is a monstrosity of language: since 'I am in pain' is not asserted, and since 'I know' is the form of words with which an assertion is made. Perhaps it is for this reason that Wittgenstein said that only as a sort of joke can I be said to know

[1] Ludwig Wittgenstein, *Philosophical Investigations* (New York; Macmillan, 1953), sections 244–6.

3-2

that I am in pain. I cannot, on this account *say* 'I know that I am in pain'.

Wittgenstein was especially sensitive to the temptation to suppose we have understood a sentence merely because it satisfies the standard criteria of sententiality and is composed of familiar words. 'It is an English sentence; apparently quite in order. That is, until one wants to do something with it...Everyone who has not become calloused by doing philosophy notices that there is something wrong here.'[1] So Wittgenstein, whose thought I have been elaborating rather than exposing in the paragraph above, would ask what ever could we *do* with a sentence 'I know that I am in pain'. But the challenge to find a normal context for its employment is less interesting philosophically than the suggestion that the disparity between the surface and the depth grammar of 'I am in pain' rules out an assertive use for it and, by default, its availability for advancing a knowledge claim. If it cannot be a knowledge claim, it cannot *a fortiori* be a *justified* knowledge claim. Then, if there is a tight connection between knowledge that *s* and justifiably being able to claim knowledge that *s*, I cannot be said to know that I am in pain. That 'I am in pain' is of a piece with 'Ouch', with cries and winces and whimpers, constitutes an elegant argument, curiously reminiscent of Berkeley's contention that we have no better grounds for supposing warmth to be a resident property of fire than for supposing pain to be: both are, or neither is; and since there is (apparently) a greater reluctance to suppose pain a resident property than to suppose warmth *not* to be one, warmth was assimilated to pain's status as an 'idea'.[2] This was a step in the direction of establishing *esse est percipi*. Berkeley apparently did not concern himself overly much with the factor which distinguishes pain, namely that pain is felt (if at all) uniquely by him whose pain it is; the *esse est percipi* theory does not require that any one percipient perceive an idea, so there would be room actually for someone else to perceive, i.e., have my pain. But that is digression. The connection here is that either 'I am

---

[1] *Op. cit.*, section 348.

[2] 'Intense heat is nothing else but a particular kind of painful sensation; and pain cannot exist but in perceiving beings, it follows that no intense heat can really exist in an unperceiving, corporeal substance'. George Berkeley, *Three Dialogues between Hylas and Philonous*, I.

in pain' is part of pain-behavior, or (say) 'Ouch' is a sentence admitting truth-values, and since there is an apparently greater reluctance to regard the latter as sentential than to regard the former as symptomatic, the former is to be assimilated to the latter. Unlike Berkeley, Wittgenstein was not concerned with wholesale assimilation, though doubtless it would be within the scale of philosophical achievement to enlarge the concept of behavior sufficiently to absorb, as symptomata, anything we would be disposed to regard as descriptive. But let us attend merely to the issue at hand.

Grammarians may be found who say that interjections are not parts of language: 'These are', writes one, 'free-floating words or meaningless syllables, that interupt the orderly progress of speech. They are accepted as evidence of emotion...since these sounds are presumably torn from the speaker without his foreknowledge, any discussion of standards would seem inappropriate.'[1] Nevertheless, some sort of line must be drawn. These cannot be appreciated *merely* in the way in which we appreciate flushes, blushes, gooseflesh, shivering, shallow breathing, and the like. These are invariant to language communities, but interjections are not. They are, for example, translatable, e.g., '"Ow!" said Pooh' comes out of English into Latin as '"Vae!" exclamavit Pu.' And this is not a mere difference in phonetic transcription or transliteration, as with the animal sounds: a dog who barks in no language whatever is described as making the noise 'Bow wow' in English, 'Wau Wau' in German, and 'Oua Oua' in French. Again, 'Ow!' expresses pain, never anger, but 'Vae!' expresses both, which, though in itself a small point, connects with a larger one. 'Ow', and 'Ouch' are responses to pinpricks, stubbed toes, bashed fingers, and mild traumas generally; but it would be blackly amusing to think of one of the ghastlier martyrdom's—that of Saint Erasmus, say—drawing a mere 'Ouch!' from the lips of the eviscerated saint: in his situation, it is wild screams or it is nothing: 'Ouch' would be a studied insult against his tormentors. Mad screams, appropriate to a martyr, would elicit remonstrance rather than sympathy if they issued from the mouth of someone who bumped into a cupboard. Someone who said 'Tiens!'

[1] Bergen Evans and Cornelia Evans, *A Dictionary of Contemporary American Usage* (New York; Random House, 1957), p. 252.

upon stubbing his toe would merely perplex a Frenchman—unless the person were exclaiming over his own clumsiness; and ''Swounds!' would sound weird today under any circumstances. There are then relatively well-defined limits and rules governing interjections: we learn manners of response, and exercise a measure of control in contrast with, say, endocrinal manifestations. But quite apart from this, *any* word, any expression of a brevity consonant with interjection, could be used interjectively in place of our somewhat restricted set of formal ejaculations: 'Coffee' may be used to express joy, pain, surprise, anger, sorrow, or, for that matter, fear. 'I am a professor' may be used to express any of these; so might 'I am in pain'. But it does not follow that this is its primary employment: it can be used to reply to a question, to remind someone of an urgency, to offer an excuse: but in performing these various functions, it is being said as something which is true by him who states it. There are many uses to which first-person reports may be put without them ceasing to be first-person reports through being used. Interjections, however rule-governed, are never in their primary function *said*. A woman who *says* 'O joy' is more likely expressing cruelty towards her lover than joy; a man who *says* 'Hooray' expresses anything but jubilation. Interjections entail, as it were, their own falsity when they are said, for consonantly with the rules that govern their employment, they cannot be other than inappropriate to their proper condition when asserted. But 'I am in pain' is not false when said, and it is wrong to assimilate it to a purely interjective role. Moreover, the sort of pain which rules out the detachment necessary for *saying* 'I am in pain' rules out in fact our saying anything whatever: it only is the extremest sort of pain which renders the assertion of 'I am in pain' self-belying. It might remain as part of something called pain-behavior, broadly construed. But by broadening that concept widely enough to incorporate it, we weaken to a proportionate degree the argument which demanded a close assimilation of it to the status of the pure interjection. And this is the important point. Every sentence we say can be called 'behavior' of one sort or another. To make this an interesting revision, however, we should have to undertake a total philosophy of man and of the relation in which men stand to their language. I shall sketch the outlines of such a philosophy in chapter 10.

V

But dismissing one class of reasons for the alleged oddness of 'I know that I am in pain'—namely, that 'I am in pain' is not assertable but only interjectable—we have not removed the oddness of it in the context 'I know that...' which is purported to be impressive to someone not 'calloused by doing philosophy'. The fact remains that we seldom utter such a sentence even in the vale of tears we inhabit, and philosophers otherwise sympathetic to the view that 'I am in pain' is descriptive, have tended to apologize for maintaining this position. For though, as Wittgenstein suggests, we might say that this sentence 'sounds all right at first', the difficulties arise when 'one wants to do something with it'. A. J. Ayer writes, for example:

If, in the course of a discussion about knowledge, or as part of a game, one were challenged to give a list of things one knew, I think it would be quite proper to give such replies as 'I know I am thinking about a philosophical problem' or 'I know that I am looking at a sheet of paper', or 'I know that I am in pain'. Indeed, this is about the only context in which sentences of this kind do have a natural use: as offering examples of what we may safely claim to know.[1]

These remarks serve to return us to the broad concern of our inquiry. I have been arguing that 'I am in pain' may be regarded in its primary function as an assertion, reporting a fact, namely that he who says it is in pain. Assertion, again, I have contended, functions as a claim to knowledge, with an implicit 'I know' accompanying it. A man is justified in asserting *s* if he in fact knows that *s*. The question now before us is whether 'I know that I am in pain' would make any assertion over and above what 'I am in pain' itself makes when asserted.[2] If 'I know' accompanies, as it were, every assertion, then these words go without saying, they merely make explicit what is taken for granted, and add nothing in their own right. But there is something curious about Ayer's example. 'I am in pain' may entail 'I know that I am in pain'. Yet 'I know that I am in pain'—in Ayer's context—does not

[1] A. J. Ayer, *Privacy* (Proceedings of the British Academy, 1960), pp. 48–9.
[2] 'From the fact that it cannot be said of me that I know I'm in pain, it will not follow, of course, that it *can* be said of me that I do not know—i.e., that I am ignorant of the fact—that I am in pain.' Roderick Chisholm, *Theory of Knowledge* (Englewood Cliffs, New Jersey; Prentice-Hall, 1966), p. 30n.

entail 'I am in pain'. For in the game he has described, 'I know that I am in pain' is virtually incompatible with 'I am in pain' being *true*. If it were true, the game would not go on. Indeed, 'I know I am in pain' if it entailed as true 'I am in pain' would virtually interupt the presentation of that list of things we could safely claim to know. Since the game is not warped, we must assume that 'I am in pain' is false when the man says 'I know that I am in pain'. There may be contexts in which, were a man to say 'I know that I am in pain', we would be right to go on to ask: 'And what else do you know?' He perhaps answers with another example, e.g., 'I know that Ulan Bator is the capital of Mongolia'. There would be something inhuman in asking for another example of knowledge in case 'I know that I am in pain' were being used in any *primary* way, however. What it means is, in the former context, that when I am in pain I *know* it. But in that context, nothing like that is meant by the other example. In the course of this little game, Ulan Bator *is* the capital of Mongolia but the man *is not* in pain. There is a use for '*I* know' in which it serves in answer to the question 'Who knows?'. But what sort of stupid situation would arise in which anyone would ask 'Who knows that he is in pain?' with, perhaps, prizes for the knowledgeable respondent? There *is* something different about 'I know that I am in pain' in that it is not just another piece of information one *happens* (*viz*., by cognitive accident) to possess. When a man says he is in pain we don't reward him for his sapience but behave solicitously and, hopefully, in mitigation of his agony. Since *our* response is, as it were, pain-relieving behavior, it is natural to regard 'I am in pain' as pain-behavior, and there is after all a peculiar problem with 'I know that I am in pain'.

Yet we should not let speech so totally usurp language. The manner in which I should know that I am in pain is no more intimate than the manner in which I know that I am *not* in pain. I seldom assert that I am not in pain, and then only in those contexts where others might believe me to be in pain. My purpose is to say that I have overcome the pain, or that the anaesthetic worked, or that they should tend to someone else since I am all right, or whatever. It is not only that, when not in pain, I do not come to know this on the basis of evidence, but that in the end I have a unique and peculiar authority which would make

'I know that I am (not) in pain' uniquely and peculiarly gratuitous. Yet it would have a role to play if people persisted in treating me as though I were in pain when I was not, or conversely. If the dentist says I am only imagining that the drill hurts, that I am under an anesthetic which aborts any pain, I would have to say 'I know that I am in pain', implying that before my knowledge in such matters, his claims must yield, including any claim he might make regarding anesthetics. And I should be reminding him of the facts. I might even monologically have to be reminding myself of such facts. For suppose I let him convince me that I am only imagining that I am in pain. Then I might have to bring myself to my senses by saying inwardly, as it were, that imagining pain is nonsense, that I *know* whether and when I am in pain, that if I am in pain I know it and am not, because I cannot be, imagining that I am so. So there is a natural use for these words, even in soliloquy. Yet I can only remind others or myself of an authority which is everywhere accepted. And it is this, to return to Ayer's example, which curiously makes 'I know that I am in pain' true whenever I say it, whether I am in pain or not. It is a standing fact that we have this authority, and it is this that is expressed by the statement. It is not so much a knowledge claim as such, but a claim about claims. It is because it is so generally accepted a fact that he who is in pain knows that he is, that no one ever is required to say that he knows that he is in pain. It is through this same standing fact that we would reject as nonsense the denial 'I don't know that I am in pain'. So in the end 'I know' is a gratuitous attachment to 'I am in pain'. But it is gratuitous in a different manner than that in which we suggested that 'I know' is gratuitous in connection with a simple assertion. For the latter would be due to a fact about language, while the former would be due to a fact about *knowledge*. Where mistakes are not allowed, 'I know' can have no use, other than to remind ourselves or others of these facts. It *is*, then, a kind of joke to say 'I know that I am in pain', as though there were something special about me, or when ascribing knowledge that he is in pain to *m*, as though there were something peculiar about *him*. But in this case 'I know that I am in pain' differs sufficiently from 'I am in pain' that it could be true when the latter is false, and cannot, accordingly *entail* the latter.

It cannot be the *general* force of the words 'I know' to remind others of my authority, since I do not have that authority in most of the cases in which I use these words, or am not accorded it automatically through the sorts of considerations which justify their use in connection with 'I am in pain'. Thus I might say 'I know she loves me', and here I can claim no automatic authority since the state of another's feelings, and especially their feelings towards ourselves, is a matter upon which we are notoriously insecure. It is, in such cases, a special achievement to have knowledge at all. It is for these reasons that first-person reports are, in their typical employments, poor examples to work with as examples of knowledge claims. 'I know' has a primary force only if 'I might not have known' is sensible, as it is not with the typical first-person report. This would be a poor reason for saying that first-person reports do not express knowledge, as poor a reason, in its own way, as the fact that I might not have known what I can significantly claim to know is a poor reason for saying that I do not know it. The cartesian tradition in epistemology, which we shall consider later in this book, often consists in a form of skepticism according to which, if I might not have known that *s*, then I do not know that *s*. Wittgenstein, whose anti-cartesianism is celebrated, inverted this to the position that if it is not sensible to suppose that I might not have known that *s*, then it is not sensible to say that I know that *s*. These positions are mirror images of one another. It is against the Wittgensteinian inversion that we must explain the efforts philosophers make these days to render 'I am in pain' somehow corrigible. As though, unless I *could* be mistaken, I could not claim to know that I were in pain. It will be useful to consider one attempt at saving first-person reports for knowledge claims before drawing some general conclusions.

The logic of the philosophical counter-instance is this. If an example can be constructed, however fanciful, which escapes through the meshes of some supposed principle, then no necessity attaches to that principle. In the present case, if there could be imagined an example in which someone learns, on the basis of evidence, that he is in pain, then it is not essential to that concept that pain be known non-evidentially by him who suffers it. In that event, though every one in fact does know that he is in pain directly, it could be otherwise. And if it could be otherwise, 'I am in pain' is vindicated as a knowledge claim, though 'I know that I am in pain'—in the sense I have given it of 'When I am in pain, I know it'—is rendered contingent, and true only if *not* entailed through the *concept* of pain. I shall proceed to sketch now a counter-instance of some supposed force against the principles we have been considering, a case similar to one once thought up by Norman Malcolm.[1]

We have an anesthetic individual *n*, who obviously has never in his life felt pain. But *n*, unlike Gautama, has not been protected from the sight of suffering people, and knows how to apply the predicate 'is in pain' to others. An astute behaviorist, he will have learned the proper things to do and say when others suffer. He himself might have learned for example, to say 'Ouch' when he bumps his head, in case he notices that he has bumped it, thinking that this is the thing one *says* under those conditions: as people say 'Pardon me' when they bump into one another. He has learned the grammar of interjection inductively. Such a man would, of course, never be especially sympathetic: there would be something cold and mechanical in his 'commiserations'. Should he become a doctor, he would be one who stands to his patients in exactly the way in which a mechanic stands to an automobile. In an important sense, though he is able as anyone to say when others are in pain, he does not know what it is to be in pain. Should someone suggest to him that pain is something interior, he would regard this as mere muddle. Such expressions as 'inner suffering' or 'unmanifested pain' would strike him as comical if barely intelligible: as though there were writhing ghosts in unperturbed machines: sheer metaphysical cant.

Let us now suppose *n*'s anesthesia dissolves one day, and waves of pain inundate him. He has feelings of a sort he has never had before, he does not *know what is happening*. But seeing that he is behaving outwardly as others behave when it is correct to say of them that they are in pain, he infers, by an analogical argument which is the precise inverse of the argument from analogy which is sometimes supposed to be the basis of our inferences to Other Minds, that he is in pain. So 'I am in pain' is an inferred sentence for him, *not* a basic sentence, and had he

[1] Norman Malcolm, 'Knowledge of other Minds', *Journal of Philosophy*, LV, 23 (1958), 969–78.

not noticed what he was doing, he would not have known he was in pain.[1] If this case can arise, the status as knowledge claims of 'I am in pain' is preserved. Before we honor it, however, a few comments are in order.

(1) Does *n*, while still anesthetic, *infer* that others are in pain when they groan, writhe, say 'I am in pain', etc.? What, then, is he inferring *to*? Having never felt pain in his own case, would not *being in pain* just *be* to act that way? That a person were acting that way would not be evidence for a distinct but connected claim that they were in pain: there would be nothing other than the behavior in which pain could consist.

(2) When pain does come to *n*, he would not infer it from the simple observation of his external behavior. For he might have learned long since to 'be in pain', e.g., to make the noises which he calls 'moans', to make the movements he calls 'writhings', etc. What he would discover in this case is that *he is not doing* these things: they are *happening to him*. At this point he discovers, in fact, that his erstwhile pain-behavior only *outwardly* resembled the behavior of those who truly were in pain. The difference between knowing what we are doing and knowing what is happening to us is one of the most primitive pieces of knowledge that we have. It would then involve a transformation of perception that he should discover that what he was manifesting but not doing was truly pain-behavior. For what *n* would have come to realize is that he, and hence others, have interiors. His perception of others, thus, would be transformed through this revelation. Learning that he

---

[1] Malcolm argues that the man has not *got* the concept under these conditions: 'Let us note that if the man gives an answer (e.g., "I know it must be pain because of the way I jumped") then he proves by that very fact that he has not mastered the correct use of the words "I feel pain". They cannot be used to state a *conclusion*. In telling how he did it, he will convict himself of a misuse.' Norman Malcolm, *loc. cit.*, p. 277. In view of Malcolm's express ambition to reduce, following Wittgenstein, 'I am in pain' to 'pain-behavior', one must wonder whether he is entitled to the use of 'use' here. We don't in *this* respect 'use' tears, limps, and the like. To be sure, verbal behavior is qualified as 'new' pain-behavior. But the distance between it and the rest is perhaps wide enough to weaken the assimilation. Moreover, in so far as we *do* allow that a woman may *use* tears, rather than merely *cry*, could we not, as it were, assimilate *used* tears to 'new pain-behavior'? The worst of it is, for Malcolm's case, that just the difference between crying and using tears is the difference which the whole of the Other Minds Problem is supposed to be *about*. So one is merely begging the question, not answering it, by the strategy of widening the concept of 'behavior'.

is in pain in this manner is not just another fact he happens to have picked up: it involves a transformation of a whole *body* of facts. It involves a transformation of himself and the world, for when he acquires an interior, so does the *world*. As a piece of learning, this one resembles more a religious conversion, e.g., suddenly to see what up to now had been merely *things* as 'divine visual language' as Berkeley described the world of objects.[1] So if it is an inference, it is not a routine, garden variety one. He has to change his whole world in order to *receive* this inference.

(3) Finally, of course, it would not merely be the new thing that the 'pain-behavior' was something he was not *doing* but which was *happening* to him: there would in addition be the *pain*, the like of which he had never felt before. Would *n* truly have inferred from the behavior to 'I am in pain?'. Well, in a sense, but only in a sense. Strictly speaking, he would not so much have inferred that he was in pain as that *it was pain he was in*. He would have made a discovery as much about language as about the world: his inferred sentence 'I am in pain' would have the force of 'So *this* is what they call "pain!"' His experience would be rather like that of a wandering tourist who finds himself in a fascinating church, say Santa Maria della Pace. In a sense he knows where he is, since he can say all sorts of things about it: but he does not yet, until he has looked it up in his guidebook, know that the church he is in is Santa Maria della Pace. So in a sense he infers that the church he is in is Santa Maria della Pace: it fits the description in his guidebook. The 'is', then, of 'This *is* Santa Maria della Pace', is identificatory. And by parity of analysis, there is a covert identificatory 'is' in 'I am in pain', e.g., 'That which I am in = pain'. But this is not the sort of inference at all which the case originally supposed.

Santa Maria della Pace *fits* the description given of it in the guidebook. But *n* has to identify his state as one of pain by correlating the inner state he is sustaining with his outward behavior. Pain, as such, is 'indescribable' in that 'pain' is one of the terms we understand only through having *experienced* that to which it applies. One cannot learn

[1] George Berkeley, *Alciphron*, IV, For a brilliant gloss on this, see Ian Ramsey, 'The Possibility of an Empirical Metaphysic', in Warren Steinkraus (ed.), *New Studies in Berkeley's Philosophy* (New York; Holt, Rinehart, and Winston, 1966), pp. 13–30.

what pain is by heeding descriptions, or by merely observing the behavior of others, e.g., by learning when to apply or withhold the
predicate 'is in pain' on the basis of behavioral criteria. In brief, 'pain'
is a *two-stage predicate*.[1] We learn one stage of its meaning by external
criteria, and the other stage of its meaning through instantiating it ourselves. But we only know, of a given two-stage predicate F, that we
are instantiating F—or that it is F which we are instantiating—in case
we have (or in case whoever teaches us the meanings of our two-staged
predicates has) already mastered the external criteria for ascribing F
to others. There must be external criteria, of course of a public sort,
or our inner states will be merely inchoate. Others, when they notice
our behavior, tell us what state it is that we are in, tell us that we are
'in F', for example, and in this way we come to a mastery of our two-
stage predicates. And in the course of living out the banal fabric of
human life, we come in the normal stages of our *educations sentimentales*
to learn the meanings of love, fear, jealousy, and the like.

Of course there may be many feelings we have which we do not, in
one sense, know we have, because we have never identified them in
any way. Nietzsche, who thought deeply about this matter,[2] believed
that all sorts of feelings for which the herd has no name would be had
by exceptional persons, but their chance of surviving, much less com-
municating these feelings to others, would decrease proportionally with
the number and intensity of these socially unacknowledged feelings—
though, like a true romantic, Nietzsche supposed we could always at
least express ourselves in poetry.[3] But the romantic's complaint that
others do not understand him is really a matter of his not understanding
himself. With two-stage predicates, unless we can apply them successfully to others, we can hardly apply them to ourselves and,[4] more
important for the case we are examining, if we are in a state which is
utterly unassociated with any external behavior, the best we could say
of it was that it was *strange*: a 'funny feeling'.

[1] See my 'Historical Understanding: The Problem of Other Periods', *Journal of Philosophy*, LXIII, 18 (1966), 566–77.
[2] Friedrich Nietzsche, expecially *Die Fröhliche Wissenschaft*, section 354. For a discussion see my *Nietzsche as Philosopher* (New York; Macmillan, 1965), pp. 116–22 and *passim*.
[3] Friedrich Nietzsche, *Über Wahrheit und Lüge in Aussermoralischen Sinn*.
[4] P. F. Strawson, *Individuals: An Essay in Descriptive Metaphysics* (London; Methuen, 1959), pp. 104 and 109.

However this may be, the inference suggested as a counter-instance to the claim that we do not infer that we are in pain does not, in fact, subvert that principle. But it does bring out a better point than it meant to establish. A man *can* be in pain and not know it: because he does not know *what* it is that he is feeling. Thus the one sensitive man in a community of anesthicals would never be able to say, either to others or to himself, what was going on within him. So the force of the principle that a man cannot be in pain without knowing it must be modified to mean: there are no unfelt pains. But there can be felt pains not identified as such. And if a man does not know what pain is, he can be in pain without knowing that he is. And so mistakes are after all possible. Thus 'I know that I am in pain' is ambiguous. Interpreted as 'When I am in pain, I feel it', the sentence is true and even necessary, through the concept—or the nature—of pain. But I can feel pain without knowing that it is pain I feel. And if knowledge requires here that I have the latter information, then 'When I am in pain, I know it' must entail 'I know what (understand what) "pain" means'. And interpreted this way, the sentence is contingent, for nothing in the concept or nature of pain necessitates our knowing how to describe or identify pains. Nevertheless, the concept of pain precludes my knowing that I am in pain on the basis of evidence; and to have mastered the concept is to appreciate that only the pain itself will tell me that I am in pain. It follows that 'I am in pain' is always a basic sentence, expressing direct knowledge on the part of him who asserts it when it is true. The claim to knowledge is automatically justified through the concept of pain itself. Justification here does not—because conceptually it cannot—consist in appeal to evidence.

VI

'I know that *s*' has the force of asserting *s*, and since *s* may be asserted without the specific employment of the words 'I know', taken merely as assertion, 'I know that *s*' may seem to reduce to the assertion of *s*. Yet even with the assertion of *s*, we must distinguish the act of assertion from the content of whatever is asserted: in a full sense of meaning, *s* does not exhaust the meaning of ⊢*s*. The Fregean ⊢*s* is read 'It is a theorem that *s*'. And being a theorem is a fact about *s* which requires explication of a context rather considerably wider than the mere contentual analysis of *s* in isolation would suggest. So too 'I know that *s*' has a wider meaning. It means, in effect, that *I am justified in* asserting *s*. And being justified requires explication of a context rather considerably wider than what the mere contentual analysis of *s* would suggest. It is our task as epistemologists to explicate this context. And it must be appreciated that since *s* may be true without *m* being justified in asserting *s*, '*m* knows *s*'—or 'I know that *s*' in case I am *m*—can be false though *s* is true. And this being so, they cannot have the same meaning.

One way in which we are justified in asserting *s* is when we have evidence for *s* which satisfies a criterion of adequacy. Another is that we are justified, as in the case of pain, through the nature of what we claim to know. And the question remains as to what justification I might give for asserting *s* when *s* is a *basic sentence for me*, when I am not justified through a concept. The question becomes crucial in cases where I could but do not know that *s* through the fact that I have evidence—where evidence is not ruled out conceptually, and where direct knowledge nevertheless is not, one hopes, conceptually ruled out either. I should like at least to suggest the *sort* of thing which is involved. I might be saying that there is a pair of relations, call these R and R', such that *s* stands in the relation R to the same thing to which I stand in the relation R'. I might, for example, say that I know that *s* when *s corresponds* to the same thing which I *experience*. Without analyzing these relationships, without specifying what it is which can at once be corresponded to by a sentence and experienced by me, this cannot be regarded as more than a *scheme* of an analysis. It is one I shall fill out in the course of this book. But merely as a scheme, it suggests that *direct knowledge* is at least a *triadic relationship* holding between *m*, *s*, and *a*, where *a* itself is corresponded to by *s* and experienced by *m*. If *a* can be corresponded to by *s* without being experienced by *m*, then, when *m* knows that *s*, *s* is a basic sentence for *m* without being a first-person report. When *s* cannot correspond to *a* without *m* experiencing *a*, then *s* is a first-person report for *m*. A first-person report is one which corresponds to something whose *esse est percipi*. But I should and shall want to argue very hard against the proposal that the entire class of basic sentences be absorbed to these—hard as I have tried in this chapter to argue that *s* may be a basic sentence, albeit a first-person report. In other words, I shall wish to argue that not everything we experience is something whose *esse* is *percipi*—which means that I can experience something in such a way that it and my experience are non-simultaneous correlatives. The astute reader will already have seen that the triadic relationship will have to be modified eventually. For consider once again '*m* is in pain'. Let this be *s*. Let *s* correspond to the state of *m*'s being in pain. There is no such thing as unexperienced pain. But there is such a thing, if our argument has been correct, as experiencing pain without knowing that it is pain one is experiencing. Would *m* know that he was in pain if this were his case? If not, the analysis must be modified.

We have, however, three relationships to clarify: (a) the relationship between *s* and its correspondent; (b) the relationship between *m* and *m*'s experienda; and (c) the relationship between *e* and *s* when *e* is evidence for *s*. In addition, we must ascertain a criterion of evidential adequacy, and must augment our analysis in a way which deflects the objection of the paragraph above.

3

BEING MISTAKEN

A man m might claim to know that s and he might in fact be wrong, or mistaken, with regard to s, but he himself cannot say 'I know that s but I might be mistaken'. It would be like offering a gift and then saying one is not quite sure it is his to give. For in view of the transitivity of knowledge, when I assert s to n, I, as it were, give n a right to assert s in his turn. But I cannot give knowledge which is not mine, and I cannot transfer a right to assert which I am not certain I myself possess. So with the sentence 'I know that s but I might be mistaken', I take away with part of the expression what I offer with the other, and at the performative level the sentence is an empty gesture. Neither can I *ascribe* knowledge to m while saying that m might be mistaken. If I ascribe knowledge that s to m, I am in effect claiming knowledge that s myself. Of course m may know things that I do not, and though I cannot specify something that he knows but I do not I can *describe* something he knows which I do not, e.g., he knows the proof of Fermat's last theorem and I do not. So here the problem does not lie at the level of performance on my part, but arises through a feature in the concept of knowledge itself. For whether or not I know what m knows, I cannot say both that he knows it and that he might be mistaken, and this must be because 'might be mistaken' is *descriptively* ruled out by 'knows' in such a manner that 'cannot be mistaken' is *entailed* by 'knows'. Finally, if this is an entailment, it must go through independently of the *manner* of knowledge, e.g., independently of any special *adverbial* information concerning the *sort* of knowledge it is. Thus 'm knows directly that s' will entail 'm cannot be mistaken with regard to s' independently of the information furnished by the adverb 'directly'. Or, if it does not, then whatever adverbial information is required for the entailment belongs to the *analysis* of knowledge, not to the specification of a kind or mode of knowledge. Hence, once again, the entailment would go through without benefit of the adverb: for if the adverb does not apply, the concept of knowledge will not apply either. So the entailment not only goes through independently of any adverbial qualification: in addition no *strength* is added by specification of the mode of knowledge. So far as exemption from mistake is concerned, this is a pure, logical feature of the *concept* of knowledge, regardless of the various types and modes of knowledge that *s*.

The entailment, however, must *itself* be carefully qualified. For whereas we will all acknowledge that, if *m* knows that *s*, then *m* cannot be in error, cannot be wrong, with respect to *s*, few of us would so readily countenance the direct contrapositive of this, *viz.*, that if *m can* be in error, *can* be wrong with respect to *s*, then *m* does *not* know that *s*. For the contrapositive has some exceedingly troubling overtones. It rings, indeed, with the noise of shipwrecked epistemologies, for it lends itself to an approach to the problems of knowledge that is traditionally commonplace and radically misleading. This consists in seeking to identify some class of *sentences* in connection with which men allegedly cannot be in error, e.g., first-person reports. This approach we owe to Descartes. It little matters that Descartes chose to discuss it in terms of ideas rather than sentences: the same problems—as we shall see later— arise in either case. The quest for *clear and distinct* ideas is, as a quest for certainty, of a piece with the quest for incorrigible sentences.

II

I shall now present an argument, the conclusion of which yields a cartesian program for epistemology.

(1) By definition, if *p* implies *q*, then *p* expresses a *sufficient condition* for *q*.

(2) By simple logic, if *p* implies *q*, then not-*q* implies not-*p*. But by definition, if not-*q* implies not-*p*, then *q* expresses a *necessary condition* for *p*. So, when *p* expresses a sufficient condition for *q*, *q* expresses a necessary condition for *p*. Necessary and sufficient conditions are 'simultaneous correlatives'.

(3) If something exists, or happens, or is the case, then all the con-

ditions necessary for it to exist, or happen, or be the case, must be satisfied. If so much as one condition necessary for *it* does not hold, then *it cannot* hold. This is a weakened version of the Principle of Sufficient Reason. It does not say that there must be a Sufficient Reason for anything whatever, except that the absence of a necessary condition is a sufficient condition for something *not* to be. And this is compatible with something being in the absence of a sufficient condition.

(4) It is a logical feature of the concept of knowledge that, if *m* knows that *s*, then *m* cannot be in error with regards to *s*. The *consequent* here states a necessary condition for the antecedent. Hence

(5) It follows from (4) and (3) that, if *m* can be in error with regard to *s*, then a condition necessary for *m*'s knowing that *s* fails to hold, so *m* does not know that *s* and, so long as this condition fails to hold, *m cannot* know that *s*.

(6) Hence, in order to establish whether *m* knows that *s*, and for *m* himself to be justified in claiming to know that *s*, it must be established that *m* cannot be in error with regard to *s*. But unless *s* is that sort of sentence with respect to which error is impossible, it is possible that *m* is in error with respect to *s*.

(7) From (6) and (5) it follows that if it is possible for *m* to be in error with respect to *s*, *m does not know that s*. For if *s* is the sort of sentence with respect to which it is possible to be in error, then *m* can be in error with regard to *s*.

(8) It follows that the only sentences expressing knowledge are those in connection with which there is no possibility of error, that is, sentences it is *impossible to doubt*. Unless there are some sentences it is impossible to doubt, then there is nothing we know, and we must resign ourselves to a forlorn skepticism.

(9) So, if we are to avoid skepticism, we must put aside '*tout en quoi (nous pourrions) imaginer le moindre doute*' and seek that in connection with which doubt is unimaginable unless, indeed, '*il n'y a rien au monde du certain*'.[1]

Since the first five lines of this argument impress me as unexceptionable, and since the conclusion strikes me as philosophically fatal, though

[1] René Descartes, *Méditation Seconde*.

that fatal conclusion follows logically from everything after line (6), I am inclined to regard (6) as containing a radical mis-step. The shift, I believe, is this: we inadvertently shift the subject of the sentences we are operating with from m to s, and pass from saying that, if m knows that s, then m cannot be in error, to saying something like, if m knows that s, then s *itself* must somehow be undubitable: as though if we found the right kinds of sentences (ideas), then these would be doubt-proof through some structural feature. I shall discuss in later chapters the structural characterization which is demanded, but for the moment I am interested in the shift from m to s, a shift which must have occurred somewhere in Descartes' thought when he set out so momentously on his search for ideas it would be impossible to doubt. Descartes, indeed, felt that if it were possible to doubt something, then it would be possible for *him* to doubt that thing, and since, if *it* were uncertain, *he* could not be certain, whatever were dubitable might as well be discounted in advance as *false*.[1] And philosophers ever since have acquiesced in this, either seeking to establish the foundations upon one or another type of incorrigibilia, or else, if more critical, denying the whole force of cartesian architectonics by finding pockets of dubitability in whatever blue-chip sentences happen to be favored by cartesians. But the unremitting search for counter-instances to candidate-indubitables is an aggravated transport of Misplaced Slyness. For it accepts implicitly the design of a program its career consists in defeating, namely that if any sentence or idea *could* withstand counter-instantial criticism, why then...But what ought to have been pointed out is that the attainment of certainty does not require that there be such sentences or ideas in the first place. Hence, even if any should be found, they would be mere curiosities, essentially irrelevant to the establishment of knowledge.

I do not wish to suggest, of course, that there might not be some sentences which, by virtue of some internal structural feature would be *un*knowable. There might, comparably, be certain actions which nobody could perform, actions inherently unperformable; just as such

---

[1] '*Je m'efforcerai néanmoins...en m'éloignant de tout en quoi je pourrai imaginer le moindre doute, tout de même que si je connaissais que cela fût absolument faux.*' René Descartes, *Méditation Seconde.*

sentences would be inherently unknowable. There exists an impressive analogy between the theory of knowledge and the theory of action, parts of which I shall endeavor to exploit. But it is just now instructive, perhaps, to consider a cartesian approach to action. Suppose there are, as I suggested, unperformable actions, or what we might think of as *necessary failures*, in that whoever tries to perform one of these fails through the nature of the action. By contrast, there are a great many actions we might speak of as *fallible*. It is possible to try these and fail. Most of what we do is in this respect fallible, that is, we could have failed rather than succeeded in what we did. Of course, if *m* does *a*, it follows that *m* cannot have failed in doing *a* (on the grounds that, necessarily, we cannot both succeed and fail). The contrapositive of this is that, if *m* can have failed in doing *a*, then *m* did not *do a*. This is conspicuously fallacious, but it is in perfect analogy with the cartesian argument we have constructed. And it leaves us with a perfectly analogous program for action, namely, to seek out actions that are *infallible* ('fail-safe'), arguing that we only truly do that in which it is impossible to fail. Hence, if there are no infallible actions, there is no action, there is nothing we ever *do*: and so we must sit down in a forlorn impotency. The argument that we can do only what is infallible is exactly of a piece with the argument that we can know only what is indubitable. Both are very bad arguments.

III

Knowledge is cognitive success as mistakes are cognitive failures; and as one cannot fail and succeed at once, one cannot know and be mistaken at once, since being mistaken is cognitive failure. So it is a trivial and conceptual truth that one cannot be mistaken with regard to *s* if one knows that *s*. But there is certainly another sense of 'can be in error with regard to *s*' which is compatible with, though hardly entailed by '...knows that *s*'. Let *s* be a dubitable sentence: one that sensibly can be doubted. I should wish to argue that every sentence is of this sort, since every sentence just in virtue of being a sentence can be false. But for the moment let *s* be any sentence, which could be false (there must be non-controversially many), and hence which can be doubted, i.e., one can doubt that it is true. Its truth-value is not, as it were, internally determined. Well, if it is possible to be mistaken in connection with *s* no matter in what relationship *s* stands to this individual or that, it follows that *m* can be mistaken with regard to *s*, just because of the kind of sentence *s* is. Now suppose that *m* knows that *s*. From *this* it follows that *m* cannot be mistaken with regard to *s*. So from our two hypotheses, we derive the conclusion that *m* both can and cannot be in error with regard to *s*, which is patently contradictory. If cartesians, we would infer either that *s* is indubitable or that *m* does not know that *s*: at any rate, the hypotheses must be inconsistent.

I contend that there is no inconsistency here because, in the *whole* arguments that appear to yield these incompatible conclusions, the word 'can' has what I shall term a different *scope*. This difference in scope is lost sight of when we isolate the conclusions of these arguments from the contexts that entail them.

Consider this analogy. If I am healthy, I cannot be sick, since these conditions absolutely exclude one another. Yet I am a human being, and everyone knows that human beings can be sick. It follows that *I* can be sick. These arguments are impeccable, with seemingly inconsistent conclusions following validly from unexceptionable premises. But who would argue that '*m* is healthy' is incompatible with '*m* is human'? It is plain what has gone wrong. The word 'cannot' in the first argument has no place in the conclusion of the argument at all. That argument should read: It is impossible that *m* should be healthy and sick at the same time. But *m* is healthy. Therefore, necessarily, *m* is not sick. The 'cannot' gives way to the 'necessarily', but the latter has reference to the relationship between premises and conclusion: its scope is the *argument as a whole*, and it no more belongs with the conclusion than the 'therefore' does. It says, in effect, that the sentence it is attached to is a conclusion, that it is entailed, but it says nothing *internally* about the conclusion. The other argument should read: Whoever is a human being can be sick; *m* is a human being; therefore, necessarily, *m* can be sick. Here the word 'can' belongs to the conclusion since it is part of the predicate. Its scope is internal, and it cannot be broken away from the whole predicative expression 'can be sick'.

But it now is simple to see that the original conclusions were not in-consistent with each other at all. They are compatible: *m* is not sick though he can be sick, since health is not our essence. Our original cartesian argument must be similarly treated. Fallibility is compatible with our essence, since we are not infallible by nature. So, though we do know, it is compatible with our nature that we are in error. But when we sort the scopes of the operative words out, we shall find no inconsistency in saying that, though we cannot be mistaken, we can be. Descartes, whose curious methodological directive we have already remarked (namely, that if *s* could be false, then it *is* false) ought, by parity of argument to have concluded that since it is possible for us to be mistaken, we *are* mistaken. And since he was aware that his was a nature with which error was compatible, he should have concluded that he *never* could be right. But how irrelevant to his quest for certainty this conclusion would have been in the end! It would be like concluding that since it is possible for me to have twenty daughters, my present apartment is incompatible with my needs, since it has not room for twenty daughters. It is an insanely bad reason to look for a twenty-room apartment on the sole ground that it is possible for me to have that many daughters. It is no less bad a reason to restrain myself from claiming to know that *s* on the grounds that I am a fallible creature, or that *s* is a dubitable sentence. It would be equally absurd to *assert* every sentence on the grounds that I can be right, or that the sentence *could* be true.

The word 'can', like the other modalities, has caused no end of philosophical problems, and apart from keeping its scope sorted out, there is a further consideration to which our discussion entitles us. From '*m* knows that *s*', what strictly follows is '*m is* not in error with respect to *s*', not '*m cannot* be in error'. The 'cannot' which appears is, as we argued, external. But the 'can' is uneliminable from '*m* can be sick' if it follows from 'Human beings can be sick and *m* is a human being'. This is not merely because 'can' is part of the predicate, but because of the kind of predicate it helps make. Notice that the sentence in question has no copulative or predicative 'is'. Were one to be artificially made, it would have to go something like this: '*m* [is such that he] can be sick' which leaves the predicate intact. That 'can' is not reducible in favor of a simple 'is' since the 'can' is what we are categorically predicating of *m* to begin with.[1]

IV

These arguments ought to be somewhat liberating, for they exempt us from the traditional epistemological task of attempting to isolate and identify a class of peculiarly indubitable sentences. Our basic sentences, thus, need not be immune to falsity through any internal feature, yet the fact that they are corrigible will constitute no fatally conclusive obstacle against our knowing them to be true. It does not follow that we cannot know that *s*, given that *s* can be false; it does not even follow from the fact that *s* has been false on an inductively impressive number of occasions.

In view of this, a great deal of importance is drained out of the controversy concerning first-person reports. Why insist that these *can* be

---

[1] The appearance of 'can' in the predicate touches upon a problem of abiding philosophical concern, namely whether 'can' is generally eliminable in favor of some such categorical equivalent as 'will...if —', or whether, in 'can F', 'can' already *is* categorical, ascribing a power or capacity to an individual. The problem is complicated by epistemological considerations, or rather, considerations of *meaning*, according to which, for example, the meaning of a sentence is more or less its mode of verification. In this case 'can F' becomes vexing, since its verification via observation is muddy unless one says something to the effect that, observing that *m* is F, or that *m* does F under condition *k*, is one with verifying the sentence '*m* can be F' or '*m* can do F'. In this case, and relative to that theory of meaning, '*m* can be F' *means* 'Under *k*, *m* is F'. But the theory of meaning here is moot, and it is not plain that the verificationist rendering just sketched in fact captures the concept of 'can'. It is not plain, for that matter, that even in its own terms, verificationism can eliminate 'cans' altogether. For consider 'cannot'. By verificationist criteria, this would mean that there is *no* condition *k* under which *m* is F. Even supposing that we exhaustively verified this, i.e., determined by observation that under no condition is *m*, F, would we have exhaustively verified that '*m* cannot be F'? Surely we would want to add that *m* would not be F under *any* condition *k*, or that there *could* not be a condition under which *m is* F. But this illicitly brings in the very notion which was to have been analyzed out. So there is a residuum of meaning in '*m* cannot be F' which is not exhausted by any conjunction of observations to the effect that *m* is not F. A single observation to the effect that under some condition *k*, *m is* F will of course, by the principle that *ab esse ad posse valet illitur*, conclusively verify that *m* can be F. The question only is whether the former is the *meaning* of the latter. If it were, then if *m* is not F under *k* would have to mean that '*m* cannot be F'—and the latter would be exhaustively verified by the former, contrary to our previous conclusion regarding *cannot*. At this point the topic becomes too complex for a casual footnote, i.e., the question becomes *inter alia* whether (*m* can be F) captures the meaning of *m cannot* be F.

corrigible in order to preserve them as genuine knowledge claims, when the fact is that neither the corrigibility nor the incorrigibility of sentences has any *special* relevance to the question of what a man might know or justifiably claim to know? Miss Anscombe has maintained that 'There is point in speaking of knowledge only where a contrast exists between "He knows" and "He (merely) thinks he knows"'.[1] And since there is apparently *no* point in saying 'He thinks he knows that he is in pain', I suppose it follows that there is no point in speaking of knowledge here at all. But it is not that there is no point in saying that someone thinks he is in pain: it is that any such claim is false, presumably through the nature of pain itself. All that presumably *could* be false is the logically distinct claim that someone incorrectly thinks that what he feels is correctly called 'pain'. The proper response to Miss Anscombe's claim is *not* to try to find cases where a man *might* properly be said to think himself in pain (and be wrong), but to emphasize that the alleged incorrigibility of first-person reports is beside the point, that the whole issue is correctly diagnosed as Misplaced Slyness. If Descartes was ill-advised in seeking incorrigibilia (amongst which he of course counted first-person reports), we are equally ill-advised in seeking to destroy cartesianism by arguing what must after all be a rather silly point, that we don't really know, that we can't really *say* we know that we are in pain. And the fact is that when a man knows something, there *is* in one respect no room—whether what he knows is that he is in pain or some other thing—for his being in error with regard to it—for his merely, in Miss Anscombe's words, 'thinking he knows'. For I take her words to mean 'does not know'.

---

[1] G. E. M. Anscombe, *Intention* (Oxford; Basil Blackwell, 1957), p. 14. Here Miss Anscombe explicitly denies 'that being able to say where one feels pain is a case of something known'. If a man complains of pain in his foot but nurses his hand, then it would be 'difficult to guess what [he] could mean'. Whereas, with a man who claims his leg is bent when it is straight, 'He is wrong in what he says but not unintelligible'. Aside from being hermetic, these remarks impress me merely as arbitrary. If we assimilate pain to pain-behavior, the first man is wrong in what he says but intelligible. And if we do not, it is hard to see what these baroque strategies come to.

V

Basic sentences have been crucial in traditional epistemological discussion for the two reasons that they seemed to be required as expressing our ultimate evidence, and that, independently of that, they seemed to be uniquely constituted as expressions of what we could safely claim to know. They could, of course, play the latter role and be utterly useless to anyone save an epistemologist morbidly fixated upon certitude. Our whole concern with basic sentences is hinged to the conception that they are not isolated in the security alleged to attach to them, but perform a function in the architectonic of cognition. Yet it is their alleged certitude that is our immediate concern; in this connection we might ask why basic sentences should be so highly regarded. Granted that, if we know that *s* directly, it follows that we cannot be wrong, this consequence, as I have argued, would follow from the bare fact that one knows that *s*, independently of the manner or mode of knowledge. So what is so especially felicitous about basic sentences?

One consideration is perhaps this. Suppose we specified a set [*k*] of conditions under which *m* knows that *s*. Then if *s* is a basic sentence for *m*, [*k*] might contain fewer elements than if *s* were other than basic, and there would accordingly be fewer ways in which things might have gone wrong. Since a basic sentence *s* for *m* is characterized as *directly* known by *m*, hence not *in fact* known by *m* because *m* has evidence *e* for *s*, there is at least no gap between *e* and *s* which must be closed by inference. And the superstition is that the fewer gaps there are, the less hollow space there is for skepticism to haunt. We are all familiar with views according to which there is true knowledge only when there is a perfect congruence between 'knower and known'—which is perhaps why first-person reports have been so particularly favored in theories of knowledge: presumably we are totally coincident with ourselves, knowers and knowns in one seamless fabric.[1] Epis-

---

[1] 'There is at least one reality which all grasp from within by intuition and not by simple analysis. This is our own self in its course through time...We can never sympathize intellectually with any other object. But we certainly sympathize with ourselves.' Henri Bergson, *Introduction to Metaphysics* (Boston; John W. Luce, 1912), p. 12. 'We are not merely the knowing subject, but in another aspect, we ourselves also belong to the inner nature that is to be known, *we ourselves are the thing in itself*...therefore,

temologists have thus been concerned to achieve a cognitive *plenum*, and have supposed that gaps must be bridged by inference, and that where there is inference there is chronic insecurity.

It is a theme of this book that there are always gaps, that these are what make knowledge possible. I cannot develop this theme until later chapters have brought us to a point where the logic of such gaps becomes perspicuous. But here we might at least ask what is so perilous about inference as such. Men do of course often infer to conclusions which are wrong, or to which their evidence does not entitle them, but one can only naively suppose an interesting skepticism could be erected upon the thesis that we might always have made an error in inference as such. For suppose one argued that, since error in inference is always possible, we can never be certain of any sentence *s* unless we know directly that *s*, unless all inference is eliminated from the conditions [*k*] that must be satisfied in case we are to know that *s*. This is not a skeptical consequence that could be established. For it certainly could not be established by *argument*, for in that case it would turn savagely against itself: if we can always make mistakes in inference, then we might have made one here. And if for some reason the particular inferences involved in this argument are secure from doubt, then the conclusion of the argument is false, since the argument provides a counter-instance to itself. Since one of the premisses must be false, what more obvious candidate for doubt than the premiss that holds that we might *always* make an error in inference? So no argument can establish this consequence and, unless by argument, it is difficult to see how it could be established. For we certainly do not know it directly. There can, then, be no general interesting argument against inference as such. Descartes, in fact, whose capacities for detecting spaces for inserting skeptical

a way from within stands open for us to that inner nature belonging to things in themselves, to which we cannot penetrate from *without*.' Arthur Schopenhauer, *The World as Will and Idea*, Supplement to the Second Book, chapter xviii. The decisive answer to these views is due to Santayana: 'Knowledge is not eating, and we cannot expect to devour and possess *what we mean*. Knowledge is recognition of something absent, it is a salutation, not an embrace. It is an advance on sensation precisely *because* it is representative.' George Santayana, *Reason in Common Sense* (New York; Scribners, 1905), p. 78. What Santayana says has application even to self-knowledge. If just being ourselves is no advantage so far as knowledge of ourselves is concerned, not being something else *need* be no *disadvantage* so far as knowledge regarding it is concerned.

wedges amounted almost to a form of genius, has an argument to establish that it is impossible for us to make a mistake in deduction.[1] This is excessive, but perhaps, since there can be no true Inferential Skepticism (as we might call it), such doubts as might be raised in connection with inference are in principle discoverable, and hence of no ultimate concern to a proper skeptic.

Philosophers wary of inference have been so not because it is inference, nor because of reservations concerning their own inferential prowess. Rather, they have doubted that inferential principles of the sort crucially required are to be met with, granted that if there were such principles, mere application of them in deductive contexts would not be impossibly hazardous. Consider, for mere illustration, the common syllogistic inference from 'a is F' to 'a is G' via the major premiss 'All that is F is G'. There is an *a priori* metaphysical theory, taken seriously at least since Hume, that no two events, nor parts of the world, nor states of things, nor stages of events—no two distinct states of the world, in brief—are so related that one of them *must* be so, given that the other *is* so. It follows that each state of the world is independent of each other state, so that whatever happens, *however* it happens, is compatible with anything else that happens, however *it* happens. So, although it is true that Socrates is mortal, since all men are and he is a man, no inconsistency in the universe would result were he instead to be immortal: at best the odds are against it. The falsity, then, of 'a is G' is always consistent with the truth of 'a is F'. Since, however, the inference to the former from the latter via 'All that is F is G' is immaculate, our only recourse is to suppose a weakness in this major

---

[1] René Descartes, *Règles pour la direction de l'esprit*, II, 'Il faut noter, en outre, que les expériences sont souvent trompeuses, mais que la déduction, ou la simple inférence d'une chose à partir d'une autre, peut sans doute être omise si on ne l'aperçoit pas, mais ne saurait être mal faite même par l'entendement le moins capable de raisonner... En effet, toutes les erreurs où peuvent tomber les hommes (et non les bêtes, bien entendu) ne proviennent jamais d'une mauvaise inférence...' This is repeated and emphasized in Règle III: 'La déduction...ne peut pas être mal faite par l'homme.' Nevertheless, intuition 'étant plus simple, est par suite plus sûre que la déduction'. Moreover, Descartes supposes that any knowledge arrived at deductively in part 'reçoit sa certitude de la mémoire'. But neither its greater complexity nor its reliance upon memory are counted by him as disqualifying, since arithmetic and geometry, which 'sont beaucoup plus certaines que les autres sciences...consistent tout entières en une suite de conséquences déduit par raisonnement'. *Règle* II.

premiss. It cannot guarantee the incompatibility of a false conclusion with a true minor premiss unless—contrary to the metaphysical theory just noted—it truly asserts a *descriptive necessity* in the world. Unless it does so, we can be no more certain of the conclusion than we are of it; and since *it* could be false, inferences from true minor premisses to conclusions, however logically proper, are never exempt from doubt. And it is descriptively necessary sentences which the inference-shy philosopher despairs of finding.

This has immediate application to questions of evidence, inasmuch as we commonly take one state of the world to be evidence for another, *viz.*, the humanity of Socrates for the mortality of Socrates. If the falsity of '*a* is G' as well as the truth of '*a* is G' are indifferently compatible with the truth of '*a* is F', there is always the long chance that we are wrong in claiming to know that *a* is G when our evidence only is that *a* is F. So how can we be justified *ever* in claiming to know because we have evidence, in case we are justified in claiming to know only when we do know, since inferential principles of the required sort are lacking? Consider, for its immediate relevance, a further cartesian program for illustration.

Descartes supposed that *all* our evidence must be drawn from states of ourselves, expressed as first-person reports. So, unless some inferential principle could be validated which could carry us from any such sentence to any sentence *s* not a first-person report, i.e., to an *s* about the *world*, then the truth and falsity alike of *s* will be compatible with any evidence *we* may have. So, for all I know or can know, *s* is false, and it may as well be false, given that neither its truth nor its falsity casts a differentiating shadow upon any state of myself. '*La raison me persuade,*' Descartes concluded, '*que je ne dois pas moins soigneusement m'empecher de donner créance aux choses qui ne sont pas entièrement certaines et indubitables, qu'à celles qui nous paraissent manifestement être fausses*'.[1] And surely Descartes was right: if, consistently with anything I know or I *can* know, *s* might be false, then I can always be in error with regard to *s* in a manner which exactly rules out my knowing that *s*. So, until he found relief in ontological argumentation, there arose for him the haunting possibility that the world—if

[1] René Descartes, *Méditation Première.*

there *were* a world—would be radically discrepant with his representation of it. Unless, of course, there is a descriptively necessary connection between world and representation: a kind of pre-established harmony.

Such a principle as Descartes sought would have to be *a priori* and not in any way based upon experience, for I cannot *experience* the congruity of representation and world, unless I occupy the space between the two where I can check the one against the other. As it happens, a thesis of the present book is that this cartesian program is misconceived, and that we are *defined* through the fact that we exactly occupy the space between representations of the world and the world. We do not, I shall argue, require a transcendental principle to transport us from evidence of the world to the world. Once within the world, an analogous problem remains of going by secure inferential methods from one state of the world to another, and so of finding anything resembling *adequate* evidence *ici-bas*.

Now it is of course an extremely bold claim that each state of the world is logically independent of each other state. It is less bold—and Hume himself argued for nothing stronger—to claim that however intimate the connection between states of the world, *we* at least can only know that as a matter of fact, certain states of the world are constantly conjoined. On the plausible view that one state of the world is evidence for another, we hardly can expect stronger evidential connections than we are in a position to suppose that we can establish *causal* connections. And given that a pair of world-states has been *always* noted in conjunction with one another, still, Hume famously argues, we have no basis for supposing they always *must* be, and his problem concerning the justification of induction is basically a challenge to those who suppose they may elevate the 'is' of conjunction into the 'must be' of entailment. What in *experience*, he asked, could correspond to this *must*?

I shall not press this query further here. I only note the consequence that if the challenge is not met, we only can justifiably claim to know what we know directly. But let us, just for the moment, entertain the fantasy that the challenge has been met, and that inferential principles are available by means of which we may proceed with impunity from *e* to *s* in such a manner that the falsity of *s* is incompatible with the truth of *e*, and that we can justifiably then claim to know that *s* because we have evidence.

VI

Imagine *m* as possessing evidence *e* for *s* such that it is impossible that *s* should be false when *e* is true. We may then say that *e* *entails* *s*, since this is what 'impossible for *s* to be false if *e* is true' must finally mean. And we shall now say that *m* may justifiably claim to know that *s* even if *m* does not know directly that *s*, providing that *m* knows that *e* and *e* entails *s*. I am not at the moment concerned to defend this characterization of knowledge of non-basic sentences, but only in stressing that in order for there to be knowledge of this sort at all, there must be a sentence, distinct from *e* and *s*, and such that, if this sentence be *r*, it is difficult to suppose *m* could justifiably claim to know that *s* on the basis of *e* if *m* did not know that *r*. Now *r* is this sentence: '*e* entails *s*'. The question before us is whether *m* knows that *r*.

It is implausible to suppose that *m* should know that *r* because *r* is entailed by some set [*p*] of premises, however characterized, which *m* happens to know. For then there must be a sentence exactly like *r*, and puzzling in whatever way in which *r* may be puzzling, of this sort: '[*p*] entails *r*'. The question then must arise as to how *m* knows *this* sentence. Nor will it serve to suppose it is known inferentially. Plainly, we have once more the sort of situation which yields an infinite regression. From that we may gather that while in fact *r* itself might have been derived inferentially from premises which entail it, not every such sentence as *r* could be known that way. And this leaves the alternative that these sentences must in some instances be basic, must be known *directly*.

I do not wish to rule it out that *r* might be known directly. It is only that it seems to differ from such paradigm basic sentences as first-person reports, for example. When we think of a sentence *s* corresponding to just what *m* experiences, we think, perhaps, of a light flashing, or of the grass in a field stirring, or a whistle sounding. These, though not first-person reports, are things a man might say he knows directly, and not on the basis of any evidence. Here we are being only as precise as our analysis to this point permits us to be. But at this crude level, there are certain claims to direct knowledge which we would disallow. For what are the limits of direct knowledge after all? There are many things I in fact know, if at all, because I have evidence for them. But the same sentence which is non-basic for me need not be non-basic as such, and though I may not, *m* may know directly that *s*. And it may be that there are sentences which, if anyone in fact knows them, he knows them non-directly and as a consequence of possessing evidence for them. Yet it is conceivable that someone might know them directly. Until we could draw a logical limit, we could not identify any class of sentences as inherently non-basic. Thus God is alleged to know not only all there is to know, being omniscient, but to know everything directly, so that every sentence *s*, of which it is sensible to suppose that '*x* knows that *s*' could be true, *would* be basic if *x* were God. 'The manner in which God knows the infinitude of propositions is utterly more excellent than the manner in which we know the few that do,' wrote Galileo,[1] 'for we proceed by argumentation and advance from conclusion to conclusion, while God apprehends through a sudden, simple intuition.' Yet this would not especially help with our problem concerning *r* and all sentences like *r*. For let us take the point of view this theological perspective affords. We go from *e* to *s* by inference from evidence. For us, *s* is non-basic. But for God, *s* would be basic, as would all true sentences. But God has no use for inferences, and hence requires no such sentence as *r*. And this is where the difficulty appears. It is not only that we need *r* because not all sentences are basic

---

[1] Galileo Galilei, *Dialogo sopra i due Massimi Sistemi del Mondo*, in *Opere* (Florence; Edi. Naz., 1929–39), I. St Thomas argues that God's knowledge cannot in general be discursive, in part because this would require knowing *first* one thing, *then* another, which is incompatible as a temporal process with acknowledged divine attributes; in part because it means going from known to unknown, and the latter category is illicit here. Thomas distinguishes between knowing something *from*, and knowing something *in* something else, the latter being the case with God: 'God sees the effects of created causes in the causes themselves, much better than we can, but still not in such a manner that the knowledge of the effects is caused in Him by the knowledge of the created causes, as is the case with us.' *Summa Theologica*, Question 14, art. 7. This means that God must know everthing directly, and any question asking how God knows, which would receive an answer of the form 'I know because...' is ruled out. The distinction, incidentally, answers to the highest and the penultimate types of knowledge recognized in Spinoza's scheme in *Improvement of the Understanding*.

for us. It is that *r*'s role seems to be that of relating sentences which could in principle be basic, but which happen not to be so for us. But is that which relates what are in principle basic sentences itself a basic sentence? It seems in some vague sense to belong to a different level than the sentences it relates. In an idiom we have used before, it does not seem to belong to the surface of language nor to describe some feature of the world. Yet it also seems strange to suppose we do not know that *r*. And if *we* know that *r*, so must God, on the standard assumption. And then *r* would have to be basic, in principle at least. But this leaves the question of how it *could* be basic for *us*, given that, for us at least, it is demonstrable that not every sentence of the same type as *r* could be known through inference.

VII

Consider once again the analogy with the theory of action. There are many things we do of which it would be correct to say we *cause* them to happen: we burn pieces of paper, we cure people's headaches, we knock over chairs, we move stones. But by contrast, there are other things we do directly: not by causing them to happen, but by doing them, as it were, without causing them to happen. These, in analogy with basic sentences, I speak of as *basic actions*.[1] Thus, I raise my arm as a basic action, or I frame a mental image of a triangle, and so forth. There are amongst us many who are specially gifted, in being able to do, as basic actions, certain things which normal agents can at best do by causing them to happen. In these respects they are *positively abnormal*. And then there are others, who only can do by causing to happen what the rest of us commonly do directly. These are *negatively abnormal*. There is no causal route which a positively abnormal agent follows in doing that in which his abnormality consists: he just does it without doing anything else which stands to it as cause to effect. Normal persons find it hard to understand this, much as negatively abnormal

---

[1] Basic actions, and the analogy between the theories of knowledge and of action are explored in my papers 'What we Can Do', *Journal of Philosophy*, xv, 15 (1963), 435–45; 'Basic Actions', *American Philosophical Quarterly*, ii, 2 (1965), 141–8; 'Freedom and Forbearance', in Keith Lehrer (ed.), *Freedom and Determinism* (New York; Random House, 1966), pp. 45–63.

persons find it hard to understand how normal agents do what they do. But it is generally the case that we are up against a metaphysical blank wall, of the most perplexing opacity, when we undertake to perform, as a basic action, something which lies outside our repertoire of basic acts. I should want, in fact, to argue that we could not sensibly even *try* this: the ability to perform basic actions is a gift, and a gift is just that: something which cannot be acquired save through having it given you.

Now comparably with all of this, there are things each of us knows or can come to know directly, certain sentences which are within our repertoire of basic sentences. There are those who are negatively abnormal, lacking 'gifts', e.g., the 'gift of sight' and so can only know by inference what others can know directly. And there are persons with what I think of as 'sixth senses', which confer positive abnormality upon them, e.g., persons who discriminate colors by touch, or can sense directly certain electromagnetic signals to which normal percipients are blind (deaf? insensitive?). We can, of course, by intermediating devices, know what recorded signals such a person gets directly, and so stand to such a person in something like the relationship in which the blind, for example, stand to us who are normal with regard to the theory of knowledge. There are questions, of course, of how far we might sensibly suppose ourselves capable of evolving in the direction of positive abnormality, but I have no way of determining what limits there are, or if there are any. Most of us would, I think, have to compute, or at least look at a long-range calendar, in order to know on what day of the week 15 February 2002 will fall. But there are idiot savants who appear to know these sorts of things directly. They answer the sort of question to which 'Friday' is an answer instantly and unthinkingly, and are always correct. So they might be said to know such things directly: they have a gift. To be sure, their brains may be equipped with rather a remarkable circuitry, but that is irrelevant to the exercise of a gift in just the way in which the fact that my arm is neurologically complex to whatever degree necessary for me to perform basic actions with it is irrelevant to my performing those basic actions. That is, I activate the nervous network by raising my arm, not the other way round. I of course can check up on the idiot savants, and nothing they know is beyond my ken except the manner in which they know it. But so again I can cause to happen almost anything which a positively abnormal agent can do, so that nothing lies outside my power save the manner in which it is done. This, I think, was close to Galileo's point. There was in principle nothing known to God which lies ultimately outside our ken, but the manner of knowledge is what separates us from divinity plus the fact that whatever we *can* know God, who is perfectly actualized, *does* know. And comparably in the theory of action, we perhaps *can* do whatever God in fact *does*, except he does directly what we must *cause* to happen.

The analogy between theory of knowledge and theory of action may be protracted to a considerable distance, but I wish to concentrate on one sector of it now. It appears that the relationship '— causes —' plays a role in the theory of action at just that point where '— entails —' plays a corresponding role in the theory of knowledge. Since the two theories sustain parallel development we might be able, by refraction as it were from the theory of action, to achieve a degree of insight into this troublesome node in the theory of knowledge.

Suppose that m does a (symbolically $m\mathrm{D}a$) and that a causes b (symbolically $a\mathrm{C}b$). Does it follow that $m\mathrm{D}b$? In other words, under the condition described, is b to be taken as an action of m's, or is b but the *consequence* of an action? We mark some sort of difference in the topic of responsibility, regarding, as a general rule, only certain of the consequences of an action of m as further actions of his. And roughly speaking, I think we make the distinction more or less as follows. If $m\mathrm{D}a$ and $a\mathrm{C}b$, then $m\mathrm{D}b$ only if $m\mathrm{D}(a\mathrm{C}b)$. But if it is not the case that $m\mathrm{D}(a\mathrm{C}b)$ (symbolically $\mathrm{N}(m\mathrm{D}(a\mathrm{C}b))$), then, even if $m\mathrm{D}a$, b is only a consequence of what he does, and not an action of his. We may represent this as follows:

$$
\begin{array}{ll}
\textrm{I} \quad m\mathrm{D}a & \textrm{II} \quad m\mathrm{D}a \\
\quad\;\; a\mathrm{C}b & \quad\;\; a\mathrm{C}b \\
\quad\;\; \underline{m\mathrm{D}(a\mathrm{C}b)} & \quad\;\; \underline{\mathrm{N}(m\mathrm{D}(a\mathrm{C}b))} \\
\quad\;\; m\mathrm{D}b & \quad\;\; \mathrm{N}(m\mathrm{D}b)
\end{array}
$$

Invariant to the two cases is that b happens because of a, and that m does a (i.e., a is an action). To an external observer, the two cases might look exactly alike, and there need be no external difference: the difference between (I) mDa and aCb and (II) mDa and $mD(aCb)$ is merely in the punctuation, as it were: the brackets do not belong to 'nature'. But let us proceed to the analogue in the theory of knowledge. We replace descriptions of events with descriptions of sentences, replace 'does' with 'knows' (D with K) and 'causes' with 'entails' (C with E). Then

$$
\begin{array}{ll}
\text{I}' \quad mKe & \text{II}' \quad mKe \\
\quad\;\; eEs & \quad\;\; eEs \\
\quad\;\; mK(eEs) & \quad\;\; N(mK(eEs)) \\
\hline
\quad\;\; mKs & \quad\;\; N(mKs)
\end{array}
$$

Here the question concerned is whether m knows whatever is entailed by what he knows, or whether only certain of the consequences of what he knows can be counted as knowledge of his.[1] And just as we supposed that a consequence of an action is an action in its own right only if the *causing* were an action, so here we suppose that the consequence of a piece of knowledge is a piece of knowledge in its own right only if the *entailing* is known. The natural question at this point is how we are to analyze the doing of a causing and the knowing of an entailing, and then whether there are any helpful analogies. But before broaching either of these, there is an important disanalogy which demands elucidation. Let us consider these schemas:

$$
\begin{array}{ll}
\text{III} \quad N(mDa) & \text{III}' \quad N(mKe) \\
\qquad aCb & \qquad eEs \\
\qquad mD(aCb) & \qquad mK(eEs) \\
\hline
\qquad N(mDb) & \qquad N(mKs)
\end{array}
$$

The disanalogy seems to lie in the fact that III′ makes sense while III does not. It does not because it does not obviously make sense to say that m performs the action of a-causing-b without doing the action a.

[1] If m knows that p, and p entails q, then m knows that q: this is a thesis of Jaako Hintikka in his *Knowledge and Belief* (Ithaca; Cornell University Press, 1962). As such it is criticized, amongst others, by Hector Neri-Castañeda, in his review of the latter in *Journal of Symbolic Logic*, XXIX (1964), 132–4. Hintikka replies that this consequence holds only in an 'epistemologically perfect world', and in ours so far as it approaches that. See his '"Knowing Oneself" and other problems in Epistemic Logic', *Theoria*, XXXII, 11 (1966), 1–13.

So the two descriptions do not seem cotenable. On the other hand, a man can know that *e* entails *s* without knowing *e*, so that the matching pair of premisses here are cotenable. Since it cracks at so crucial a point, the analogy we have been spinning out fails to help where it is needed. But since the analogy impresses me as too extensive to be jettisoned carelessly, I should like to suggest a way in which it could be naturally rehabilitated.

First of all, consider under what conditions a man is most plausibly held responsible for the consequence *b* of an action *a*. I think the simplest set of conditions are these: he must know there is a connection between *a* and *b*, and he must act in the light of that knowledge. You cannot act in the light of knowledge you do not have, but you can have knowledge in the light of which you don't act. At any rate, we might now replace $mD(aCb)$ in III with the conjunction $mK(aCb)$ and $mAK(aCb)$—where the right-hand conjunct reads '*m* applies the knowledge that *a* causes *b*'. There is, then, a cognitive element in action. But then there is an actional element, as we may call it, in cognition. For once more, we might distinguish knowing that there is an entailment relationship between *e* and *s* and acting in the light of that knowledge, in this case actually drawing the inference from *e* to *s*. And we might then replace $mK(eEs)$ with the conjunction $mK(eEs)$ and $mAK(eEs)$, where the right-hand conjunction is to read '*m* applies the knowledge that *e* entails *s*'.

Now let us return to III. It still describes an impossible situation. If *m* knows that *a* causes *b*, then he cannot both apply that knowledge and not do *a*. It then is false that $mD(aCb)$ if it is the case that $N(mDa)$. But in III' we now find an exact parallel. For *m* may know that *e* entails *s*, but he cannot both have and apply this knowledge if he does not know that *e*. So III' is ruled out in whatever way in which III is ruled out: it is false that $mK(eEs)$ and $mAK(eEs)$, in case $N(mKe)$. So by analyzing more or less what is involved in 'doing a causing' we are able to restore the analogy in a fairly natural way.

But now the question faces us as to where all this *bricolage* has brought us, and it is not precisely easy to say. Yet there is one thing which bears some comment. It is that in our action—theoretical expansion of III, we have what appears to be an instance of knowledge which does not give way to an analogy in which the K is replaced by D. Its un-assimilability to the description of an action is conspicuous because of the context of D's. Its counterpart in III′ is *inconspicuous* because it appears in a context of K's. So perhaps we are dealing here with knowledge of rather a different sort than might at first have appeared, and its difference would be revealed through the analogy. Certainly, if in the case of III we would say that it was knowledge *in the light of which m acts*, it seems plausibly symmetrical to propose that its counter-part in III′ is knowledge *in the light of which m knows*. And this at least would suggest that it is of a different type than that which we might know *in* its light.

VIII

It remains to be seen how useful any of this is. To conclude that we are dealing here with 'knowledge of a different type' is at best suggested by an analogy which many might find unpersuasive, and by a metaphor i.e., 'in the light of' which many might find merely picturesque. I shall propose an analysis at a later point which I hope will be persuasive. But it is worth noting *en passant* that should we find in the course of an analysis that we require a form of knowledge which as a type is demonstrably incapable of being inferred and, again as a type, it seems anomalous to suppose could be known directly, it is very natural to the philosophical temper to conclude we are dealing with knowledge which is *innate*. So much is suggested by the expression 'in the light of' which is redolent of the so-called 'natural light'—the *lumière naturelle*— appeals to which are made at critical junctures, for example, in *Méditation* III. For knowledge which we have and which cannot easily be supposed as acquired would seem *somehow* as though it would have had to be born within us. That would be a deep consequence of our argument, and I am not philosophically an adversary of such an idea.

Nevertheless, it is unplausible to suppose, when we turn to our analogy with the theory of action, that the knowledge in the light of which we act may commonly be appreciated as a deliverance of the *lumière naturelle*. When I tap an egg in order to crack it, I apply my knowledge that eggs, when tapped sufficiently forcefully, will crack. It can hardly be the natural light which guides me here. And when one uses an analogy seriously, as I have done, one is obliged to use it consistently.

The analogy is weakened in some measure by the consideration that we have made use of the notion of 'responsibility' which is, perhaps, too legalistic and too much an institutionally varying one, to be of any absolute philosophical utility. Thus a man might be held responsible for doing *b* when he does *a* and he *believes* that *a* causes *b*. His belief was right, as it happened, but the point is that standards of assigning responsibility are sufficiently permissive that we can be said to act in the light of beliefs, and be said to do whatever is a consequence of what we do, in case we believed it would be a consequence. But nothing like this will work for knowledge. For how could we propose that *m* knows that *s*, given that *m* knows that *e* and even given that *e* entails *s*, if *m* does not know but only *believes* that *e* entails *s*? Certainly *m* would hardly be justified in claiming, under those circumstances, to know that *s*. For in saying that he merely believed that *s* follows from what he knows, he is placing, as it were, a form of disclaimer on *s*, which conflicts, as a performance, with assertion of *s*. Well, he might none the less be said to know. Then here would be a case where a man knows but is not justified in claiming to know. But perhaps this is as good a point as any to take up the topic of belief and its connection with knowledge. We may be better fortified then to shoulder the difficult questions which have latterly been exercising us.

4

KNOWLEDGE AND BELIEF

I

It has been standard in epistemological texts to offer an analysis of knowledge which consists of a psychological, a semantical, and a doxastic component, e.g., *m* knows that *s* if, and only if, (1) *m* believes that *s*, (2) *s* is true, and (3) *m* possesses adequate evidence for *s*.[1] The component (2) has been commonplace in philosophy more or less since Parmenides, and will not be queried here. Latterly the adequacy of the Standard analysis (as I shall term it) has been questioned,[2] in large measure because of the independence of (2) and (3); but whether this means that a fourth component should be added, specifying that the connection between (2) and (3) is not absolutely contingent, or whether this should be built into our conception of evidential adequacy, has yet to be determined by advocates of the Standard analysis. For that matter, there ought comparably to be a question of the connection between (1) and (3), inasmuch as we may moot the claim that *m* knows

---

[1] 'We know *p* when (1) *p* is true and (2) we believe *p* to be true...[and] (3) There must be complete evidence that *p* is true.' John Hospers, *An Introduction to Philosophical Analysis* (Englewood Cliffs, New Jersey; Prentice-Hall, 1953), pp. 146–8. Roderick Chisholm, in his *Perceiving: A Philosophical Study* (Ithaca, New York; Cornell University Press, 1957), offers the analysis: '"S knows that *h* is true" means: (i) S accepts the hypothesis (or proposition) that...; (ii) S has adequate evidence for the hypothesis (or proposition) that...; and (iii) *h* is true.' p. 16. And in the sense of 'believes' which has the same sense as 'accepts': 'knowing entails believing'. p. 17. Similar tripartite analyses may be found in J. O. Urmson, 'Parenthetical Verbs', *Mind*, LXI, 244 (1952), 480–96; Jaakko Hintikka, *Knowledge and Belief* (Ithaca, New York; Cornell University Press, 1962), pp. 19–20. One or another variant on the same structure might be called The Standard Analysis. It is at worst contended that these will constitute a necessary if not a jointly sufficient condition for '...knows that...'. See next note.

[2] Edmund Gettier, 'Is Justified True Belief Knowledge?', *Analysis*, XXIII, 6 (1963), 121–3. Gettier's paper has released a string of ingenious counter-proposals and augmentations See Michael Clark, 'Knowledge and Grounds: a Comment on Mr Gettier's Paper', *Analysis*, XXIV, 1 (1963), 46–7; Ernest Sosa, 'The Analysis of "Knowledge that P"', *Analysis*, XXV, 1 (1964), 1–3; John Turk Saunders and Narayan Champawat, 'Mr Clark's Definition of "Knowledge"', *ibid.* 3–7. Keith Lehrer, 'Knowledge, Truth, and Evidence', *Analysis*, XXV, 5 (1965), 168–75; Gilbert Harman, 'Lehrer on Knowledge', *Journal of Philosophy*, LXIII, 9 (1966), 241–7.

that *s*, given that he possesses adequate evidence for *s* and believes that *s*, unless he believes it *because* he possesses adequate evidence. It is ingenuous to suppose that possessing adequate evidence *compels* belief, and inasmuch as a man may then, consistently with possessing adequate evidence, not believe or even disbelieve *s*, there is plainly room for supposing that he might believe *s*, only for quite extrinsic and fortuitous reasons. Well, we might say even so that he knows that *s*, but in that event the requirement that (1) figure in the *analysis* of *m knows that s* comes up for question.

With these deep matters I shall not for the present be concerned. Rather, I shall settle for the weak observation that the Standard analysis is but one of a class of what I shall designate as Compatibilist theories of the relationship between knowledge and belief, Compatibilism being defined through its holding only that the *denial* of '*m* believes that *s*' is *not* entailed by '*m* knows that *s*'. The strongest version of Compatibilism is that in which '*m* believes that *s*' is entailed by '*m* knows that *s*', *viz.*, as part of the meaning of the latter. Such is the case with the Standard analysis of the preceding paragraph, where the entailment is perhaps not as interesting as it might be if (1) were entailed by '*m* knows that *s*' because (1) were entailed by (3).

I am concerned to identify the Compatibilist status of the Standard analysis, only because of some exceedingly traditional philosophical views, according to which the *denial* of '*m* believes that *s*' *is* entailed by '*m* knows that *s*', so that '*m* believes that *s*' is incompatible with '*m* knows that *s*'. All such theories I shall designate as Incompatibilist. Incompatiblism has been a philosophical commonplace since (at least) Plato, and I am inclined to suppose that philosophy itself begins with a distinction between knowledge and belief which borders upon Incompatiblism. It begins here, rather than with pronouncements that the world is made of water (or fire, or gods), although perhaps is encouraged by the incompatibility of the latter sweeping claims with common sense. For if these claims are true, the world must really be different from what it appears, and the distinction between knowledge and belief may then have been introduced to explain the discrepancy. Belief and knowledge would then be incompatible to the degree that appearance and reality are construed to be.

But these historical speculations to one side, we hardly can be said to have much clarity with regard to the concept of knowledge until we have ascertained whether Compatibilism in some form, or Incompatibilism in some form is correct. A concept which at once is said to entail another concept, *not* to entail that other concept, and to entail the negation of that concept, cannot be regarded as conspicuously lucid. And while it may be argued that all the obscurity here lies in the concept of belief, the fact remains that the two concepts have so long a history of association that any darkness or opacity in the one must cast a shadow upon the other, so I shall attempt, within the compass of this chapter, at least to raise the shadows slightly.

II

Incompatibilists have, I believe, been impressed by the fact that knowledge and belief appear to be *alternative* concepts. In English, thus, '*m* believes that *s*' and '*m* knows that *s*' appear to be equally suitable answers to the grammatically intelligible question, 'Does he believe or does he know that *s*?' We must be wary of using what may prove merely parochial features of a local language as evidence for philosophical theories of any magnitude, but there is impressive support for my claim in the treatment of knowledge and belief in the tradition. A necessary condition for *alternativity* is that the alleged alternatives have a recoverable common grammatical structure, which '...knows ...' and '...believes...' appear always to have. It then becomes a matter of determining that place in the structure, alternations in which determine which, if any, of a set of alternatives is true. Thus it is differences in color which determine which of '*a* is red' and '*a* is blue' is true. The question now is: What is it, variations in which determines the difference between knowledge and belief? And this, I argue, is a question whose sensibility presupposes parallel grammars for '... knows...' and '...believes...'.

Two main kinds of answers have been given, depending upon whether knowledge or belief has antecedently been taken as the clearer of the two. Thus, it seems to many thinkers incontestable that belief is a state, probably a psychological state of persons, so that in saying that *m* believes that *s*, we are ascribing some condition to *m*. Now, if we accept the tacit assumption that knowledge and belief have parallel grammars, we shall equally be supposing that, in saying that *m* knows that *s*, we shall be ascribing some condition, perhaps a psychological condition, alternative to belief, to *m*. But whereas it is likely that belief *is* a state or condition of individuals, it is doubtful whether *knowledge* is.

The theory just sketched I shall designate the Subject theory. Another sort of theory is this. It has seemed to many thinkers that knowledge is a *relation* between individuals and something recognized as the *object* of knowledge. To know that *s* is then to stand in some relation R to some object *o*, where *o* is what makes *s* true. If knowledge and belief are alternates, i.e., determinates of the same determinable, then belief, too, must be a relationship, and there must accordingly be *objects of belief*. That the difference between knowledge and belief might consist in *different* relations to the *same* object—the object of knowledge and of belief depending upon which of these relations were satisfied— would be a plausible account if there only were *true* belief. But there is false belief as well which, if belief is relational, must have *its* object. Presumably this will not be the object of knowledge, and so, speaking crudely, the idea that it is relations which alternate gives way to the view that it is *objects* which alternate: knowledge differs from belief as *objects* of knowledge differ from *objects* of belief. This I shall term the Object theory.

The Subject and the Object theory have been held, in various forms, by deep and serious thinkers. Each theory has one intuitive datum in its support, *viz.*, it is intuitive that belief is a condition of individuals and that knowledge has objects. But since each theory is committed, apparently, to the alternativity of knowledge and belief, each is also committed to a quite *unintuitive* consequence, namely, for the Subject theory, that knowledge is a condition of subjects, and, for the Object theory, that there is a class of objects of belief. And so we find two parallel and, I submit, futile quests, one for the cognitive states, i.e., internally recognized conditions of individuals which are states of knowledge; and the other for *objects* of belief, objects which, as we shall see, are invariant to the differences between true and false belief.

Neither quest need ever have been undertaken had it been seen that knowledge and belief do not alternate, and that, surface linguistic evidence notwithstanding, they lack parallel grammars. But recognition of this has been inhibited by the introduction into the literature of what we might call a theory of 'second intensions', which has had a powerful recent influence. According to this, knowledge and belief are not alternatives in any sense whatever, but the *sentences* 'I know that *s*' and 'I believe that *s*' are used for alternative and, indeed, incompatible performances. So this is another form of Incompatibilism, albeit at the level of language: with 'I know' I give my word,[1] whereas with 'I believe' I refrain from giving my word. This, in effect, was the brilliant suggestion of Austin. I shall term it the Socio-Linguistic theory, for reasons I shall briefly mention.

If Austin were correct, the quests for states of knowledge and objects of belief would have been radically misguided consequences of philosophers having taken 'I know' and 'I believe' to be descriptive, rather than performative utterances. Once shown otherwise, there remains only the problem—not a deep one and essentially an empirical one—of describing the conditions under which it is suitable to *say* 'I know' and 'I believe' respectively. And this is but a matter of determining when, in the words of A. J. Ayer, 'I have the right to be sure and hence the license to say "I know"'.[2]

Against the Socio-Linguistic theory, whose program I otherwise regard as unexceptionable, I shall argue that 'I know' and 'I believe' are descriptive, even if also (and irrelevantly) performative. So the problems of defining knowledge and belief remain. But I can simplify the philosophical task by showing that we do not require objects of belief nor states of knowledge, for belief *is* a state and knowledge not, and knowledge *has* objects while belief does not. Neither the Subject nor the Object theory is correct because knowledge and belief are not alternatives. And since they are not alternatives, they are not *incompatible* alternatives. We may then decide at leisure which form of Compatibilism is correct, or at least likeliest.

[1] J. L. Austin, 'Other Minds', in his *Philosophical Papers* (Oxford; Clarendon Press, 1961), p. 67.

[2] A. J. Ayer, *The Problem of Knowledge* (London; Penguin Books, 1956), pp. 31–5. That one should have the right to be sure, for Ayer, is a necessary condition for knowledge and it, together with *s* being true and *m*'s being *sure* that *s*, forms a sufficient condition. I balk at 'being sure'. But that, with the other two, gives us perhaps the right to *say* 'I know'.

III

I am going to suppose that few will disagree that the sentence '*m* believes that *s*' may be true invariantly as to whether *s* itself is true or false, so that if the difference between true and false belief here is only the difference between the truth and falsity of *s*, then *m* may believe that *s* under whatever variations in truth-value of *s* there may be. Comparably, '*m* believes in *n*' may be true invariantly as to whether *n* exists. So just as one may believe what is false, one may believe in what is not, without there being any internal difference between these cases and those in which we believe what is true and believe in what is. In contrast with '*m* knows that *s*' and '*m* knows *n*' which respectively entail the truth of *s* and the existence of *n*, '*m* believes that *s*' and '*m* believes in *n*' do not. So I shall regard the latter, unlike the former as *semantically indifferent*.

In view of this, it is not unnatural to regard 'believes that *s*' and 'believes in *n*' as predicates which may be taken as absolutely true of *m* when it is true that *m* believes that *s*, or *m* believes in *n*. That they may be so taken was first suggested by Quine, who writes: 'The verb "believes" here ceases to be a term and becomes part of an operator "believes that" or "believes[ ]", which, applied to a sentence, produces a composite absolute general predicate whereof the sentence is counted an immediate constituent.'[1] I shall concentrate on 'believes that *s*', though a parallel analysis may be given for 'believes in *n*' if wanted; and I shall acknowledge the abnormality of the predicate's containing a sentential shape by designating the *class* of predicates, which it exemplifies, as *sentential predicates*. The identification of sentential predicates is, unfortunately, not a mechanical matter; for '*m* knows that *s*' looks dangerously as though it were predicating 'knows that *s*' of *m*. Whatever the case, it is not unnatural to suppose that, in predicating belief-that-*s* of *m*, we are ascribing to *m* some absolute condition. And so the Subject theory will appear unexceptionable, so far as its intuitive aspect is concerned. But then the Object theory for belief is not altogether hospitable to our treating 'believes that *s*' as a sentential predicate, inasmuch as *it* requires belief to be a relation. So we are obliged at this point to justify our move.

[1] W. V. O. Quine, *Word and Object* (New York; John Wiley, 1960), p. 216.

One convenience of treating it so connects with a trait of sentences in which beliefs are ascribed to persons. This concerns the so-called *referential opacity* of terms which occur in *s* in such a manner that, were the latter to have been a free-standing sentence, i.e., not occur embedded in a predicate, those terms would have conspicuously referential status. In the free-standing state, it is generally held that if *t* is a referential term in *s*, then any term *t'* co-referential with *t* may replace it, leaving unaffected the truth-value of *s*—the latter depending upon satisfaction of reference without regard to differences in meaning. The principles implicit here license uninhibited interchange of co-referential terms in given sentential contexts, a license indispensable for algorithmic work. But it is notorious that this privilege does not extend to sentences when these occur in sentences ascribing beliefs: if true that *m* believes that...*t*..., it is not necessarily false but certainly not automatically true that *m* believes that...*t'*..., co-referentiality of *t* and *t'* notwithstanding.

It is not altogether clear why this should be so, and I can see the temptation for ruthlessly overriding it. One might argue that if a man believes that...*t*..., well, he just believes that...*t'*..., and our reluctance to suppose otherwise must be due to some tacitly held, perhaps metaphysically suspect, theory of belief. Thus there is no requirement that we must report upon a man's beliefs in terms he would have used to report them, and often we must use terms he *could* not have understood. Mo Tzu believed that ghosts exist, and that he did so is an historical truth of Chinese philosophy, but he could not, since the language had not yet been invented, have understood this straightforward English description of what he believed. This ruthlessness is appealing, but will not survive some implausible consequences. It would require Mrs Newton's neighbors to have believed, since they believed that Isaac Newton would not survive the first six months of his life, that the author of *Principia Mathematica* would not survive the first six months of his life.[1] At such junctures, the most uncompromising extensionalist might allow an exception, rather than allow our intuitions regarding beliefs to go so completely under. So it is something of a

[1] This is an example of what I designate as *narrative sentences*. See my *Analytical Philosophy of History* (Cambridge; University Press, 1965), especially chapter VIII.

relief not to have to do *either*. For the principle of co-referential inter-change will apply to terms only when they occur in non-predicative positions anyway, and in counting '...believes that...*t*...' as a (sentential) predicate, we have removed it from exposure to the principle to begin with. So in effect the principle encounters here no exception whatever, and our intuitions regarding beliefs remain intact.

As we shall see, this happy resolution is only a temporary respite, but the coherency we are allowed to preserve by means of the sentential-predicate analysis of sentences which ascribe beliefs, is some presumptive evidence in favor of the correctness of that analysis.

IV

These advantages may be thought trifling in contrast with certain others of a more strikingly metaphysical order. If...believes that...is taken as a relational predicate, the question becomes pressing regarding *what m* must be related to when '*m* believes that *s*' is true. Notice that, whatever this relatum may turn out to be, it must be neutral relatively to the truth or falsity of *s*, since '*m* believes that *s*' is by common con-sent true even when *s* is false. So the problem is not so simple as in the case of '...knows that...'.In the latter case, when it is true that '*m* knows that *s*', then *m* may be related to whatever makes *s* true. Let this be *o*. Then if *o* does not exist, the relation collapses and '*m* knows that *s*' is just false. Trivially, there is no false knowledge, but part of our problem is to account for false belief, so the relatum for *m* when *m* believes that *s* cannot be the same, or even of the same type, as that which serves for knowledge.

The demand that belief be relational, together with the collateral demand that belief-sentences be semantically neutral, forces us to furnish semantically neutral *objects* of belief, e.g., intensions, essences, proposi-tions, abstract actualities (which remain whether there are concrete actualities which correspond to them or not), and comparable onto-logical monstrosities, the nature of which is determined in advance by the problem they are manufactured to solve. They are always, by a nice convenience, outside of space and time and corruption, and there, whatever the semantical vagaries of the beliefs that take them as objects.

The temptation to postulate such entities is aborted, however, when 'believes that' is not taken as relational, but as predicable absolutely of single individuals one at a time.

To be sure, a mere shift in philosophical grammar leaves the universe as it is, and there may indeed *be* just those entities, those objects of belief, in some crooked corner of a universe ontologically more generous than our mingy imagination would credit. Well, the loss will then be ours. But since the only reason we have for supposing there are such entities is an antecedent view that belief is relational, we can hardly use the possibility that they may exist as support for the relational interpretation. It is not as though we were talking about nefrits or hammer-toed clams!

The stock arguments in favor of relationalism descend from *Theaetetus* 189b,[1] where Socrates proposes that to believe is to believe something —since to believe nothing is not to believe—and implies that there must therefore be an *x*, which *m* believes, when it is true that *m* believes '...*x*...'. Minor quantificational prophylaxis might preserve what is intuitive while eliminating what is dubious in this account, but there are subtler arguments and less compromising ontologies than those traditionally proposed in response to the socratic demand. Israel Scheffler,[2] thus, generates a relational theory of belief from three philosophical theories, each of which, though contestable, possesses an undeniable philosophical power. (1) The Nomological–Deductive Theory of Explanation, which requires, of every valid explanation, at least one general law in its premisses. (2) The Want–Belief Model of Explanation for human actions, according to which we explain a man doing *a* with reference to his wanting *b* and believing that *a* is a means to *b*. But then by (1) there must be a general law (roughly) to the effect that, whenever men want *x* and believe that *y* is a means to *x*, then they do *y*. But (3) by a Principle of Ontological Commitment, we are committed to the existence of objects of belief if we must quantify over objects of belief, since the existence of whatever is a value of a variable we are constrained to bind is something *we* must then countenance. Obviously there *is* no constraint if (1)–(3) can be gotten round, but Scheffler has

---

[1] Cf. Plato, *The Republic*, 477–8.
[2] Israel Scheffler, *The Anatomy of Inquiry* (New York; Knopf, 1963), pp. 88–110.

arguments which are not to be dismissed lightly, and he has, moreover, some genial candidates for objects of belief, namely *inscriptions*. Inscriptions are homely objects to be found the time-space world over, and, furthermore, it is easy to furnish samples of them, so all we need to do now is to analyze belief as a relationship between a person and an inscription.

Scheffler's theory is vulnerable chiefly through its extreme artificiality, and though naturalness is not an overriding criterion for accepting or rejecting philosophical theories, if we can find a natural theory of belief which is not conspicuously incompatible with (1)–(3), then we may regard ourselves as having outflanked Scheffler's position and hence the obligation to deal with it directly. Moreover, the relational conclusion is, setting aside the problems of inscriptions, inconsistent with aspects of the psychology of the concept of belief.

There are various psychological accounts of belief, ranging from the view that belief is something (purely) internal—a modification of a *res cogitans*, an imprint upon a *tabula rasa*, a certain (unanalyzable) feeling accompanying certain impressions—to the view that beliefs are dispositions to behave, habitual patterns of behavior, and the like. In large measure, we are going to have a different analysis of belief as we move to a different view of the mind–body problem, with various shades and compromises exactly reflecting the shades and compromises on the latter question. Yet it is common epistemological ground throughout this range of positions that, in order to ascribe a belief to *m*, it is sufficient to make observations upon *m* alone, and that, if there should be an uncertainty attaching to any such ascription, this will at least *not* be due to the fact that there is something *other* than *m* upon which we ought to be making observations. Thus, if a belief is a mental trait, observable solely on account of *m*'s infallible reflective introspection, then *m* and *m* alone can say with certainty what he believes and that he believes it. Or if belief is a habitual pattern of behavior (and dispositions are not hidden springs which cause tendencies, but tendencies as such), so that *m* is in no specially privileged, and perhaps even in an unfavorable position, and must, as you and I, read his beliefs off the surface of his behavior, it remains *m* alone upon which observation must be made in order to certify ascriptions. Of course, it will be in response to various items of the *environment* that *m*'s beliefs will be activated, but none of these can be regarded in general as *objects* of belief in the sense required by the relational theory, for we still would have to account for false and semantically vagrant beliefs, and the objects of belief would have to exist invariantly as to the truth or falsity of the belief. So that there should be things, external to *m*, which activate beliefs, his relation to the object of belief would *not* be his relation(s) to *these* objects, and in the relevant respect it remains *m* alone upon whom observations are to be made. But if there *are* objects of belief, then we must observe something other than *m*: we must observe the objects and determine whether the relation is satisfied in any given instance. And this is incompatible with (perhaps) the (one) common ground under the various psychological theories of belief. These theories, *as a class*, re-enforce the view that it is solely facts regarding *m* which are relevant in ascribing beliefs to individuals. Compatibility, then, with the entire class of psychological theories regarding beliefs is some evidence in favor of a non-relational theory, inasmuch as relational theories are incompatible with them as a class. So we have here a notion which captures another intuitive sector of our antecedent beliefs about beliefs.

v

The fact that we can use terms which the believer would be prohibited through linguistic ignorance from using, while at the same time we are severely restricted in descriptions he might have had the linguistic equipment for understanding but lacked the requisite knowledge to apply, suggests that we have liberty of interchange for synonymous terms (expressions) in sentential predicates, though not for non-synonymous but co-referential ones. This, however, is hasty. As we shall see, there are restrictions upon intra- and inter-linguistic interchanges of synonyms which are quite instructive.

Let us now recall our *Sinn–Bedeutung* distinctions, and turn from referential matters (*Bedeutungsfrage*) to matters of meaning (*Sinnsfrage*). Surely, one wishes to say, a term does not suffer modification of *meaning* when shifted into predicative position, even though it is referentially emasculated. And surely, again, reference to one side, interchange of synonymous expressions must leave unaffected the truth-value of the context. But it is not by any means clear that we have license even of synonymy interchange in sentential predicates. Let us suppose that 'is a widow' means 'has survived a legal husband' and let *m* believe, in consequence of a series of jolly adventures with women ostensively identified as widows, that widows are merry women. It plainly is not automatically true that *m* believes that women having survived their legal husbands are merry, and indeed he may not believe this at all, having had a series of dismal encounters with women ostensively identified as having survived their legal husbands. This *could* be taken as evidence that the expressions are not synonymous. But why then not have said on similar grounds that the pair of terms in our earlier example are not co-referential after all? Besides, such strategies are dangerous. It is always possible to find contexts in which interchange of synonymous expressions will alter truth-values without our wishing to say, because of this, that they are after all not synonyms. Consider, thus, quotations. If *m* says '...*t*...' then it is false that *m* says '...*t'*...'. Yet one would hardly wish to argue that *t* and *t'* must therefore *not* be synonyms. An incapacity to sustain truth-values by interchanging terms in quotational contexts leaves undetermined the synonym-status of these terms, and we don't want to let the existence of quotational contexts serve to subvert the possibility of establishing synonymy. So at least we have to decide whether contexts formed by sentential predicates are like quotational contexts or not and, if not, then why interchange of synonymy breaks down. Whatever the case, sentential predicates appear not only referentially opaque, but meaning-opaque as well. Yet it is difficult to suppose that we can explain this latter opacity as we explained the former: the former, it seemed plausible to think, would be due to the fact that being relocated in a predicate rendered a term a-referential; a term does not become a-meaningful in consequence of such transportation, and the plausible assumption would be that it retains its meaning, and so its synonymy kinships, in and out of sentential predicates.

Of course there are some prophylactic strategies available. One is that terms embedded in sentences which are, in turn, embedded in sentential predicates, do not occur there in a sufficiently loose state that interchange is possible. Suppose *m* believes that widows are merry. Then we will be predicating '. . . believes-that-widows-are-merry' of *m*. Here the hyphens are punctuational reminders that the terms have been melted down, so to speak, to form simple, seamless lexical units, which must be taken as wholes; and the erstwhile words are reconstituted virtually as syllables. But we have no license for the interchange of syllables, much less for speaking of synonyms for syllables, and the only substitution licit would be with the sentential predicate *as a whole*. If we are at liberty to make predicates out of names, we need hardly balk at transforming words into syllables!

This strategy nevertheless is intuitively artificial, and I shall endeavor now to explain the source of what I feel as philosophically queasiness in connection with it. Typically and in principle, the meaning of a term is independent of its reference in much (or just) the same way in which the meaning of a sentence is independent of its truth-value. We may, in principle, understand a term, just as we may understand a sentence, independently of any consideration of *knowledge*, i.e., independently of the establishment of any epistemic relation between ourselves and the referendum of a term, or between ourselves and whatever conditions, external to a sentence, confer upon it a truth-value. I shall not argue this claim here but merely advance it, pending later argument, acknowledging that there are problems, at one end, with terms the meaning of which it is sometimes said we cannot get unless we have experienced instances to which they apply and, at the other end, with sentences, the meaning of which is said to determine which truth-value they are to bear. In the general case, I should argue, *Sinn* is logically independent of *Bedeutung*, or, in other terms, *Bedeutung* varies in independence of *Sinn*. But it is implausible to suppose that *Sinn* may vary in this way. A term retains its meaning in and out of quotational contexts, and so, one would believe, does it retain its meaning in and out of predicative contexts. We *understand* it invariantly as to contexts of these sorts and, in view of this, altering its status from a term *simpliciter* to an ersatz syllable in a hyphenated neologism, appears to leave meaning and understanding unaltered.

In addition to this, the strategy raises serious linguistic problems. For we must now be accorded the same generative powers for *terms* as we possess for sentences, and a definitive dictionary becomes impossible in principle: it would be like asking for a finite *phrasikon* of all the sentences in a language. Doubtless we *do* have the ability to generate infinite terms, *viz.*, by means of subscripts and the like. But these will not be spontaneously intelligible to speakers of the language as are the infinite sentences we may generate. And *these* terms are not somehow invented: they seem accessible to exactly those mechanisms of understanding which enable hearers to take in and comprehend sentences never before encountered. Well, we could continue to regard the terms as terms and merely rule that interchange between them and their synonyms will not be allowed. But this is philosophically unsatisfactory. Is it merely a *rule* that we will not allow interchange of synonyms in quotational contexts? We want some sort of an *explanation*.

VI

When a man says or writes something, he produces what I shall un-ingratiatingly call a *wordthing*. Sentences, for example, are wordthings, made of ink or of soundwaves. A quotation of a wordthing is, as it were, a picture of it, standing to it in a replicative rather than a descriptive relationship. So a quotation says nothing about the wordthing it replicates, though the fact that a given wordthing should be quoted at all says something obliquely about it: not just everyone gets his portrait painted. The reason, then, that we have no liberty of substitution in quotational contexts is that, if we replace a portion of it with a synonymous portion, it may retain its meaning, but it collapses as a replication. It is a misquotation at best, and at worst a bit of editorializing on the part of the quoter, whose business it is to show what a man said without comment. The license we have with word-things, then, extends only to replacement of portions with other portions which may, by conventions of portraiture, stand in the same replicative relation to the original as the replaced part, *viz.*, if we replace cursive with uncial or move from the *written* to the *spoken* word.

The ethics of quotation have a certain direct interest. The wordthings produced by a man are *his* property and *his* responsibility. When I quote, I take responsibility only for replicative accuracy: so I am not to be attacked for quoting *m*'s words '*n* is a swine' to *n*:—for it is not *I* who so says. Neither am I to be praised for some especially striking sentence which I quote, and if I do not make it plain that I am quoting and not saying, I have stolen another man's words, pretending that they are my own. This is in general a self-confession of internal inadequacy: I should *like* to have produced the wordthing, but was not capable of it. So in pretending the words are *mine*, I in effect masquerade as a different person than I am.

Of course it is difficult sometimes to tell whether a given wordthing is original or replication, inasmuch as the replication of a wordthing is often an exact copy of its original, and the two are, just as wordthings, indiscernible. It is difficult similarly to tell (or can be) whether a given paintthing is a copy of a paintthing—a copy of a Poussin, say— or is an original artistic statement by Poussin himself: a difficulty compounded when Poussin is his own copyist (and we all quote ourselves on occasion, like Socrates). A paintthing will belong in a quite different history, and require to be judged by vastly different criteria, depending upon whether it is an original artistic statement or but the exact copy of one; and quite distinct talents are called for in either case (imagine Jackson Pollock having to *copy* one of his things). Some men may be able to paint anything already painted, but have no capacity for original artistic statement. And with words it is the same: a man might have phenomenal ability to recover the words of others, and have nothing to say himself.

Consider now the wordthing *s*—a sentence originated by *m*. As wordthing, *s* is a part of the world, as much so as a stone, and like the replication of a stone, the quotation of *s* will picture one of the world's minor components. Let now S as it occurs in 'S' replicate *s*, i.e., share parity of structure with *s* conformably with the conventions of word-portraiture. Merely taken as a wordthing, *s*, no more than a stone, is true or false. Neither, of course, is S in 'S' true or false, quotations never being true or false, only accurate or inaccurate. They cannot be true or false primarily because nothing is *said* with them. Now let us suppose that *s* is true, that is, that it satisfies a truth-relation with another part of the world, say *o*. There is no reason why *o* should not be another wordthing, e.g., an English sentence. Since *s* is true, we shall suppose that *s* says '*o* is an English sentence'. But this will be replicated by S in 'S' which has the shape '*o* is an English sentence'. But while *s* is made true by *o*, 'S' is not: 'S' is semantically neutral, saying nothing but only showing *s*.

Typically, of course, *o* will *not* be a wordthing, for we do not commonly speak about the components of the world which are made of words. My concern has only been to stress the different sorts of relationships which hold between *s* and *o*, and between 'S' and *s*. It is a difference which has some collateral interest for the philosophy of language. There are famous episodes in the history of that subject wherein an ideal language was considered ideal through the manner of its relationship to the world. It was to *show the world forth*, standing to it in the relation in which 'S' stands to *s*. In order for it to succeed, there had to be supposed an isomorphism between language and the world, a parity of structure which virtually demanded that the world not merely contain but that it consist of wordthings. For wordthings replicate but wordthings, and so are indiscernible from one another as the accuracy of the one approaches optimality. So the world, which is made of facts, could as readily be taken as a picture of its language. The ideal language truly *says* nothing: it only *shows*. So in satisfying the one relation—the relation of 'S' to *s*—it is precluded from satisfying the other—that of *s* to *o*—just because it *does* not say. The ideal language is curiously mute, a mere reflection, the accuracy of which we check against the world. And presumably the world itself is mute: for there is nothing other than it, about which it could talk. And there are deep Tarskian reasons why it cannot talk about itself. It could only talk about its language.

The same wordthing can be used to say or to show. But in showing it does not say, and in saying it does not (except incidentally and irrelevantly) show. A Correspondence theory of Truth does not require —if anything, it requires that there be not—a replicative relationship between language and the world. In some special circumstance, perhaps, a sentence can show what it wants to say something about, but showing accurately and saying truly would be different relations only freakishly satisfied by the same sentence. And in the general case a sentence may be true, quite independently of whether it shows whatever makes it true. But our concern lies with the topic of belief, from which we may appear to have wandered.

VII

It is beyond controversy that the world contains wordthings, bits of itself in sentential shape, for example. Why should it be implausible to suppose that, as bits of the world ourself, we should not be constituted, in part, of wordthings? Let me recklessly speak now of men as being in certain *sentential states*. We shall obviously wish to distinguish being in sentential states from such extrinsic happenstances as bearing tattoos or startling birthmarks: I shall think of sentential states as *internal* to men: but the time for precision is not yet here. I shall now suppose that in predicating 'believes-that-*s*' of *m*, we are asserting that *m* is in a sentential state. The sentence *s*, embedded in the predicate, serves to individuate the sentential state ascribed to *m* by being, literally, a picture or quotation of that state. We now may say that '*m* believes that *s*' is true if, and only if, *m* is in a sentential state *o*, and *s* replicates *o*. Since *s* functions quotationally, *showing* the sentential state in question, this would explain the opacity of belief-contexts not only with regard to reference but with regard to meaning as well. For quotations may do neither more nor less than replicate the wordthings they mean to quote. Thus '...said "*s*"' is true of *m* if, and only if, '*s*' replicates what *m* said. There are certain problems with *oratio obliqua*, perhaps, but the sole liberties which may be taken with this form of quotation are grammatical, matters affecting the inflections of nouns (so far as the language permits a distinction between nominal and accusative cases) and in moods of verbs, and the like.

It may at this point be asked whether it is any more felicitous to postulate sentential states than merely to rule out substitutions of co-referential and synonymous expressions in belief-contexts. My reply is that these opacities are genuine discoveries, and that sentential states would at least provide an explanation of the facts which they reveal. Let me now marshal some further support for the theory in which sentential states function as quondam theoretical entities.

(1) Let *o* be a sentential state of *m*, and let *s* replicate *o*. Let *t* be a

89

term in *s* and *t'* a synonym for *t*. By replacing *t* in *s* with *t'* we get the sentence *s'*, which we may henceforward regard as a sentence synonymous with *s*. Still, it would be false that *m* said that *s'* when he said that *s*, for *s'* fails to replicate his words. But so would it be false that *s'* replicates the sentential state *o* in case *s* replicates *that* state. Still, the question remains as to whether the falsehood of *m* believes that *s'* is entailed by this fact, and the answer to this is No: neither the truth nor the falsehood of this is entailed by the truth or falsehood of *m believes* that *s*. And the reason for this is plain. It simply does not follow from the fact that, if a man is in one sentential state, he must be in another, any more than it follows from the fact that a man says one sentence that he must say another. This is so even if the states (and sentences) in question are replicated by synonymous sentences. A man believes that *s*. So he may or he may not believe that *s'*. In our earlier example, *m* will believe that wives with one dead husband are merry, given that he believes that widows are merry, providing that (at least) he (i) knows that the terms are synonymous and (ii) has applied this knowledge in the present instance. But there is no need that he should ever have connected things up. It is, then, physically possible that he should at once believe that *s* and disbelieve that *s'* even where there is a rule of language where *s* and not-*s'* is inconsistent—and even where the man in question knows the rule of language. Granted, he ought, knowing that rule, to believe that *s'* if he believes that *s*. But the theory of sentential states gives a natural explanation of why he need not. For the sentential states which *s* and *s'* replicate would be distinct sentential states of *m*.

(2) Similar considerations apply when we replace a term *t* in a replica of some sentential state with another term co-referential but non-synonymous with it. It is usually just a matter of fact that a pair of terms should be co-referential, e.g., that Lady Murasaki should be the author of *Genji Monogatari*. It is possible to know that person without knowing *who* she is, and it is a fact that many who knew Lady Murasaki did not believe that she was the author of *Genji*. It is natural, because of certain natural facts about knowledge, that we should have opacity in replicae of sentential states, it being a natural fact regarding knowledge that even though one knows something under one

description, one need not and perhaps *cannot* know it under another description, *viz.*, one could not be in a certain sentential state, given the causal conditions under which one is in another.

(3) In our casual remarks on the ethics of quotation, the suggestion emerged that there is an intimate connection between a man and his words. We can quote his words, but in so doing our relation to those words is thoroughly external. They no more are *our* words than they would be the words of a recording tape which played them back. Yet we can steal the words in the sense of pretending that they are ours and, in so far as there is the intimate connection between a person and *his* words, we are, as I suggested, in effect pretending to be a different person than we are.

Now in addition to stating a fact, i.e., in addition to being true, words may *express* a fact about him who says them, and indeed, they may express *this* fact whether they are true or false. Suppose I know that Lady Murasaki wrote *Genji*, and say as much. Then I give *you* a fact about Oriental literature, and you have a right henceforward to assert it as something which you know: another exotic fact. The fact itself does not express a trait of either of our personalities, but *that I should have* this knowledge *might* express a trait of mine. Thus my having this knowledge could be due to a passionate interest in Oriental literature. And *this* I do not transfer to you along with the knowledge which I transfer. For it may be a dominating internal trait of mine that I am involved with this literature, whereas with you the knowledge is only an external ornament. You could, of course, pretend that the knowledge here expresses an internal trait of yours, but all that is expressed here is the internal trait of wanting to be like me.

Knowledge itself is transitive. I cannot speak of *my* knowledge in the way in which I speak of *my* beliefs. Nor can I transfer my beliefs the way I transfer my knowledge. I transfer knowledge easily, since *s* is detachable from *m* knows that *s*. But *s* is *not* detachable from *m* believes that *s*. When I know that *m* knows that *s*, then *I* know that *s*. But if I know that *m* believes that *s*, I only *might* believe that *s*. When I transfer my knowledge, I teach. But when I transfer my beliefs, I indoctrinate. To transfer my beliefs is to transform the persons to whom I transfer them into my own image. For when they acquire a new belief, they acquire a new sentential state. And when thenafter they *state* that *s*, they are expressing an internal trait of themselves, whether what they state is true or false.

(4) That a man's statements of belief, when sincere, express traits of himself which it is natural to regard as sentential states, may be underscored by the slight degree of control we often have regarding what we are to believe. Under inquisitorial pressure, I can pretend that certain beliefs are mine, but the beliefs I avow notoriously can remain hopelessly external. I may *want very badly* to believe them. I may pray in the hope that the sentences I want to believe should become part of me, and so internal. Should this happen, and it is suitably regarded as an exercise of grace when it does, then in a very profound sense the person to whom it happens is changed and, in his own eyes, reborn. It is not clear that by a mere act of will, we can make a certain belief *ours*. When, as Al Ghazali marvelously put it, 'the glass of [one's] naive beliefs is broken', then 'This is a breakage which cannot be mended, a breakage not to be repaired by patching or by assembling of fragments. The glass must be melted once again in the furnace for a new start, and out of it another fresh vessel formed.'[1]

But we may find more domestic examples of this. Consider any sentential predicate '...believes-that-*s*' which is not true of you, e.g., '...believes-that-babies-are-brought-by-storks'. I think I understand how someone may believe this, and I think I understand well enough to believe false the sentence embedded in the predicate. What I cannot do is achieve an *internal* understanding of what it is to instantiate the predicate myself, what it *would be like to hold* this belief.[2] I cannot imagine, even, what it is like, for in imagining myself to hold this belief, I at the same time know that the belief is not mine, and there is always a distance intervening, as it were, between the belief and me. This distance is never a part of him who holds the belief. The only way to know what it is like to hold this belief is in fact to hold this belief naively, and the conditions which are presupposed for successful

---

[1] Al Ghazali, 'Deliverance from Error and Attachment to the Lord of Might and Majesty', from W. M. Watts (trans.), *The Faith and Practice of Al Ghazali* (London; Allen and Unwin, 1953), p. 27.

[2] See my 'Historical Understanding: The Problem of Other Periods', *Journal of Philosophy*, LXIII, 18 (1966), 566–77.

imagining rule out imaginative success. No: a new vessel would have to be formed: I should have to be a different person from what I am for this belief to be mine.

(5) It may be an interesting fact regarding *m* that *m* believes eccentrically that storks bring babies: but *m* does not take this to be an eccentric autobiographical fact but rather an uneccentric fact about the *world*. He does not refer his beliefs to himself but to the world, and in effect, to change one's beliefs is to change one's *world*. The world for him who believes that storks bring babies will have to be different from the world for him who holds the ordinary generative-obstetrical beliefs: a belief is not an isolated thing, but functions in a system, and to change a belief is to change a system, and one's system of beliefs defines one's *world*.

Now this would have a natural explanation if beliefs were sentential states. For sentential states are, since replaceable with sentences, to be regarded as sentences themselves, and sentences are *representations*. Obviously, 'representation of *x*' is an absolute property of a sentence, it is the meaning of a sentence, not a relation *between* a sentence and *x*. A sentential state is thus not merely (say) a grammatical ornamentation on the ghostly flanks of a *res cogitans*. Sentences mean to be about the world, and *my* world is defined by my representations of the world, whether these be true or false. It is for this reason that to change a belief is to change one's world. And it may be for this reason that one cannot by a mere act of will change one's beliefs: for since they are referred to the world, it is presumptuous of me to suppose that by an act of will I can modify the world. If a belief is held, it is because he who holds it believes it to be true; and it may perdure, even when he knows it to be false—a fact which may be explained in terms of the difficulty of erasure once one's soul has been scored with what later proves to have been a semantically vagrant sentential state.

VIII

Israel Scheffler regards the relata of individuals who stand in the belief-relation as believers, to be inscriptions. Inscriptions are interesting entities, perhaps, but philosophically unexceptionable ones, being in space and time, and easily generated as *graffiti*. It is this metaphysical responsibility which is especially appealing about Scheffler's position, and one might say that, after all, sentential states are *exactly* inscriptions. So the sample inscriptions, which Scheffler ingeniously suggests, will serve their role in virtue of being replicae of sentential states—portraits, as it were, of the relata of believers, *showing* what *saying* that they believe *describes*. Thus far, then, postulating sentential states removes a measure of artificiality from Scheffler's account by means of a proto-scientific strategy which Scheffler must consider congenial. This being so, it may be wondered why we ought any longer to insist upon the absolute predicative status of '. . . believes-that-*s*'. Why not now regard the decision as between a relational and a non-relational analysis of belief as a matter of no special philosophical moment? For if the sentential state is the relatum of believers, who are so called because the relation is satisfied, then this relation holds independently of the semantical-value borne by the sentential state (read: inscription). So there can be none of the sorts of objections there were before to 'objects of belief'.

This objection cuts deeper, I think, than it intends, for it touches the quick of *categorial grammar*. Consider any sentential value of φ*x*, *viz.*, '*a* is yellow'. Here we could be talking about a relationship between a particular—*a*—and the color yellow, considered as an entity, the universe containing *a* and *yellow*, at perhaps different levels, with the copulative 'is' standing for a complicated participatory relationship between them. We then would have a general license for recasting anything which now stands as an absolute predication as a relational one, the decision turning only upon extra-grammatical and perhaps extra-logical considerations of what sorts of entities we were prepared to budget for in our ontologies. This is not a matter I can go deeply into here, except to remark that since the entities involved would be of different 'levels', so the relations between them would then be inter-typical, and so themselves relations of a different sort than the intra-typical relations which hold amongst entities of the same level. And so bit by bit we should find reinstated all the old distinctions, and the gain in making entities out of properties would have to be paid for elsewhere, as though there were some principle of the Conservation of Distinctions operative over philosophical revisions. But again I press past this fascinating suggestion to what is immediately of relevance here.

The yellowness of *a* is, in some not easily formulated sense, sufficiently an internal character of *a* that we would want to say that *a* were different, that *a* itself were changed, should *a* lose its yellowness (it being interesting to reflect that yellowness would not change were it to lose *a*). But relations are external. If *a* is next to *b*, there is no internal change in *a* if *c* is inserted between it and *b*. The *world* will have changed, for a relation will have collapsed, but the terms of the relation are what they are in and out of the relation. Now I have proposed that a man's beliefs are in something like this sense internal to him, in that when he changes his beliefs, *he* changes. So, unless the relationship in which it is proposed that believing is to consist may be counted an internal relationship, penetrating its terms or at least one of its terms, I should want to persist in regarding believes-that-*s* as an absolute trait of *m* when '*m* believes that *s*' is true. It is a trait which depends upon no other thing than *m* himself, who satisfies, as it were, all the truth-conditions required by the sentence. For as was momentously recognized in the first great pages of modern philosophy, our beliefs might be just as they are, representing the world just as they do, whether or not there *exists* a world for them to represent truly or falsely. So I might be just the person I am, with just the beliefs I have, though nothing beside me existed.

I am not now concerned with those epistemological agonies engendered by this latter consideration, using it only as a mechanism here to underscore: if those agonies are possible, beliefs have to be internal properties of individuals, considered one at a time. To say that is, perhaps, not to say much, and for the reason that I am convinced of a fundamental difference between persons and things, I am convinced that I possess (or am possessed by) my sentential states in a different way than that in which a thing possesses (or is possessed by) its properties. For after all, one might say that a piece of paper or of recording gear, or a tattooed skin or—to use a more traditional example—a wax tablet may bear inscriptions and so be regarded as in sentential states. Yet they are so in a manner too external to capture the intimacy I wish to suggest.

But perhaps bearing inscriptions or imprintments in these cases *is* an external relationship between media and inscriptions. A tape is restored to itself, retaining its integrity minus an irrelevant measure of wear and tear when its messages are erased. So perhaps what I wish to say is that *I am my sentential states*, that (perhaps) I contain them not as a book contains sentences but as a *story* does: the story is made of its sentences, whereas the book is only inscribed with the sentences of the story which it houses.

I am made of sentential states, but not wholly made of them. For then I should be but a set of inscriptions. Rather, I think, believing involves *assenting* to a representation of the world, and assenting to *s* involves something more than a linear juxtaposition of *s* and Yes. The connection, rather, is like the ⊢ of Fregean notation, which serves to assert the sentence it operates upon. The assertion of *s* consists, then, not in *s* alone, but rather in an *action with s*. And so, I suggest, a belief is a kind of action with *s*. The connection between an action and what the action is done *with* is at once philosophically crucial and philosophically complicated, and while I have ideas regarding its analysis, I shall make no effort in this book to further them. A sentence is part of me as an arm is part of me, namely, when I am able to perform an action with one. There is no lifting of an arm without an arm, as there is no assenting to a sentence without a sentence. And it is the latter, perhaps, which is all that is required to capture and domesticate the socratic claim that when I believe, I must believe something. There are no *pure* beliefs, no sententially unqualified beliefs.

IX

Sentential states may be regarded as theoretical postulations, inducing a natural explanation of conceptual features of the phenomenon of belief. So we verge here upon science. I have no evidence that there are sentential states, only persuasive arguments in their favor. But in the end my theory is an empirical one. Why should we not suppose that some day sentences might serve to individuate neural states, so that we might read a man's beliefs off the surfaces of his brain? We could find out *what* he believes in this manner. But that he should believe what we have decoded is another and a deeper matter, whose understanding requires not the progress of science but the deepening of philosophy. It concerns the nature of action, and I must postpone further analysis of it. I only have sought a theory of belief plausible enough to render implausible a theory requiring *objects* of belief.

X

If the Object theory of belief is wrong then we cannot suppose knowledge and belief incompatible alternatives on the basis traditional in platonistic philosophy, namely that the objects of knowledge and the objects of belief must be disjoint. In *Republic* 477–8, for example, Plato —or Socrates—proposes that knowledge and belief are distinct powers, and as distinct powers must have distinct objects, and so the objects of belief cannot be the objects of knowledge. Belief, in such a case, must be relational, and it must naturally have been puzzling what the objects of false belief are—a problem Plato must have found vexing, for he takes it up again in the *Theaetetus*. But I shall pursue the matter no further: if there are concepts of belief which are relational, they must simply have no bearing upon the concept of belief we have been analyzing.

Meanwhile, it is awkward to suppose that knowledge should be a sentential state, or that 'knows that *s*' or 'knows *a*' should be taken as predicates, true absolutely of *m* if '*m* knows that *s*' and '*m* knows *a*' are true. For as observed, the latter entail respectively the truth of *s* and the existence of *a*, and it cannot easily be accepted that we could, if knowledge were an absolute property of an individual, by a mere examination of *m*, deduce that *s* is true or that *a* existed. For in the typical case, the truth-conditions for *s* and the existence-conditions for *a* will be independent of features which are *m*'s absolutely, and we are obliged to range afield in order to determine whether *s* is true and whether *a* is. So the Object theory, which seems unacceptable for belief, has in its support the fact that 'knows' resists treatment as a sentential predicate, and may be taken as irreducibly relational. And then the other term in the relation, whatever it may prove to be, may be the object of knowledge. With this, we capture what is intuitive in the Object theory of knowledge. But the Subject theory, which worked so well for belief, now seems unacceptable for knowledge. It must therefore be interesting to explain why anyone ever should have supposed the Subject theory of knowledge *correct*.

XI

Let us turn to Prichard, who held the Subject theory in a fascinating form. He writes: 'We must recognize that whenever we know something, we either do, or at least can, by reflecting, directly know that we are knowing it, and that, whenever we believe something, we similarly either do, or can directly know that we are believing it and not knowing it.'[1] In support and in explanation of this claim, Prichard writes that knowing and believing are so transparently distinct that confusion of one with the other is all but impossible.[2] So, by merely reflecting upon *myself*, I know or can know whether mine is a condition of knowledge or of belief.

If by reflection is meant the sort of inward glance by which we are alleged to discover our own internal (mental) conditions, then, unless *s* should have as its truth-conditions features exclusively of ourselves which are accessible to reflection, Prichard's theory seems just false. Let *s* = the sentence that 'The magnetic moment of the nucleus lies between -6 and $+2$ nuclear Bohr magnetons'. We ask a physicist whether he knows that *s*, or merely believes it. He answers that he knows it. Perhaps this is an excessive claim, but he makes it, and asked to justify his claim, let us suppose, he produces no evidence but merely announces that he has reflected, found his to be a condition of knowing, from which the truth of *s* follows. I don't think we would accept this justification, but any difficulties we might have with it would have been as obvious to Prichard, who was hardly a fool. So what could he have meant? A clue to his intention, perhaps, lies here: 'We should only say that we know something when we are certain of it, and conversely, and...in the end we have to allow that the meaning of the terms is identical; whereas when we believe something, we are uncertain of it.'[3]

---

[1] H. A. Prichard, *Knowledge and Perception* (Oxford; Clarendon Press, 1950), p. 86.
[2] 'We cannot mistake belief for knowledge, or vice versa.' *Ibid.*, p. 88.
[3] *Ibid.*

Well, the difference between knowledge and belief *could* be only the difference between certitude and incertitude. But are we to allow that the question whether or not we are certain can be resolved by reflection? Reflection will admittedly tell a man whether he *feels* certain. But then '*m* knows that *s*' cannot be synonymous with '*m* is certain that *s*' if the former is to entail *s* and the latter means that *m* *feels* certain: for the feeling of certainty is notoriously compatible with the falsity of that in which one is confident. Or, if we are to preserve the entailment, then we would withdraw our concurrence in the proposal that whether or not we are certain is a matter open to reflection. So it is just a distraction to shift from knowledge and belief to certainty and uncertainty. But again, Prichard was intelligent enough to have seen this for himself. So there must be a point of some importance submerged under the obvious vulnerabilities of the argument. If Prichard was misled, it must have been for reasons powerful enough to have blinded him to surface fact.

Prichard very likely thought, as many others have, that when we believe something, we in the nature of the case know that we believe it, as though there were something constitutionally impossible in supposing that *m* believes that *s* but does not know that he believes it. But should this view prove true, then all that is required for him to do is reflect on himself, and this should tell him directly that he believes what he does. Currently, such a view of belief is in very low favor, but however we arrive at knowledge of our own beliefs, whether these are revealed in our behavior or whatever, it is not just the inadequacy of Prichard's views on *belief* that raises difficulties. It is the assimilation of knowledge to a presumed condition of ourselves, something we can exhaustively determine about ourselves whether through reflection, or through observation of our own behavior or whatever. But let us follow this through. Consider once again the physicist. Faced with our reprimand, he might come forth with an ingenious proposal. If we are asking, he would say, how he knows that *s*, well, he has a great deal of evidence, and he could explain it to us providing we were interested in mastering sufficient physics to be able to follow his proof. But he thought our question was not how he knew that *s* but how he knew that he *knew* that *s*. That is a different matter. He certainly has nothing like the same sort of evidence for this that he has for *s*. We had confused knowing and *knowing that one knows*. And perhaps 'I know that *s*' is always a first-person report, perhaps it is always a basic sentence for me, even if *s* itself is not a basic sentence: after all, that *s* should be non-basic does not in any way entail that 'I believe that *s*' is *not* basic! And just as with belief, when I know something, perhaps I in the nature of the case know that I know it, as though there were something constitutionally impossible in my knowing something and my not knowing that I know it. Or, again, in case I should know without knowing that I do, a moment's reflection will settle matters. It is, then, *knowing that we know* which is the critical issue here, and upon which the Subject theory rests. We have encountered the concept already, and might take the opportunity to advance our understanding of it. For it is not as though Prichard were the only philosopher to hold that there is no knowing unless there is the knowledge of it.

XII

I should like to take up a somewhat stronger version of Prichard's theory that, if *m* knows that *s*, then *m* knows that he knows that *s*. This version is due to Jaakko Hintikka, who has argued that the two sentences '*m* knows that *s*' and '*m* knows that *m* knows that *s*'—or, in his notation, K*ms* and K*m*K*ms*—are 'virtually equivalent'.[1] As I understand this, we would say that P and Q are *virtually equivalent* when we cannot, either with P and not-Q or with Q and not-P, consistently describe any state of affairs. This means that P cannot be true jointly with not-Q nor Q with not-P: so P and Q would have to be true together if either of them is true at all. So if K*ms* and K*m*K*ms* are virtually equivalent, there is no state of affairs we can consistently describe either with the pair K*ms* and NK*m*K*ms*, or the pair NK*ms* and K*m*K*ms*.

That no state of affairs can consistently be described with the latter pair admits of a trivial proof. Let us suppose ourselves entitled to make some uniform substitutions in Hintikka's formulae. Replace K*ms* with

[1] Jaakko Hintikka, *Knowledge and Belief* (Ithaca, New York; Cornell University Press, 1962), p. 104.

r. This yields the pair N*r* and K*mr*. But by common consent, K*mr* yields *r*. We now conjoin N*r* and *r*, which is not a virtual contradiction, but a contradiction. So no state of affairs can consistently be described with this pair. Such an informal proof of this half of Hintikka's thesis differs, as it happens, from his. He constructs a set of rules which prevent the pair of sentences from forming part of the same formal system, so his method is more general and powerful than mine. But proof here seems scarcely to matter, it being more or less the common sense of the matter that if a man does not know that *s*, he can hardly be thought of as knowing that he knows that *s*! It is the other half of the thesis that is more vexing and rather less adjudicable by common sense. And here my style of *grosso-modo* proof yields nothing untoward: all we get for putting *r* in place of K*ms* in the formulae K*ms* and NK*m*K*ms* is the innocuous pair *r* and NK*mr*. These seem compatible unless *m* knows everything, which is (in the typical case) false. True, it is out of the question for me to *say* '*s*, but I don't know that *s*'. This would be another inconsistent performance of the sort which our analysis keeps turning up. We apparently are able to say '*s*, but *he* does not know that *s*'. Still, that we can in general say this—without an inconsistent performance—does not entail that we in particular can say 'He knows that *s* but he does not know that he knows that *s*'. That particular conjunction may after all be incapable of consistently describing any possible state of affairs. So we must not too readily lean on semi-formal proofs buttressed by common sense. For Hintikka has a proof that this pair is not co-tenable.[1]

The notion of what Hintikka calls a *model set* is that of a set of sentences that together describe a possible state of affairs or *partially* describe one. If two sentences cannot together enter the same model set, there is no possible state of affairs they may jointly describe. Hintikka deduces a contradiction from his rules together with the assumption that K*ms* and NK*m*K*ms* are entered in the same model set, and concludes that no possible state of affairs could sustain a description consisting of their conjunction. It quickly follows that K*ms* and K*m*K*ms* are virtually equivalent: there is no possible state of affairs which the one can describe and the other not. Hintikka's discussion is obviously sophisticated

[1] *Ibid.* p. 105.

and subtle, but since it is relatively simple, as I shall show in chapter 6 and have already suggested in chapter 1, to provide an *actual* state of affairs that is correctly described with K*ms* and NK*m*K*ms*, something has either to be wrong with Hintikka's rules or he is using a defective translation of the expression 'knows that', no genuine connection holding between it and his K, which allegedly represents it. This would not matter but for the fact that Hintikka has indicated his intention to capture usage.[1] So I shall argue that he has failed. He would certainly have failed, for example, in case K*m*K*ms* were to have a truth condition distinct from the truth conditions for K*ms*, and satisfaction of the latter were not automatically to satisfy, or entail the satisfaction of the former. In Prichard's analysis there is, for example, room for that: K*m*K*ms* would have as one truth-condition that *m had reflected* on the condition described by K*ms*: and the latter does not have this act of reflection as one of *its* truth-conditions. So for Prichard it is at least possible that K*m*K*ms* is false when K*ms* is true. One may say that this does not mean that Prichard is right. But my point will be that the very fact that there is a *disagreement* constitutes an internal argument against Hintikka.

It is somewhat important to stress that Hintikka has proposed that his demonstration is achieved by purely logical devices, independently of any tacit psychological assumptions of the sort by which Prichard was allegedly misled. It is not a matter of my knowing that I know when I in fact know, through some feature of the psychology of knowing, as Prichard thought, but rather the two sentences '*m* knows that *s*' and '*m* knows that *m* knows that *s*' are merely different forms of words for the same state of affairs. Hintikka endorses a thesis to this effect by Schopenhauer.[2] Well, if they have the same meaning, there of

---

[1] 'I hope to suggest that the results of our general considerations largely agree with the way we naturally use the verbs "to know" and "to believe"', *ibid.* p. 10. Hintikka hopes, indeed, to show that what he has formulated 'really captures the basic logic of knowledge and belief'. p. 60. But there remains always a question not merely whether Hintikka captures ordinary usage, but whether, in so far as philosophical usage may be distinct from this, he has captured even philosophical usage. But as Chisholm suggests, 'We should remind ourselves, of course, that the sentence that is thus demonstrated may not be the one with which philosophers have been concerned when they have asked "Can we know without knowing that we know?"' See Roderick Chisholm, 'The Logic of Knowing', *Journal of Philosophy*, LX, 25 (1963), 784.

[2] Jaakko Hintikka, *Knowledge and Belief* (Ithaca, New York; Cornell University Press, 1962), pp. 110–12.

course can be no possible state of affairs described with the one and not with the other. But once again, Prichard did not think they meant the same: he thought they described interesting, metaphysically interconnected but essentially distinct facts. After all, who would argue that '*m* believes that *s*' and '*m* knows that *m* believes that *s*' are virtually equivalent, or that they are but different forms of words for the same fact? That would entail all by itself an important cartesian thesis, and make it trivially impossible that we should not know what our beliefs are. So '*m* believes that *s*' and '*m* knows that *m* believes that *s*' have distinct truth-conditions. Why should it be different with knowledge? Prichard did not think it *was* different. And perhaps he was wrong here. But I repeat that if he was wrong, so is Hintikka. That there can be a disagreement about the meaning of the *word* 'knows'—as evidently there is—that is enough, as I shall hope to prove, to refute Hintikka's thesis, and ultimately the general thesis that K*ms* entails, much less that it is equivalent or virtually equivalent to, K*m*K*ms*.

XIII

Prichard not only believed that we each can know in a direct way whether we know or whether we believe that *s*. He also held a thesis which either he did not distinguish from this one, or which, had he done so, he would surely have offered in explanation of it, namely, the thesis that knowing and believing are simple and unanalyzable conditions of an individual. When I know (to reconstruct him), I know directly that I know because nothing tells me that I know except the very fact that I do know (since knowing is a simple and unanalyzable condition). Let me document these views as Prichard's. That our knowledge of knowledge is *direct* is stated here:

The knowledge is...in both cases direct; we do not know, for example, that our state is one of knowing that the noise we hear is loud indirectly, i.e., by knowing that it [N.B.: the knowledge, not the noise] has some character other than knowing—such as that of being a clear and distinct perceiving; we know directly that it is of the sort that knowing is; and so, too, with our knowledge that our state is one of believing.[1]

[1] H. A. Prichard, *Knowledge and Perception* (Oxford; Clarendon Press, 1950), p. 89.

And that knowing, like believing, is simple and unanalyzable is suggested here:

In knowing that some state in which we are is one of knowing or of believing . . . we are necessarily knowing the sort of thing which knowing is, and the sort of thing which believing is, even though it is impossible for us or anyone else to define either, i.e., state its nature in terms of the nature of something else.[1]

These two points are connected in Prichard's polemic against Descartes, which is what animated the essay where he set forth the views we have been airing. He wants first to say that nothing tells me that I know that *s* except the fact that I do know that *s* and, accordingly, that *no criterion* (as we would say these days) *is needed, or that no criterion is possible*. So there is nothing such that I must first ascertain whether it holds before I can say whether or not I know that *s*. But secondly, and rather more interestingly, Prichard wants to say this. Even if there were some criterion for knowledge, I would have to know what knowledge is before I could *apply* the criterion. So I at the very least always know what knowledge is, whether I know in any other instance. In asking about knowledge, as Descartes did, he at least knew what he was asking about: he at least knew what knowledge was. So a *generalized* doubt is impossible. Suppose, thus, that I say I know nothing whatever, but only have beliefs, any or all of which may be mistaken. Well, I must at least know what beliefs are, Prichard argues, so it is false that I know nothing. Indeed, if it were true that I knew nothing at all, if I at least knew just *that*, then I would know something. So I never could know nothing, and if I know anything, I know what knowledge is. So it is after all not exactly a case of knowing that I know when I do know, which was of interest to Prichard: it was rather his thesis that in saying I know—or that I don't know—I always know what knowledge is. And *that* I know by reflection, e.g., on the meaning of the word 'knowledge'.

Descartes, of course, was a past master of that style of argumentation. Consider only his besting of the *malin génie*. Descartes proved he could not always be mistaken. He could not because, in order to make a mistake, a man has to *assert* something. If you do not venture an

[1] H. A. Prichard, *Knowledge and Perception* (Oxford; Clarendon Press, 1950), p. 89.

assertion, you never are wrong (though of course never right either). So, on the hypothesis that I am always mistaken, it follows that I am always asserting something. So I cannot doubt that I make assertions (= think). So there is at least one thing about which I am not mistaken on the hypothesis that I am always mistaken, and that hypothesis, accordingly, is self-defeating. Against this the *malin génie* is helpless. But to what does such an argument come? It does not entail that I ever make a *correct* assertion, or have a *correct* thought, save in this one utterly irrelevant case where I assert something about assertions, or think a thought about thinking. So the argument brings cold comfort. And so it is with Prichard's. His point is that I automatically have an instance of knowledge in the mere wonderment whether or not I have knowledge: I know what I am wondering about, and hence the wonderment is self-gratifying. Merely to have the idea of knowledge is at once to have something which instantiates it, an observation vaguely reminiscent of the Ontological Argument. But this at best works in the one case, where what we know as a result of knowing what knowledge is, is just that. If *comprendre, c'est savoir* works at all, it does so just where it is *savoir* which is the object of *comprendre*. And this the *malin génie* may accept with a measure of equanimity. He grants that he knows what knowledge is. So much is required for the intelligibility of his own position. But it is compatible with his knowing this one thing that he should know nothing else of the slightest interest.

And now it should be clear where Prichard has gone quite astray. He has confused *knowledge*, in the epistemologically relevant sense, with *knowledge* in that sense of the term which means, in effect *understanding*. It is knowledge in the sense of knowing how to use a word or expression correctly. But *understanding*—even understanding what 'knowledge' means—can be, and very likely is a sentential state of persons. At least 'understands *s*' may plausibly be taken as a sentential predicate. So all Prichard will have shown is that understanding and belief are states of ourselves to which we have access through reflection. Now it may be wrong that reflection tells me that I understand, for the question of whether we understand is very often a matter of whether others understand *us*, but Prichard's main claim may be allowed to stand, namely that it is very difficult to suppose that *belief* and understanding are not distinct and unmistakably different conditions of ourselves. For after all, we understand a great many propositions which we do not believe. And perhaps I could understand everything and believe nothing, as Descartes felt himself at one point dangerously close to having to accept.

Now of course Prichard may have believed that, in order to understand a term, I must have had experience of something to which the term correctly applies. So, if I understand 'knowledge' I must have had access to an instance of it, from which theory and which fact it would follow that I cannot at once understand 'knowledge' and pretend I have no instance of it. But this is a dangerous principle to adopt, and at its best it would mean that I could only understand *simple* and *undefinable* terms through having had access to something to which they correctly apply, and Prichard's claims notwithstanding, it is far from plain that 'knowledge' is a simple and undefinable term. And there is pretty good evidence that Prichard himself could not have understood it very well, inasmuch as he thought that knowledge must be a simple, unanalyzable condition of an individual. At the very least it is a simple and unanalyzable *relation* between individuals and 'objects of knowledge', and the point stands, so far as arguments against skepticism are concerned, that one cannot tell, through merely reflecting upon oneself, that this relation is satisfied. It is, as we shall subsequently see, a quite external relation indeed.

Should '...knows that...' prove relational, then of course, 'knows that *s*' is not a sentential predicate, nor is knowledge-that-*s* a sentential state of persons. This may be obscured by the fact that many of the logical features which make the theory of sentential states so natural are exhibited by knowledge. Thus, as the reader may ascertain for himself, there are just the same opacities of meaning and reference for '...knows that *s*' as for '...believes that *s*'. This could easily be accounted for if, in order to be said to have knowledge, an individual must be in *some* sentential state, without it having to follow that the sentential state is knowledge. If, as the Standard analysis proposed, knowledge-that-*s* entails belief-that-*s*, this would explain the opacities nicely. That one must be in *some* sentential state which *s* replicates when one knows that *s* does not entail that one knows that *s* when one is in that sentential state—for then, from the mere fact that we were in the required state, we could deduce *s*. And it is part of my thesis that there is no state of ourself which guarantees the truth of any sentence about the world.

To hope to find, in some absolute condition of oneself, a condition sufficient for the truth of a sentence about something *other* than oneself, is a very typical and very tragic philosophical hope, which I shall later discuss as exemplifying a *quest for certainty*. The fallacy in it, of course, is not restricted to sentences regarding something other than oneself. Thus the sentence *s* may be about myself, without it following that my being in some absolute sentential state *o* is a sufficient condition for *s*, and without it following either that, in having access to *o*, I need do nothing further in order to know that *s*. Self-knowledge is no privileged instance of knowledge.

XIV

I wish to consider one further attempt to rehabilitate the thesis which Prichard apparently confused with the thesis he actually held. I prolong the discussion chiefly because there are some further philosophical points which the analysis I want briefly to examine raises, and these bear upon problems central to our general inquiry. The analysis now before us is due to Norman Malcolm.[1]

According to Malcolm, there is a strong and a weak sense of 'know' and, if we stress the strong sense, then we have something reasonably close to Prichard's claim, so close that that claim may be reconstructed by considering the criterion for the strong sense of 'know'. The *weak* sense appears to be this. The man *m* asserts *s*, and upon investigation, *s* turns out to have been true. We then allow that *m* (in the weak sense) knew that *s*, though, had *s* turned out false, we would say instead that *m* only believed that *s*: 'believe' alternates with 'know' *only* in the weak sense of the latter, and in that sense it must be stressed that nothing about *m* himself marks the difference between knowing and believing. The difference is wholly external, and concerns just the difference in truth-value of *s*. 'As philosophers', Malcolm writes, 'we

[1] N. Malcolm, 'Knowledge and Belief', *Mind*, LXI, 242 (1952).

may be surprised to observe that it *can* be that the knowledge that *p* is true differs from the belief that *p* is true only in the respect that in the one case *p* is true and in the other false. But that is the fact.'[1] Malcolm leaves no room here for a difference between true belief and knowledge, but that is of less concern to me than the fact that there should be, according to his analysis, no subjective difference between (weak) knowledge and belief. It follows that, by mere reflection, I cannot possibly determine whether I know or believe: whatever reflection discovers will be some condition neutral with respect to the distinction between knowledge and belief. For the 'weak' sense, then, Prichard was wrong, and perhaps it was our mistake in criticizing him that we had in mind the weak sense. If *he* meant instead the *strong* sense, the argument was at cross purposes.

A man employs the strong sense when, in claiming to know that *s*, he will allow nothing to count in counter-evidence to *s*. He would not, according to Malcolm, 'call anything evidence against it. The person who makes the statement would look upon nothing whatsoever as evidence against it.'[2] He himself might not be able to *show* that a certain piece of allegedly counter-evidential stuff was not so in fact. But he would rule it out that it really could be counter-evidence. Now a measure of support for this account may be found in the fact that there *are* many things we claim to know and such that we would never permit it to be seriously proposed that there might be impressive evidence against them. We know that all the classic problems having to do with ruler-and-compasses solutions will not ever be solved in the required terms; that no one is going to square the circle, duplicate the cube, or trisect the angle by those means. Proofs of varying degrees of ingenuity rain down upon mathematics departments and popular scientific journals, but it is merely charity upon whomever's part it is that would undertake to examine these, to point out the flaw. They know in advance that there must be a flaw, the question being only whether it is worth the trouble to identify it. In much the same way, we know there will be no perpetual motion machines, whatever collaterally interesting pieces of information might turn up in seeking to build or design one. Again, I once found a simple proof in logic

[1] N. Malcolm, 'Knowledge and Belief', *Mind*, LXI, 60 (1952).   [2] *Ibid.* p. 62.

that if P and Q are any pair of propositions which are incompatible, then, if R is compatible with P, Q and R are incompatible. Out of such discoveries rather intricate metaphysical edifices take their rise, but at the time I counted it only a parlor *divertissement* for philosophers, at its best a further refinement on the paradoxes of material implication. A colleague, however, realized that if I were right, every non-euclidian geometry had to be inconsistent if euclidian geometry was consistent. But there is a famous proof of Klein's to the effect that every non-euclidian geometry has a model in euclidian geometry, so all are consistent if it is. Knowing now that there *had* to be a flaw in my argument, he was now sufficiently motivated to nail it down.

These cases only illustrate a state of affairs Malcolm has described without illustrating the strong sense of 'know'. For in the cases cited, it is not a matter of not *allowing* anything to be counter-evidence. We know there can be no counter-evidence, in that we know that whatever is *incompatible* with what we know is false, and we know there are no ruler-and-compasses solutions to the classic geometrical problems, etc. If any one turned out to be false, we should say, I suppose, that we had only believed. It merely happens that these things are true, and for that reason there is no *serious* counter-evidence. So let us consider Malcolm's own examples, to see what they bring out.

Malcolm claims strongly to know that $2 + 2 = 4$. He knows this, he says, not because he has a proof, nor, for the matter, because of anything. He simply knows it, as everyone does. Proofs for it can be found, but these do not bring, as it were, a sigh of relief that an old, familiar, but conceivably dubitable proposition had finally been vindicated. Rather, they merely illuminate the foundations of mathematics, and should any proof appear to go *against* the proposition, that, as Malcolm suggests, would be a reason for rejecting the proof. We will not allow that there can be a proof more certain in its premises than we are that 2 plus 2 equals 4. And this is not because the sentence in question happens to be a piece of mathematics, nor a tautology, nor *a priori*, nor analytical in some doubt-impervious way. For there are other sentences, equally certain with this, which are none of these; and yet other sentences, which are mathematical, analytical, *a priori*, if they are *anything*, and yet we would hesitate to say we knew these in the strong sense at all. This part of Malcolm's discussion is interesting and important, for it cuts across a distinction which, certainly at the time when his paper was published, and scarcely less so today, was considered impermeable.

The basis of the difference, I think, is this. In both arithmetical calculation and in the testing of empirical hypotheses, there are what we might term 'checking procedures', simple operations by means of which we finally determine whether or not an empirical claim is true, or whether or not a computation is in error. In checking a calculation, I break it down into the simplest steps I can, e.g., nearly as simple as 2 plus 2 equals 4. This is *about* as simple as I can get: 2 plus 2 equals 4 is not, in the ordinary way of number manipulation, calculated. It is in terms of repeated steps, themselves uncomputed, that computations are checked, e.g., as by a machine. In the sense in which a man might make an error of computation, there is no way in which he is subject to such an error with 2 plus 2 equals 4. So, with such sentences, *one* kind of error is excluded. But comparably, suppose I claim (using Malcolm's own example) that an inkpot is to be found in the dresser. I can be wrong in this, not knowing whether I really am wrong or not until I—or someone—has checked up. Checking up here consists in looking in the dresser and seeing an inkpot. If I see one, my original claim is vindicated. Now nothing stands to this checking procedure as it stands to the initial claim. All empirical checks are perhaps reducible to such simple operations as looking in a certain place and seeing. And with these simple checks, nothing further is to be done. These are the steps with which checks are made, and any way in which we might check up on these would involve other operations of just the same sort. How could one coherently trust *those* if, for whatever reason, *these* are deemed untrustworthy? Such doubts are incoherent.

There are disanalogies between empirical claims which are shown false and calculations which have been shown erroneous, but the analogies here are striking and important. Yet it is absolutely necessary, Malcolm's thesis (which I have tried to reconstruct) notwithstanding, that we emphasize that these simple checks do not guarantee us against being wrong. They guarantee us only against a *certain way of being wrong*. It is only that, whatever other or further kinds of errors there might be, these *cannot* be discovered nor rectified through repeated checking operations of the sort which makes appeal to these simple cases. It would have to be altogether a different sort of error. So Malcolm would not have shown that error is impossible with these, but only that it would not be discoverable in ways like those which the simple checking procedures reveal.

Now it may very well be that, as the notion of evidence is construed, there would be no sense in saying that *evidence* could count against such sentences as 'Here is the inkpot' or 'Two plus two is four'. For these are just the sorts of sentences with which we *express* evidence, at least ultimately. Now contrast these sentences with the following. 'Every non-euclidian geometry has a model in euclidian geometry'; 'It is mechanically impossible to derive energy from bodies by cooling them below the temperature of the surrounding object'; 'A straight line cannot be constructed equal to any given arc of a circle'. These sentences (amongst others) are appealed to in connection with our claims to know that the circle cannot be squared, that perpetual motion machines are impossible, that 'Danto's theorem' is false. And it was the latter which I pointed to as cases where we know that nothing is going to count as serious overriding contrary evidence. We appeal to the former sorts of sentence as evidence for these. Yet it makes *sense*, because these sentences do not express *ultimate* evidence, to speak of evidence going against them. It is only that we know such evidence cannot be taken seriously. The sense in which I claim to know, therefore, that the circle cannot be squared is perhaps different from the sense in which I might claim to know that 2 plus 2 equals 4, or that I see an inkpot. I know the former perhaps because I have evidence, but I know the latter for a different reason: perhaps because they *are* evidence. In both cases I know evidence cannot go against my claims, in the first because the evidence is too strongly in favor of it, in the latter because of the way in which 'evidence' is characterized. The question before us now is whether these 'checking procedures' constitute knowledge in the strong sense.

Now let us consider the difference between the two cases of ultimate evidence, i.e., the two kinds of checking procedure of which Malcolm gives us examples. If a man were told he was wrong in claiming that

2 plus 2 equals 4, he should at least know that it cannot be because he has miscalculated. But if *not* miscalculation, then it is not easy to see in what his error could consist. Were someone to argue against him that 2 plus 2 equals 5, the one who so argued could not insist that *he* had computed correctly and revealed an error. At best he would be working with a different base, or using one of the terms differently from the rest of us, or employing some novel operation. No fact other than this could be relevant, not even the possibility of a *malin génie*: for reference to the latter merely repeats the charge that I could be in error without specifying how anything I have said is put in doubt. So we are left just with a difference in the use of terms. By contrast, consider the beholding of an inkpot, an ultimate check in the domain of experience. There could be an analogous disagreement, e.g., if someone were to use words differently, using 'apple' for 'inkpot' and so saying that I am seeing not an inkpot but an apple. But there is another possibility here which does not arise in the case of 2 plus 2 as equal to 4. I can reach for the inkpot and *find that my hand closes on nothingness*! Malcolm considers this possibility. He meets it by saying that he would dismiss the latter as an hallucination, not the former. He would persist in saying that he saw an inkpot. He will now not allow his grasping of nothingness as contrary evidence. But surely, in point of ultimate evidence, grasping is of a piece with seeing. Both are of the order of ultimate checks. So you cannot by fiat, as it were, decide that one is to count as evidence and the other not. For then you are going against your original characterization of ultimate evidence. Now one cannot appeal to *evidence* in order to decide a case where there is a conflict amongst the sentences which ultimately *express* our evidence. The doubts are not resoluble in that manner. But to point this out is not to defeat a skeptic who has found ultimate evidence unsatisfactory, since it is exactly his point that the sentences which express ultimate evidence may come into conflict, and when they do the entirety of the sentences expressing ultimate evidence are corrupted as a base for certitude. Well, you can *decide* to accept one such sentence and to reject the other. But you cannot justify the decision you appeal to, and you surely have no guarantee that you have made the right one. The fact of the matter is that even with our ultimate checks, we can be wrong,

so here we are in the end dealing with knowledge in the weak sense, and reference to checking procedures is a diversion.

The issues here are serious in epistemology, and I have some obligation to consider them at a later stage in my discussion. I wish here merely to emphasize the relevance, as Malcolm sees it, of his remarks to the Subject theory of knowledge. It is this. We can by reflection know that we are using the word 'know' in a strong sense, as ruling out by decision anything which conflicts with what we want to say, in this sense, that we know. So perhaps we can. But in this context it is not interestingly controversial whether I can know by reflection what I *decide*. The point is that I cannot know by reflection whether what I have decided is true,[1] and hence whether I know it in the sense of 'know' which has the logical feature that '*m* knows that *s*' entails *s*. As Richard Taylor has pointed out,[2] there are many who are so strong in their faith that they will let nothing count in evidence against the claim that God exists. Do they really 'know' that God exists? Well, perhaps they do, but you cannot deduce from the fact that they will abide no contravening evidence that He *does* exist. For we then could find adequate evidence for the existence of God in the heart of any true believer. But by the same criterion, we could in the heart of every true disbeliever find adequate evidence for the non-existence of God. The point is that the strong sense of 'know' is compatible with the falsity of what one claims, in that sense, to know. Only the *weak* sense is incompatible with the falsity of what one claims to know. For the weak sense is precisely defined in terms of the *truth* of what one claims to know. But whether what one weakly knows is in fact known is not open to reflection to decide. And where it is open to reflection to decide the truth of what is claimed is not entailed. With the weak sense, finally,

---

[1] Malcolm attempts to rescue Prichard afresh in his revision of the 1952 paper which appears in his collection *Knowledge and Certainty* (Englewood Cliffs, New Jersey; Prentice-Hall, 1963), p. 71. He points out that 'reflection can make us realize that we are *using* "I know it" in the strong (or weak) sense in a particular case'. In fact I think, from my own analysis, that Prichard was entitled to no stronger thesis than one about the use of words, e.g., the meaning of 'knows'. That is, of course, different from knowing how *I* use a word, or what *I* mean. And I am not sure the latter is even interestingly relevant here.

[2] Richard Taylor, 'A Note on Knowledge and Belief', *Analysis*, XIII (1953) and his 'Rejoinder to Mr Malcolm', *Analysis*, XIV (1954).

there is no subjective difference between knowledge and belief. In the strong sense, there may be: there may even be a sentential state. But with the strong sense, we lose the logical connection between knowledge and truth. So Malcolm's emendations are unavailing, and we must consider the Subject theory of knowledge as false. We have good grounds for supposing the Subject theory of belief as plausible. But knowledge and belief as *mutually excluding* conditions of an individual is ruled out if knowledge is not a condition to begin with.

XV

It follows from our analysis that when *m* claims to know that *s*, he cannot be describing a condition exclusively of himself, nor can he be held to assert with 'I know that *s*' a sentence, all the truth-conditions for which are satisfied by himself. It is at this juncture that the novel theory of Austin acquires a certain interest, for Austin maintained that 'I know that *s*' has a performative rather than a descriptive use, and that to suppose that it is an assertion *about* myself is to have lapsed into what Austin termed '*the descriptive fallacy*, so common in philosophy'.[1] If performative, the force of the words is exhausted in the action I perform by means of them, and Austin struck a marvelous point in suggesting an analogy between the form of words 'I know' and the form of words 'I promise'.[2] When I use the latter words, I do not describe something in which the promise consists and which I do: the promising is just the using of these words in the right place and with the right qualifications. If 'I know' can be emptied of its descriptive implications, and appreciated solely as a performative expression, then the quest of philosophers from Plato to Prichard to find out what it describes, what condition of the individual is correctly reported with 'I know', will have been demonstrably a pointless search for a phantom state, a fact of grammar misread as a state of being. This would have been a singular discovery of Austin's had he been right, which I do not think he was.

To begin with, it does not follow from the falsity of the Subject theory that 'I know' is not descriptive. It only follows that it does not describe an absolute feature of the individual of whom it is asserted

[1] J. L. Austin, *Philosophical Papers* (Oxford; Clarendon Press, 1961), p. 71.
[2] *Ibid.* pp. 66–71.

or who asserts it of himself. After all, who would doubt that 'I believe' plays a performatory function? We have time and again noted its role in softening or even withdrawing an assertion of the sentences to which it is attached. But nothing in our analysis, nor for that matter in Austin's own view, entails that 'I believe' is not descriptive of a state of the individual who asserts it of himself. The case of 'I believe' then suggests that an expression may be at once descriptive and performative, and it has accordingly to be independently argued that 'I know' is not descriptive, since that will now not follow from the fact that it is performative. Whatever may have been the Descriptive Fallacy, it could hardly have been as disastrous as what one might call the Fallacy of the Single Function as a theory of linguistic utterance. And Austin himself must have seen this: as he writes in the final paragraph of his paper on Truth, 'to say that you are a cuckold may be to insult you, but it is also and at the same time to make a statement which is true or false'.[1] And why should 'I know' not in principle be vested with a like versatility? Austin's criterion for descriptiveness was, I believe, merely that a sentence should admit of truth-values, not that there should be some specific thing denoted—or described—by the sentence held to be descriptive. Austin was professionally interested in sentences which were not descriptive in his sense:

When is a statement not a statement? When it is a formula in a calculus; when it is a performatory utterance; when it is a value-judgement; when it is a definition; when it is part of a work of fiction—there are many such suggested answers...It is a matter for decision how far we should continue to call such masqueraders 'statements' at all and how widely we should be prepared to extend the uses of 'true' and 'false' in 'different senses'. My own feeling is that it is better, when once a masquerader is unmasked, *not* to call it a statement and *not* to say it is true or false.[2]

But it is my argument that 'I know' has not been exposed as a pretender to descriptivity by having been identified as (also) performatory. And I am insisting that restoring it to descriptivity does not commit us to the Subject theory of knowledge. That we should want to keep it descriptive, without, for the present, concerning ourselves with what, if not a subjective condition, 'I know' describes, is in part dictated by

[1] *Ibid.* p. 101. [2] *Ibid.* p. 99.

our wish to preserve those logical connections between '*m* knows that *s*' and *s* which requires the former to be false if the latter is false, and the latter true if the former is. It behoves us therefore to consider for a few pages the analogy between 'I know' and 'I promise', and in doing so I shall assume, correctly or incorrectly, that 'I promise' is *purely* performatory,[1] not merely not describing a promise but not admitting the sensible assignment of truth-values.

(1) The analogy is, as Austin noticed, not a perfect one. He observed that when I do not keep my promise after having said 'I promise', it still is true that I promised, whereas if what I said I knew—*s*—turns out to have been false, it is false that I knew. Austin explains this away by saying that the crucial consideration is that I *said* 'I know' when I ought not to have, and it is true that I made the performance when the performance was unjustified.[2] And so the analogy is restored. There are, however, some rather more damaging discrepancies. Let us suppose in what follows that promising consists in either *saying* the words 'I promise' or performing some other equivalent act, at any rate *doing something* which is recognizably making a promise by the rules of a society which has the institution of promising (as what society does not?).[3]

Promising is something we do for our own part, usually, so that the natural grammatical person for voicing a promise is the first person. The only tense in which it is suitable to make a promise is the present tense. Thus 'I promised' or 'I will promise', whatever performatory employment they may enjoy, are not used to make promises with. If anything, they make assertions, and what they assert is that he who asserts them will, in the future, or has, in the past, perform(ed) a promissory action, e.g., he will say, or has said, the words 'I promise', or whatever equivalent action is socially defined as making a promise. The rules which define promissory actions thus logically require that 'I promised' and 'I will promise' be descriptive. *Some* act, of a binding

---

[1] As a matter of record, it was Hume who seems first to have advanced the performative account of promising. See *A Treatise of Human Nature*, Book III, Part II, section 5. Of course, Austin extended this to 'I know'—not to knowing!—and we are probably much indebted to him for realizing what Hume may have been saying.

[2] Austin, *Philosophical Papers* (Oxford; Clarendon Press, 1961), p. 69.

[3] The deepest discussion of this is perhaps in Nietzsche's *Zur Genealogie der Morale*.

sort, is amongst the truth-conditions for either of these assertions if to promise consists in the execution of a binding act.

But none of this holds for the presumably non-performatory 'I knew' or 'I will know'. Neither of these entails, by any set of rules, the execution of a performance of any sort comparable to the conceded promissory action. It is common ground between Austin and myself that there are no cognitive actions, but I am saying that the truth-conditions for the past and future uses of 'to know' in the first person do not require, for their satisfaction, my ever saying the words 'I know' or performing any action tantamount to the action I should perform were I to say 'I know'. What they do entail, if true, is that there will be a time, or that there has been a time, when 'Danto knows' *is* true of me. If they are descriptive, then 'Danto knows' has at some future or past time to be descriptive, that is, true or false. Again, this is not to say what they do describe, or what it does. But given that it is descriptive, why should I not be able to describe whatever it describes: and with what form of words should I describe it if not 'I know'?

'I knew that *s*'—let us confine ourselves just to the past tense—entails that 'I know that *s*' would have been true had I said it. But Austin holds that 'I know that *s*' has the force of *giving my word*.[1] The truth of 'I knew' does not entail that I gave my word, however: it does not entail that I performed any relevant action. It does not even entail that I would have given my word had I in fact *said* the words 'I know'. Suppose I refer to an episode in which everything came clear to me, and truth lay revealed. Then I might have said in exultation 'I know that *s*'. Someone overhearing me might have said 'He knows'. But I did not give him my word. He could have drawn the same inference, for example, had I (say) read aloud the document which revealed to me the truth. I am, comparably, under no obligation to one who *hears* me promise. I can promise myself something, to make a pilgrimage or break a foul habit. But how can I give myself *my* word? And yet I can say, for no one's benefit but only because it is the fact, that I know something. 'I know', in a social context, underscores, as it were, the transitivity of what it is attached to. If I say I know something, he

---

[1] 'When I say "I know", *I give others my word: I give others my authority for saying that* "S is P".' J. L. Austin, *op. cit.* p. 61. His italics.

to whom I say it knows it as well. Or he does so if what I said is true. And I have no right to give my word when I do not know it to be so.

(2) I may have known something for years, as indeed I may have been under a promised obligation for years. I report the latter fact by saying that I am under such and such a promise. This means that at the beginning of that period I said the words 'I promise' or performed some equivalent action. That action instituted the period, which will last until the promise is fulfilled: breaking the promise does not remove me from the obligation. No analogous action instituted the interval during which I can be said to know something, and there is nothing I do which terminates this period, though of course knowledge may decay. During the period throughout which I know something I can say 'I know', reporting, as it were, this fact. But I cannot while under the obligation to which a promissory act commits me say 'I promise' for I do not report a fact with these words, I make a fresh promise. I can report the fact that I am under a promise, but not by using *the words* 'I promise'. Perhaps the words 'I know' have the force, as Austin suggests, of giving my word, my authority. Each time I say them, I can do this. But in addition I report a fact, the fact, namely, that I know.

(3) It is easy to find examples in usage where a man cannot be giving his word when he says 'I know'. Thus A says 'I no longer love you' to B and B replies 'I know you do not'. B cannot be giving A his authority here! Here he is acknowledging that the words 'I love you no longer' are not needed. C says to D that A no longer loves B, and D says 'I know she does not'. Here he is not giving C his word. He is saying that C brings stale news. I can say 'I know' and express so many things with it: impatience, resignation, sorrow, sympathy, e.g., 'I know that you are suffering deeply over the loss of love'. Then, too, I can give my word. There are all these extra messages which can be conducted by the one set of words, whose common *descriptive* meaning is nevertheless the same.

(4) No one can say that I have promised unless it is true that I have performed a promissory action. But someone can say that I know without my having performed any ritual action whatever, and certainly without my ever having said the words 'I know'. But why should people be able to say of me what I cannot say of myself? It is not like

people saying that I am dead, or saying something of me such that the circumstances of what they say being true rule it out that I should say the same thing of myself and have it be true. It is (I shall show) the fact that I may know something without knowing that I know it, and others then can say of me that I know that *s* but do not know that I know it, while I cannot say as much about myself. But nothing which contributes to the logic of such a circumstance can rule it out that I should ever be excluded from knowing that I know! And what words should I better use to describe the fact that I know except the words 'I know'?

(5) Of course, Austin might have wished to argue that not only is 'I know' not descriptive through the fact that there is no special subjective condition of a subject which it describes: it is not descriptive through the fact that there is no such thing as knowledge. But then '*m* knows' would be false. So would 'I know' be false. Under these conditions, it could never be a justification for making a knowledge claim that he who makes it should know. Yet we want to be able to say to a person that he had no right to claim to know something which he did not. This case would be the universal one on such an analysis. But surely no one wishes here to argue that there is no such thing as knowledge. Perhaps one would want to say, as Austin suggests, that *m* knows that *s* only on the condition that *m* believes that *s* and is right. This is a distinguished and, as we began by remarking, widely supported view. It does not make '*m* knows that *s*' non-descriptive, however: it specifies an analysis of '*m* knows that *s*' which will make the latter true when *m* believes that *s* and is right. So why should I not then be saying when I use the words 'I know that *s*' the same thing? Does Austin really suppose that 'I am right that *s*' would not have the same transitive force as 'I know that *s*'? Surely it would. But then Austin certainly believed 'I am right that *s*'—or '*s* is true' was descriptive! His analysis of truth, which I shall discuss in my final chapter, bears this out.[1]

---

[1] This is unduly *ad hominem* perhaps. Austin's indirect contribution to epistemology is immense, even if he is wrong at every turn. His most celebrated thesis is not even mentioned in his *How to do Things with Words* (Oxford; Clarendon Press, 1962), and it is not unlikely that he by then thought better of it. As evidence (admittedly weak) for this, see the question marks on p. 161, and the suggestion, p. 90, that 'I know' and 'I believe' are 'quasi-performative'.

In general, then it impresses me that the socio-linguistic account, ingenious as it may be, is irrelevant in its conclusions and mistaken in its premisses. 'I know' may be performative and descriptive. And if our rather long exploration has any result, it is that what 'I know' describes is at the least a relationship between him who asserts it and something else. And it is this, I think, which in the end makes the Subject theory so hopeless and so enticing. So long as there is a relation, one of the truth-conditions for '*m* knows that *s*' must in the general case be satisfied by something independent of *m*. So long as this is so, there is something *m* himself has no control over, something which lies outside himself, and hence there is room for doubt. To claim to know is to claim to have gone outside oneself, but if only there were a sure subjective mark which was the state of knowledge, we could make claims about things outside on the basis of some internal fact, and so, somehow, have achieved external reference with internal security, circumventing the skeptic. This is a primal philosophical wish, to which Prichard and others, better and worse philosophers than he, have succumbed. But it is an impossible wish. Without access to an object, we are never justified in claiming to know if we are justified in claiming to know only when we do know. For we *know* only when a relationship holds, and the analysis of this relationship is our task. It ought, however, to be said that if knowledge involves a relationship, then to know that we know involves knowing that the required relationship holds. And this cannot generally be a matter of reflection. Since, however, the relationship can hold without our knowing that it does—without our evidently even knowing that it must hold if we are to know anything at all—it hardly can be true that we must, if we know, know that we do so. But this will, I hope, be proven in the chapter after next. It is, however, a conclusion to be established by analysis, in contrast with a corresponding thesis that, if we believe that *s*, we must not (or we need not) know that we believe that *s*. For this thesis, unlike our other one, depends upon the truth of a theory of philosophical psychology. One achievement of this chapter should have been a de-psychologizing of the concept of knowledge.

Philosophically fascinating as the theories discussed in this chapter have been, none of them entails an exclusivity between knowledge and belief. So we may conclude that '*m* knows that *s*' is after all compatible with '*m* believes that *s*'. That is fairly weak, of course, and the pressing question now is whether, in addition to being merely compatible with it, '*m* knows that *s*' is incompatible with its *denial*. It would be the latter if '*m* believes that *s*' were entailed by '*m* knows that *s*', as the Standard analysis requires. I am not ready yet to decide between these respectively weak and strong relations. Let me say, however, this. I do not see how a man can *know* that he knows that *s* and not believe that *s*. So it is possible that, in *some* manner, '*m* believes that *s*' could perhaps be entailed by '*m* knows that he knows that *s*'. It then would be entailed by '*m* knows that *s*' if the latter entailed '*m* knows that *m* knows that *s*'. But if a man knew, without knowing that he did, it seems plausible to suppose he might even disbelieve what he in fact knew. The question then is whether one may know without knowing that one does, a question which now becomes critical even for the analysis of knowledge. I shall hope soon to answer this in the affirmative, in which case the weaker relation between knowledge and belief will have to seem rather the more plausible.

5

ADEQUATE EVIDENCE AND RULES

Suppose that *m* knows that *s* but *only because m* knows that *e*, where *e* is evidence for *s*. What criterion of adequacy must *e* satisfy in order that what we have just supposed should ever be true? If we are to persevere in holding that the truth of *s* is entailed by '*m* knows that *s*', then we have no choice in the matter at all. The evidence *e* cannot be adequate if *s* can be false while *e* is true. I shall therefore propose that, if *e* is evidence for *s*, then *e* is *adequate evidence* for *s* only if the falsity of *s* is incompatible with the truth of *e*. Nothing weaker can serve. It cannot because, if the falsehood of *s* were compatible with the truth of *e*, then *m* cannot be said to know that *s* only because he knows that *e* where *e* is evidence for *s*. Under those conditions, he cannot be said to know that *s* at all if, consistently with those conditions, *s* can be false.

Exactly the same criterion of *inadequate* evidence is entailed by our resolution to keep a tight connection between justifiably claiming to know that *s*, and knowing that *s* as such. If a man proposes to justify, through the evidence *e*, his claim to know that *s*, then again, *s* cannot be false when *e* is true. Of course, nothing constrains us to persevere in this connection between knowledge and knowledge claims nor, for that matter, in the connection between the knowledge that *s* and the truth of *s*. It is only that, if we wish to keep these connections, and suppose, moreover, that men can know only because they have evidence, then nothing weaker than this condition for adequate evidence will do.

Now it may be urged that this is too high a price to pay, that in the interests of conceptual tautness we have lost touch with the common realities. For what will be the use of imposing a criterion of evidential adequacy which cannot be satisfied? What point is served by setting the criterion of adequacy so high that in fact it never is attained, so that men simply cannot know something only because they have evidence for it, or justifiably claim to know something on the grounds that they possess evidence? I shall speak to this objection in a moment, but perhaps I can somewhat mitigate the force of it by considering some analogous aspects of the concept of explanation.

Commonly, we explain the occurrence of states of things, or of events generally, by reference to other states of those or other things, or to other events. In the typical case, we suppose ourselves to have explained these matters successfully when we show that something was caused to be, or that it was caused to happen, by the other state or the other event to which we have referred. There are many difficulties and high technicalities with this account, none of which we can afford at this point to discuss. But there is a question of what we might term *explanatory adequacy* which bears a useful analogy to our topic. Suppose we explain the occurrence of an event *w* with reference to another event *v*. I think we would want to say that our explanation is *inadequate* if, given that *v* occurred, *w* might not have, everything else being equal: that the non-occurrence of *w* is compatible with the occurrence of *v*. Imagine, for example, that on some occasions, events in every respect like *v* took place, but nothing like *w* then took place. Then, I think, we would want to know why *w* happened *this* time if it has not happened on other occasions when *v* has. And reference to *v* seems hardly explanatory if its occurrence is compatible with both the occurrence and the non-occurrence of *w*: if anything, this suggests the relative causal independence of *w* from *v*. Comparably, if the truth as well as the falsity of *s* is compatible with the truth of *e*, that is as much as to say that *s* is independent of *e*. Now all of this suggests that the *form* of an explanation should be *deductive*. For how better represent the fact that if *v* occurs, then *w* must, than by the consideration that '*w* happens' cannot be false if '*v* happens' is true? And when two sentences are so related that the one cannot be false if the other is true, this is in effect to say that they are related exactly as the premiss and conclusion of a valid deductive argument. Obviously, no one is saying that this semantical criterion is a sufficient condition for an explanation: thus '*w* happened' cannot be false if '*w* happened' is true, but we would plainly not regard reference to *w*'s happening as an explanation of *w*'s happening: we will not accept an explanation in which the explanandum collapses into the explanans. This is just a *necessary* condition. But it *is* necessary; and its being so follows from a universally admitted feature of explanatory inadequacy.

The deductive model of explanation is most prominently identified as that of C. G. Hempel, and though much under attack in recent years, I regard it as sound[1] and even, as I hope to have suggested by my reconstruction, in harmony with our common views on the matter of explanation. But then it might be argued that the requirement of deductivity is too strong. For when, after all, do we have in fact the required certitude that *w* cannot but happen when *v* does? Are we not supposing as constant so much, indeed, that specification of all the conditions required cannot be assured? So that in point of fact, perhaps, no one has really ever provided an explanation which we can be certain satisfies the model? But this is not an argument against the model. It reflects rather on our presumptuousness in supposing we have actually provided adequate explanations when we have not. The critical feature follows, after all, from something we demand in an explanation, not something Deductivists have imposed upon us from without. We could debase the concept of explanation, should we wish to, and bring our model into line with actual practice. But what would be served by this inflationary move? It would merely be *flattery* to scientists to say that they had *really* explained an event when the fact is that it could have happened otherwise under the very conditions they propose as explanatory. Our task as philosophers is not to offer consoling messages, or breed conceptual contentment, or to offer explications of concepts which satisfy the vanities of men.[2] Rather, we must ascertain what is logically required, and if the realities fail to live up to this, then we have at least a fitting sense of our shortcomings. And as in explanation we

[1] Its status as deductive follows, I argue, from the common pattern for *rejecting* explanations. The chief architect, whatever may be the historical priorities, of the deductive model of explanation, is Professor C. G. Hempel. The classical source is his and Paul Oppenheim's 'The Logic of Explanation', in H. Feigl and M. Brodbeck (eds.), *Readings in the Philosophy of Science* (New York; Appleton-Century-Crofts, 1953). It has been contested, especially from the viewpoint of historical explanation: for a defense and references, see my *Analytical Philosophy of History* (Cambridge; University Press, 1965), chapters x and xi. For the most recent review of the issues, Hempel's *Aspects of Scientific Explanation* (New York; The Free Press, 1965), is authoritative. The polemical literature here is vast.

[2] That would amount only to sophistry, which Plato fitly stigmatizes as cosmetic flattery. *Gorgias*, 463 ff.

cannot get adequacy without the Deductivist criterion, so in knowledge we cannot hope to preserve the connections we want with anything weaker than our Incompatibilistic criterion of adequacy.

I believe we can do more than merely note these parallels between adequate evidence and adequate explanations. We can say that m knows that s if (but not *only* if!) m is able to explain why s is true. Then e would be adequate evidence for s if e explains why s is true; and it would follow from the fact that e is the explanans for s that the falsity of s is incompatible with the truth of e. And there can be little doubt indeed that, if e is truly an explanans for s, then, if m knows that e, m will *ipso facto* possess evidence adequate for s. I shall not attempt to specialize the various sorts of explanation that there are, since it seems to me a common feature of all possible explanations that they must fail if the explanans is true and the explanandum false: for what then has been explained? And as I shall not concern myself with what features, in addition to these, an explanation must exhibit in order to qualify as one, so I shall not concern myself either with what, in addition to producing e, one must do in order to explain why s is true. For while it is plain that more is required for e to explain s than that the falsity of s should be incompatible with the truth of e, nothing in my argument will depend upon these further and crucial factors. All that I wish to say for the moment can be cast just in terms of the Incompatibility notion of adequacy.

II

Let us, now, briefly indicate that it is no argument against our notion of adequacy that in an absolute sense *any* sentence for which we might have evidence *might be false*, whatever degree of adequacy our evidence reached. There are sentences which, in virtue of their modal status, might always be false, which means only that they do not enjoy the modality of necessity. But were we to claim justifiably to know that s because we have adequate evidence, it would be a sophistry to say our claim is unjustified since, independently of our evidential support, s might be false as an absolute modal fact. This is just irrelevant. It first would restrict justified knowledge claims to necessary truths, and secondly it would render any reference to evidence otiose: for necessity is determined by satisfaction of criteria which have nothing to do with evidence, e.g., a sentence may be counted necessary only if it is analytic,[1] and with analyticity we need but appeal to the rules of grammar. Moreover, a modal criterion of might-be-false would rule it out that we should ever have adequate evidence, since the modal status of such a sentence would be independent of any considerations having to do with evidence: it would be impossible to provide adequate evidence unless this modified the modal status of the sentence—and then there would be a question if it was the same sentence. No, if we have adequate evidence, then we know that *s*, for which we have it, cannot be false, *whatever may be* its modal status: indeed, we know that in the modal sense *s* might be false, for otherwise evidence for *s* would be irrelevant. So one can in the same breath, as it were, say that *s* might be false and that it might not be, providing one were making distinct references, once to its modal status, and once to its epistemic status relative to the evidence which we might have.

Earlier, we remarked upon the illicitness of proceeding from the unexceptionable sentence, 'If *m* knows that *s*, then, necessarily, *s* is true' —which reflects a conceptual feature of knowledge—to the conclusion 'If *m* knows that *s*, then *s* is necessarily true'. The inequivalence of these is plain. Thus '*s* might be false' as a modal characterization of *s* is incompatible with '*s* is necessarily true'. Hence, in conjunction with the *second* sentence, it entails that *m* does not know that *s* if *s* might be false. But '*s* might be false' is perfectly compatible with '*s* is true'. And so it does not entail the falsity of the latter, and hence, in the first sentence, is quite compatible with '*m* knows that *s*'. That *s* must be true if *m* knows that *s* is perfectly compatible with the modal possibility that *s* might be false. Once more, the scope of the word 'necessarily' must be decided, i.e., whether it pertains to the conclusion absolutely, or merely to the drawing of the conclusion. That *s* might be false is not only compatible with our knowing that *s*, but it is compatible with

---

[1] C. I. Lewis and C. H. Langford, *Symbolic Logic* (New York; Century, 1932), pp. 160 ff. They write 'That *p* is necessarily true means "The denial of *p* is not self-consistent".' Cf. Carnap, *Meaning and Necessity* (Chicago; University of Chicago Press, 1956), pp. 174 ff.: for Carnap, N*p* is true if, and only if, *p* is L-true. For brilliant animadversions, see W. V. O. Quine, *Word and Object* (New York; John Wiley, 1960), section 41.

our having adequate evidence for *s*. Some philosophers in the empiricist tradition have argued that if the modal status of sentences is that of possibility, as (they further argue) must be the case with all empirical sentences, we can pretend to no certainty with these. But on at least conceptual grounds this is a bad argument.

An analogy with explanation would again be helpful. It is perhaps a metaphysical truth that any event might, just as such, not have happened, there being no reason why there has to be something rather than nothing. So, of *w* we might in metaphysical honesty say that *w* might not have happened. This suggests that *w* is not a necessary occurrence, as indeed it may not be. But it is no argument against our having explained *w* with reference to *v* that, in this metaphysical sense, *w* might not have happened. For given the sort of event which *w* by hypothesis is, that would rule out every explanation as inadequate *a priori*, and entail, moreover, that we cannot explain contingent events. But once again, the contingency of *w*, from a metaphysical point of view, is perfectly compatible with *w* being necessitated, given that *v* in fact occurred, even if *v* is contingent in its own right. Not even in a deductive system must every theorem and every axiom be a necessary truth! So it would be compatible with a world of contingent events that everything which happens is necessitated. Hence it is compatible with a deterministic universe that whatever happens could have happened otherwise than it does happen. It is thus no argument against a determinist to prove in some absolute way that a man who does something under a given set of conditions could, under those conditions, have done otherwise: for that is quite compatible with determinism, and even with Necessitarianism.[1] In metaphysics, such considerations are merely irrelevant. Hence a stronger argument would be required: it must be shown, for example, that not only could a man have done otherwise under certain conditions, but that this is true of him in such a way that he could not have been necessitated to do what he in fact

---

[1] G. E. Moore, *Ethics* (London; Home University Library, 1912), argues, in chapter VI, that determinism is compatible with the truth of 'M could have done otherwise'. His reasoning is not characteristically transparent there. For some comments and discussions on compatibilism, see the papers in Keith Lehrer (ed.), *Freedom and Determinism* (New York; Random House, 1966), especially papers by Chisholm, Lehrer, and myself.

did. Then, in an important sense, his action could not in principle be explained. Comparably, to revert to epistemological matters, it would not merely be necessary to show that a sentence is contingent, but that it is so in such a way that it cannot be known, or that there cannot be adequate evidence for it. The *mere* contingency of a sentence entails no such consequences.

III

It may, moreover, be argued that any criterion of adequacy weaker than ours is incompatible with the concept of knowledge in general. I take this to be the force of the type of example introduced into recent discussion by Professor Gettier.[1] Thus suppose we have some notion of 'good evidence' which is weaker than adequate evidence as I have defined it. Then a man may have good evidence for a sentence *t*; *t* may entail *s*; *s* may be true; yet we would hesitate, since *t* is false, to say that the man really knows that *s*. Suppose I believe that the bell now tolls for Smith on the rather good evidence that I have knifed Smith. Smith is the husband of the woman who is my mistress. I am justified in believing, then, that the bell tolls for a man married to my mistress, this being entailed by the bell tolling for Smith, who is married to my mistress. My mistress, unbeknown to me, is bigamous, and in fact the bell tolls for Jones, her other 'legal' mate. So the bell tolls for a man married to my mistress after all. But can I be said to know this? Can, for the matter, I even be supposed justified in *believing* this? It is only by a lucky hit that the proposition I do believe is true, but its being true is independent of any evidence *I* have. Gettier argued, with his examples, that knowledge perhaps ought not to be analyzed as justified true belief.

Gettier's cases are not mere transports of irrelevant philosophical ingenuity. They attack the Standard analysis, as recorded at the head of chapter 4, in such a way that the wound they open appears incapable of staunching until some tight connection is established between the semantic component—'*s* is true'—and the doxastic component—'*m* has

---

[1] For references, see chapter 4, p. 73, note 2. For a brilliant gloss on the Gettier cases, see Brian Skyrms, 'The Explication of "*X* knows that *p*"', *Journal of Philosophy*, LXIV (June 1967).

adequate evidence for *s*'. There exists an important literature on rational belief, wherein attempts are made to let believing *s* be rational if *s* itself is 'acceptable', where acceptability is commonly defined in terms of the probability of *s* relative to a body of evidence. Evidence may be regarded as adequate (in this literature) when it renders *s* *acceptable* to a rational believer. So *s* is acceptable, and *e* adequate for *s*, when the probability of *s*, given *e*, is greater than $1 - n$, and the latter is 'high', *viz.*, greater than 0·51.[1] There are difficulties and paradoxes in connection with this account,[2] but the relevance of it to *our* discussion is that unless $n = 0$ (and supposing that '*s* is probable to degree 1·0' means the same as '*s* is true'), the falsity of *s* is always compatible with the acceptability of *s*, and it is always possible to believe rationally what is not the case. However acceptable *s* may be, and however adequate the evidence through which its acceptability is determined, the truth-value of *s* is independently determined, and may accordingly vary in complete independence of any variations in the adequacy of evidence. So it is always a contingent and external matter that what it is rational to believe should be true. So rational belief cannot be the same with knowledge, and it is doubtful whether a rational belief which is also *true* should be

[1] The sensible suggestion that *s* is acceptable in case the probability conferred upon it by its evidence is greater than 0·5 may be found in Roderick Chisholm, *Perceiving: A Philosophical Study* (Ithaca, New York; Cornell University Press, 1957), p. 28. Chisholm employs the term 'adequate evidence' in a radically weaker sense than I have given it. Thus *m* has adequate evidence for *s* if it would be unreasonable for *m* to accept non-*s*. It is unreasonable to accept non-*s* if *s* is 'more worthy of belief than non-*s*'. *Ibid.* p. 5. Presumably, 'more worthy of belief than' is a relation which does not depend upon absolute features of *s* and non-*s*, i.e., it is logically possible that with shifts in evidence, *s* and non-*s* may change positions in the relationship. Perhaps it is unreasonable to believe that non-*s* will be more worthy of belief than *s*, in case it is unreasonable to accept *s*, but I only am saying that it is logically possible for this to happen, given the weakness of adequate evidence in Chisholm's definition. Of course, Chisholm leaves 'more worthy of belief' undefined, but I mention these matters here only to indicate the following difficulty. If we substitute into Chisholm's definition, we find that *m* has adequate evidence for *s* if *s* is more worthy of belief than non-*s*. And this *may* be vitiated by circularity; for if *s* is not more worthy of belief than non-*s* because of the difference in *evidential strengths which bear on each*, it would be somewhat puzzling whence it would derive.

[2] The difficulties appear chiefly due to the multiplication of probabilities which, when taken in conjunction with some plausible premises, entail one or another version of the so-called Lottery Paradox. See Keith Lehrer, 'Knowledge and Probability', *Journal of Philosophy*, LXI (1964), 368–72; and R. C. Sleigh, 'A Note on Knowledge and Probability', *loc. cit.* p. 478.

counted knowledge, since the belief would be equally rational if the belief were false. And this, I think, is what the Gettier cases dramatize.

It is to the closing of this gap that the complicated professional literature commenting upon the Gettier cases has been devoted: to finding some internal connection between the doxastic and the semantic component of the Standard analysis, e.g., in Peter Unger's phrase, it is an instance of knowledge only if 'it is not an *accident* that a man's belief is true'.[1] But this has about it so pronounced an odor of entailment that I should be surprised were the discussion to terminate with anything weaker, though perhaps in something more subtly formulated, than the criterion of adequacy advanced by us. For I take it that 'it is not an accident that *s* is true' must mean that there is a non-accidental connection between whatever is taken as evidence and whatever makes *s* true—and non-accidental sounds like a hedging concession to necessity. Gettier's cases, after all, arise primarily through what one takes as evidence, and what makes *s* true, belonging in independent causal *series*, which happen only, as though by pre-established harmony, to co-ordinate. So it is natural to suggest that it is knowledge only if the evidence for *s* and what makes *s* true belong in the same causal series. But I shall not speculate here on the nature of the connection wanted, though I shall have something later in this chapter to say about it.

Suppose that the Standard analysis were augmented and strengthened along the lines anticipated, and there were a connection now between *s* and the evidence *e*, and that *e* indeed is adequate for *s*. Would *m* not have to know of this connection in order to know that *s*? He must know of this connection if he is to know that he knows that *s*. This is a rather intuitive reason for supposing that knowledge that *s*, at least where it is knowledge of the sort defined through the Standard analysis, cannot be supposed automatically to entail knowing that one knows. But would *m* know that *s* if he did not know the connection between *e* and *s*? I think one almost must *decide* what one wants to say here, though perhaps the analogy with action may be of some help in making

---

[1] Peter Unger, 'Experience and Factual Knowledge', *Journal of Philosophy*, LXIV (1967), 172. For comment, see Gilbert Harman, 'Unger on Knowledge', *Journal of Philosophy*, LXIV (1967), 390. Alvin Goldman's suggestive paper, 'A Causal Theory of Knowing', *loc. cit.* pp. 357–72, develops the idea that the 'non-accidental' connection may be a *causal* one. I regard this as sound for non-direct knowledge.

this decision. We earlier asked whether, when *b* is a consequence of *a* and *m* does *a*, *b* is to be regarded as his action as well. Now we can, by imposing tight criteria of liability, decide that it is his action. But it is not a matter for decision at all that *b* is his action when he does *a* and both knows that there is a connection and applies this knowledge. And similarly with knowledge itself. If a man knows that *e*, and both knows and applies the knowledge that there is a 'non-accidental connection' between *e* and *s*, then certainly he knows that *s*. Here no decision is needed. So whether it is knowledge in the other case, just as whether it is an action in the corresponding case, is perhaps only a matter of what would be the philosophical advantage of regarding it one way rather than the other. This, if so, would require us to augment the Standard analysis in some such way as this: if *m* knows that *e*, then *m* knows that *s* only if *m* knows that there is a non-accidental connection between *e* and *s*, and *m* applies this knowledge. This may sound uncouth, inasmuch as the word 'knows' appears twice in the analysis. In one case, where *m* knows *e*, it may be counted a piece of direct knowledge. But the other case, which is the one we were left with at the end of chapter 3, remains to be clarified.

There is an intermediate case to be marked between the two we have just considered. That is the case where *m* knows that *e*, believes there is a connection between *e* and *s*, and applies this *belief*. Then, I think, he could be said to know that *s* only if there *were* this connection, and if *s* were true *because* this connection held. There is an analogy in the theory of action to this as well. If a man does *a*, believing that there is a connection between *a* and *b* and applying this belief, then he may be said to have done *b* only if there *were* this connection, and *b* happened because this connection held. So once again, unless we can establish connections, we can speak with certainty only of direct knowledge and direct action.

This may be dramatized through observing that there is conspicuous room in the theory of action for a class of cases structurally of a piece with Gettier's cases in the theory of knowledge. This is where a man does *a*, believing that there is a connection between *a* and *b* and acting in the light of this belief, but where there is *no* connection except that *b* happens anyway. It happens independently of what the man does.

Thus I switch a light switch, believing that the light will go on by this means. But the electrical system has been changed, the live switch is in another room, the one I flick is a dead one, the live switch is flicked by uncanny coincidence at the exact moment I flick the dead one, and I credit myself with having turned on the light by flicking the switch. Here the light's going on is not an action of mine at all, since it did not happen because of anything I did. Since we can exclude this case as an action only because of the *absence* of a connection, the *presence* of a connection must be an element in any case except that of direct action, if it is to be a case of action. And so again with knowledge.

IV

The question very naturally arises at this point whether we ever have or ever can have adequate evidence. I here proceed with some caution, edging my way into this exceedingly treacherous topic by means of the orienting analogy between the concept of knowledge and that of action. Consider, in the latter domain, the performance of a *significant action*, or a gesture, e.g., executing a benediction through raising one's hand, or making a salute by raising a clenched fist. Here, one blesses *by* raising one's hand, or one salutes *by* raising a clenched fist, there being nothing one must do in addition, in order that a benediction or a salute be achieved. In effect, saluting or blessing must count as basic actions. Even so, something further is required in order that these basic actions be transformed into significant gestures, namely a *system of rules* under which such basic actions are *constituted* benedictions, salutes, and the like. There are, of course, complicating questions here as to who is permitted or required, and under what circumstances, to perform such gestures, but these pertain to local issues in the topic of action, and do not affect the structure of these cases. It is thus enough that a qualified individual raise his hand in order that a blessing be performed: he need not, for example, whisper benedictions in his heart.

In raising my hand I *apply* a rule which transforms my hand-raise into a gesture of benediction. Of course, *different* rules will entail different such transformations; so the transformation is achieved only for those who *accept* the rule, who have entered a convention under which they are bound to recognize suitable hand-raises as benedictions. Now something quite analogous to this is to be found in the domain of knowledge. We might, in other words, speak of a *significant cognition*. There is a case in which to know that *e* is to know that *s* if there is a rule which transforms knowing *e* into knowing *s*. Consider knowing that a certain mark has the shape *t*. To know that what has this shape is the miniscule letter '*t*', is simply to understand a rule to the effect that to be the shape *t* just is to be the miniscule letter '*t*'. There is, as with the examples in the theory of action, a special asymmetry. I can raise my hand without executing a benediction if I do not know or do not accept the transforming rule. But I cannot execute the benediction without raising my hand. So again, I can know that something has the shape *t* without knowing that it is the miniscule letter '*t*'. But I cannot know the latter without knowing the former. Not, that is, if I accept the transforming rule. Of course there are other things which a mark of this sort can mean or be, in the respect that there are other rules and other conventions possible. But that is irrelevant here. If I accept the convention, something cannot have this shape and not be the letter '*t*'—even if it is not being *used* so in a given inscription of itself. Thus I used it to exemplify the sort of *shape* I thought someone might know a mark had, who did not know, either because he did not know or did not accept the rule, that it was the miniscule letter '*t*'.

When I know what letter a certain shape is, I am applying a rule. And knowledge of the connection between shapes and letters must be simply *understanding* a rule. It is a kind of knowledge which, as we saw, Prichard confused with 'knowledge' in the epistemological sense. Knowledge of a rule is but *knowing how* to read or to interpret a mark *under a set of rules*. It is being party to a convention. Now providing one accepts the relevant rules, then, knowing something to be a certain mark is to have adequate evidence that it is a certain letter. It is to possess what Wittgenstein spoke of as *a criterion*.[1] I want to stress that

[1] In the MSS. known as, and published under the title *The Blue and Brown Books* (New York; Harper's, 1958), Wittgenstein makes a distinction between 'criterion' and 'symptom'. Thus (roughly) a criterion is a *defining* symptom (see especially p. 22). But Wittgenstein's intent here has remained obscure, and generated some exegetical literature. See especially Rogers Albritton, 'On Wittgenstein's Use of the Term "Criterion"', *Journal of Philosophy*, LVI (1959), 845–57; and Carl Wellman, 'Wittgenstein's Conception of a Criterion', *Philosophical Review*, LXXI, 4 (1962), 433–47.

we have adequate evidence only relative to a rule, and only if we accept that rule. For without the rule, it of course can be that 'This mark has the shape *t*' can be true while 'This mark is the letter "*t*"' is false. There is no inconsistency unless and until one has agreed to the convention. The convention is what constitutes the one thing as evidence, or even adequate evidence, for the other. It is not *part* of the evidence. Since Lewis Carroll at least,[1] we have been aware of the impossibility of incorporating the rules of evidence into the body of evidence, or the rules of inference into the inference they must stand outside in order to license. The system of rules here constitutes that 'knowledge' *in the light* of which we know. The rules of meaning can be counted knowledge, however, only in a very restricted sense. For rules are neither true nor false. That is why this sort of knowledge is not knowledge in the epistemological sense but is, rather, just understanding. And understanding can be taken as knowing *how*, not as knowing *that*.

Let us advance to a more ambitious class of cases now, leaving our analogy behind at this point, where it is apt to be excessive baggage. I think we can say that to understand something is to bring it under a rule—Kant spoke of the Understanding as The Faculty of Rules—and so to be able to explain what it is. Understanding is interpreting. But some rules are more complicated than those we have just considered. Take, thus, the case of scars. Certain shiny marks on the skin, of various colors from red to white, and of all manner of shapes and sizes, are called 'scars'. What they have in common, apart from the tissue of which they are composed, is that they are caused, one and all, by lesions of the skin. Nothing is a scar, but only is scar-like, if it was not so caused. So, to know something to be a scar is to have adequate evidence that the flesh so stigmatized suffered a lesion at the place where the scar now is. Now the rule which transforms these marks into scars is one which permits application of a term only on condition that certain causal presuppositions hold. There are many such terms, and many such rules in our language. It is always possible that the thing to which we apply the term 'is a scar' is not one. It is only that it is not possible it should be a scar and not caused by a wound.

---

[1] Lewis Carroll, 'What the Tortoise said to Achilles', in *The Complete Works of Lewis Carroll* (Garden City, New York; Garden City Publishing Company, 1942), pp. 501-5.

There is a form of causal skepticism, according to which no state of the world logically requires the existence of any other, so that every state of the world is compatible with every possible state, including all actual states. It is a trivial application of this skepticism that the present state of the world is compatible with any past state whatever, including, in the extreme case, that state in which there was no state of the world at all: so that what we refer to as *this* state of the world is the whole of the world's states to date. So no one now in the world ever need have suffered lesions, albeit all who bear those red or white shining skin marks would bear them just the same. They might even be called 'scars'. Yet it would be false that they *were* scars if they were not caused, or were caused by other than wounds. So this form of skepticism must be reinterpreted to mean that there are certain descriptions of the present state of the world, which do not logically presuppose as true any statements about the past. So described, the present state of the world is compatible with any past state of the world including there not having *been* a past state. But then, all of those descriptions of the present state of the world for which this does not hold could be false, for all we can tell from mere examination of *this* world-state: it could *look* just as it does, with all the same items which on the normal presuppositions it does have, but none of them would, for example, be scars. Now I am not concerned to grapple with this form of skepticism,[1] but only to point out that nothing can be evidence against it inasmuch as any *relevant* evidence would be constituted as such only by appeal to some rule of interpretation which the skepticism calls in question. The *relevance* of this form of skepticism is that it disqualifies us from interpreting the world by means of certain rules, and hence of understanding the world as we do. It underscores the extent to which our language is *constituted* of terms whose meaning is given by just such rules as these. Indeed, since referring to certain things as 'effects' and to others as 'causes' is exactly applying a rule of this sort: to rule out these terms is certainly to rule out any term which presupposes their applicability, *viz.*, of certain paintings as 'Rembrandts'. Language would be unaffected, save that it could not be applied. And we should for this reason

[1] I treat of this in *Analytical Philosophy of History* (Cambridge; University Press, 1965), chapter v.

be unclear about what things are because we could not interpret or understand *them*. The world, though remaining just as it is, would be unintelligible since the rules of intelligibility would have collapsed. I shall not speak here about how these rules got established, or how much observation and correlation and experience is capsulated in their having —or giving—the meaning that they do, inasmuch as this form of skepticism requires that terms should have just the meaning they do have, even though there is no history of meaning: the world might have come abruptly into being, with us speaking the language as we do, and having just the rules we have.

These rules of meaning would hold whether there were any occasion for applying them or not, which is why we can regard them as 'inference licenses',[1] becoming laws of nature only if they can be applied. I mean that, whether or not there *are* scars, it is a *matter of meaning* that scars are caused by wounds; but it is a *matter of fact* that scars are caused by wounds only if *there are* scars. It is the transition from questions of meaning to questions of fact, from matters of understanding to matters of knowledge, which must properly concern us here. I shall turn to this quite soon. But let me attempt before doing so to make quite clear what I take the character of the problem to be. We have found it important, in order to frame some response to the question

---

[1] 'A law is used, so to speak, as an inference ticket (a season ticket) which licenses its possessors to move from asserting factual statements to asserting other factual statements.' Gilbert Ryle, *The Concept of Mind* (New York; Barnes and Noble, 1949), p. 121. Ryle nevertheless regards 'law statements' as 'true or false'. It is only that 'they do not state truths or falsehoods of the same type as those asserted by the statements of fact to which they apply or are supposed to apply'. (*Ibid.*) A more radical view is advanced by Stephen Toulmin: 'A law...[is] something of which we ask not "Is it true?" but "When does it hold?"'...In this respect, laws of nature resemble other kinds of laws, rules, and regulations.' *Philosophy of Science* (London; Hutchinson's University Library, 1953), p. 79. For a location of this view on an array of possible ones, see N. R. Hanson, *Patterns of Discovery* (Cambridge; Cambridge University Press, 1958), chapter v. For difficulties in the notion, see C. G. Hempel, *Aspects of Scientific Explanation* (New York; The Free Press, 1965), pp. 354–9. Ernest Nagel, in *The Structure of Science* (New York; Harcourt & Brace, 1961), p. 67, writes that a law is regarded as a rule on inference when it has the 'status of a law which we are not prepared to abandon merely because occasionally there are apparent exceptions to it. For when such a premiss is replaced by a rule of inference, we are along the road to transforming the meanings of some of the terms employed in the premiss, so that its empirical content is gradually absorbed into the meanings of those terms.' How close this begins to sound to Malcolm's 'strong-sense' of knowledge!

whether there is adequate evidence, to introduce rules of meaning or, briefly, to insert *language*. A language, for our purposes, may be regarded as a network of rules of meaning; and to be master of a language is in so far to know how to interpret by bringing under rules. It is simplistic to suppose that only one rule is involved at a time: in applying any rule, we of course activate a whole sector of a language. But these are complexities which need not detain us now.

Philosophers have tacitly conceded the status of rules in their revisionist programs in the theory of meaning. Thus factual statements have at times been characterized as rules for the anticipation of experience,[1] and then the sentences which formulate 'experience' are taken as the 'meaning' of the former. Or else they are rules which connect the latter with the former, as in the theories of C. I. Lewis. Lewis regarded 'factual sentences' as 'non-terminating propositions', the meaning of which must be given in an infinite conjunction of 'terminating' propositions.[2] We might note, as an incidental fact, that Lewis felt that we could never attain to theoretical certainty regarding factual, or non-terminating propositions—or judgments, as he preferred to call them—which would mean that concerning the former, we could not have adequate evidence. But ironically, he actually specified the conditions under which we *would* have adequate evidence for them. Lewis tended to think of the set of sentences, which formulated experience and which provided the evidence for factual sentences, as 'translations' of the former. If a translation, then truth-value would have to be preserved, since if *s'* is to be a translation of *s*, then *s'* cannot have a *different* truth-value than *s*; and it follows that, if the set of terminating judgments is true, the corresponding factual sentence *cannot* be false; so if the former are evidence for the latter, they *have* to be

---

[1] 'Every synthetic proposition is a rule for the anticipation of future experience.' A. J. Ayer, *Language, Truth and Logic* (London; Gollancz, 1950), p. 101. Such a view would have been common property of Pragmatism and Positivism in the 1930s.

[2] C. I. Lewis, *An Analysis of Knowledge and Valuation* (Lasalle, Illinois; Open Court, 1946). Lewis writes: 'The truth of an objective empirical belief has consequences which are inexhaustible and are such that there is no limited number of them whose determination theoretically and absolutely precludes a negative result of further tests and hence *deductively* implies all further and as yet untested consequences' (p. 177; Lewis's italics). Again, 'The statement of this objective belief must be translatable into terms of passages of possible experience, each of which would constitute some partial verification of it' (p. 189). I discuss this thesis below, pp. 222–30 ff.

adequate by my criterion. Of course, we might not be able to complete all the tests required to establish the truth of the conjunction of terminating judgments. But then while *we* would be uncertain of factual propositions, this would be because we were finite, not because *they* are factual, and so the *principle* must be accepted that adequate evidence for factual propositions can be attained. There is perhaps a further point to be made here. If it is to be a *telling* objection that *we* cannot perform an infinitude of tests, then it must be equally telling that we cannot perform an infinitude of translational entries either, so that our understanding of these propositions will be proportionate to our capacity for executing tests. To be sure, we may never then fully unpack their meaning, but to the degree that we understand them, to *that* degree we may have adequate evidence.

It is, I believe, a mistake to regard the relation between evidence and that for which it is evidence as translational, though that is a popular image, and in *some* measure a justified one, since a translation may be regarded as an instance of an interpretation, and rules of meaning are, after all, rules of interpretation. But is the rule of translation suggested by Lewis a terminating judgment or a non-terminating one? In fact it is neither: it belongs in neither of the languages he acknowledged. In fact, it pertains to understanding rather than to knowledge; and in a sense, it specifies the conditions under which a factual sentence may be known. It specifies, indeed, if you *accept* Lewis's rules, just what would be adequate evidence for his factual propositions, providing that the rules can be *applied*. And this brings me to the threshold of the problem of knowledge.

Whether we have knowledge is essentially a question of whether we can *apply a language*. And here we may revert to our schema. If there is a rule, which m accepts, under which e is adequate evidence for s, then, if m understands this rule, m knows that s only if m can apply the rule. But to apply it, it is required that m knows that e. Of course m may know that e and not know that s. For he may not understand nor accept the rule; but if he *does*, then to know that e is to know that s, and to suppose that e can be known and s not is, contrary to hypothesis, to raise a question of meaning. This holds even for those who look for acceptable hypotheses under the logic of confirmation. At the moment, of course, there is no clear agreement on the meaning of 'acceptable hypothesis'. But once this is explicated, there will remain a question of *applying* the rule of meaning, in order to assign whatever index of confirmation it is under which the hypothesis is acceptable. And one may indeed then have adequate evidence that some sentence is an acceptable hypothesis, even if it remain open whether the sentence in question is true.

Now if we are to apply rules, we must have direct knowledge. Knowledge that e is required if there is to be knowledge that s; and as we saw, there is an infinite regression unless there is direct knowledge. One may know that e without applying the rule, but one cannot apply the rule without knowing that e. It is for this reason that direct knowledge is the most contested area in the philosophy of knowledge, and that point at which skepticism becomes illuminating and interesting. It does so because, if there is no direct knowledge there is no knowledge: because, if there is no *applying* language there is understanding at most, but not knowledge (leaving it for the present open whether there is *at least* understanding if there *cannot* be knowledge). I turn, therefore, immediately to the relationships between understanding and knowledge, and thence to skepticism proper. The remarks here made on language must be regarded as perfunctory were my task a different one than it is. But *my* interest in language is only in its application. Unless we can apply it to the world, and so interpret the world and render *it* intelligible, language as such can hold no interest for us as philosophers of knowledge, however otherwise great its philosophical interest may be.

6

KNOWLEDGE AND UNDERSTANDING

I

In an earlier chapter I proposed that *m* may be said *directly* to know that *s*, and that *s* is then a *basic sentence for m*, when *s* stands in the (as yet undefined) relation of *correspondence* with *a* and *m* knows *a*. This characterization escapes circularity inasmuch as the expression 'knows *a*'—which describes a relation between *m* and *a*—is taken as having a meaning different from '*m* knows that *s*', in the analysis of which it happens to figure. I shall think of 'knows *a*' as taking 'experiences *a*' as one of its cases, and for the sake of congruity with an important philosophical tradition, concentrate upon this case. In our discussion thus far, we have established that neither 'knows that *s*' nor 'knows *a*' can be regarded as predicates, true absolutely of *m* when '*m* knows that *s*' or '*m* knows *a*' are true; and since we also have established the latter to be descriptive, we have little choice but to regard 'knows that' and 'knows' as relational predicates. And since relations require terms, I shall speak of *a*, in our characterization of direct knowledge, as an *object of knowledge* or, in the special case upon which we are to focus, as an *object of experience*, or *experiendum*.

There is a deep question as to whether the relations are *external*, in the sense that, when the relation holds between *m* and *a* (for example) it leaves unaffected the terms of the relation in as far as they *are* terms in the relation. There is a question, on the one side, whether, in knowing *a*, there is an *internal* penetration of this upon *m* and, on the other side, whether, when *m* knows *a*, this makes an internal difference to *a*. Does knowledge of the world change the world? It is easy to ride roughshod over these questions. *Of course* knowledge of the world makes a difference to the world: knowing the causes of malaria, I stamp them out: dry up swamps, eliminate *Anopheles*—and flowers bloom, people prosper! *Of course* I am a different man in virtue of the knowledge I acquire: wrecked when I learn of perfidy, exalted at the knowledge that love is reciprocated. We must, to attain knowledge of the world, put Nature on the rack; we *must* change the world in order to understand it; and in altering the world we alter ourselves, emerging from such transactions different men than when we entered. Philosophical reputations have been made, and philosophical systems have been made out of such banal observations. But undeniable as they are, they are irrelevant to the question of whether knowledge is an external relation. It is, to take an analogy, irrelevant to the externality of the *truth* relation to point out that language may interact causally with the world, that language bears the scars of such encounters, and that the truth will make us free. To say that truth is an external relation between a sentence and the world is only to insist that sentences bear no internal mark which testifies that the relation is satisfied, and the world itself is indifferent with regard to whether a sentence about it is true or false. It is by comparison with the indifference of sentences to the question whether they are true or false—'truth' not being, as we may say, an absolute property of sentences—that I want to say that *m* may be just the individual he is indifferently as to whether he satisfies the relationship of knowing *a* or not. So when we know *a*, it is not in virtue of bearing some *internal* mark of doing so, as would be the case if the relation were internal.

It may be objected that, if knowledge is, as I insist, external, then it becomes a pressing question as to how a man, who would then be the same whether he knows *a* or not, should ever know that he knows *a*? How should he know that so external a relation in fact holds? However we may wish finally to answer this question, I want to point out that the externality of the relationship exludes only one class of answers, *viz.*, that he should know this by *examining himself.* The externality of the relationship does not entail that we cannot know that we know, but only that we cannot know this if *all* that we can know is ourselves. Moreover, if *experiencing a* is a case of *knowing a*, it equally follows that experiencing is an external relation and, once more, one cannot know that one is experiencing merely through examining oneself as one term of the relationship. And this is true even if (which is true) we are modified by our experiences, and emerge from them different from what we were before we entered them. Even if we are in fact products of our experience, this fact is irrelevant to the externality of experience as an epistemological relationship.

Now it is, of course, in spite of these considerations, a correct claim that, unless certain conditions are antecedently satisfied by *m* (as by *a*), the relationship of experience cannot be satisfied by them. Thus, no matter what sorts of relations may hold between a pair of stones, they are not ordinarily credited with experiencing one another, even if experience should be an external relation. Stones are not *open* to experience. Again, whatever relations there may be between a pair of *numbers*, there is no relationship of experience between them because numbers are not objects of experience. Both these claims are based, of course, on gross metaphysical assumptions: stones may be dully sensate, and experience the world after all; numbers may be experienced, albeit through a special, sixth sense. But notice that I have not excluded numbers as objects of *knowledge* in saying what I have: not even as objects of *direct* knowledge. There may be extra-experiential cases of direct knowledge: intuition, visions, mystical cognitions, and the like. I am merely not to be concerned with these ways, if they are ways, of instantiating the knowledge relation, since, as we shall see, the logical features we are to be focused upon are invariant to all the cases. The crucial questions of epistemology have not so much to do with questions of whether there are cases of knowledge outside the range of human experience as with whether the knowledge relationship ever is satisfied within experience. And this essentially is the question whether we are ever terms for the experiencing relationship in such a way that we are subjects of the verb 'knows' in true sentences of the form '*m* knows *a*'. This, of course, is the issue of skepticism, and if we can settle this issue to our satisfaction, it is a luxury problem then to go on to determine whether there are extra-experiential cases of direct knowledge. As we saw before, the determination of the limits of direct knowledge is not easy. But fortunately, neither is it crucial.

II

The classical empiricisms upon which we all cut our analytical teeth, and which made so much of the concept of experience, are really more likely theories of understanding than of knowledge. They were concerned with how the mind acquires the ideas with which we find it to be stocked, and experience was primarily invoked in explanation of how we came to have the ideas we have, and hence of understanding what we do. Not every idea, to be sure, need have been caused by experience (external or internal), since some ideas are fabricated by imagination out of the primitive stock experience has provided. And, in order to be recipient of a given class of primitive ideas, which are ideas somehow incapable of internal or imaginative manufacture, we must be open to a given mode of sensibility. And those lacking in a given mode would then be irremediably defective in that sort of understanding which alone is possible when the mind is stocked with ideas which are primitive relative to the mode in which they are deficient. Thus the blind are invincibly uncomprehending of '*a* is red'.

This general theory of understanding, which was instituted by Locke in argument against the possibility of *innate* ideas, is, as a causal theory, subject to the skepticisms endemic to (perhaps because logically co-implicated with) causal theories as such. No logical necessity attaches to it, so its logical opposite is, on grounds empiricists were obliged to favor, logically thinkable. Hence the mind might be stocked quite as it is stocked, though in fact none of the causal episodes insisted upon by empiricists was ever undergone. Thus, to take one such heady possibility famously suggested by Bertrand Russell, for all we logically can say to the contrary, the universe might, with us in it and all our ideas in us, have been created instantaneously five minutes ago. In that case very few indeed of our primitive ideas would have in fact been caused by experience. Well, for our purposes this would very little matter, for we are concerned not with the acquisition but the application of ideas. And we should have all the same problems of establishing the knowledge relation—or the experience relation—between ourselves and the world, even if it, and we, were but five minutes old. The age of the world is logically irrelevant to the questions of direct knowledge except in such cases as memory, in case we think of memory too as an external relation between ourselves and the past.

One somewhat weaker possibility than Russell's might be considered here. It has been suggested, by Peter Unger, that it is logically and perhaps technically possible that an individual *m*, whose knowledge, let us suppose, is acquired precisely as empiricism holds, may be artificially duplicated by another individual *m-ii*, so that every state and trait of *m* is replicated in *m-ii*. This does not undermine the classical theory completely, since the original pattern will have to be established through experience, but my interest in the case lies elsewhere. Although every sentential state of *m* may be duplicated in *m-ii*, so that *m-ii* *understands* everything understood by *m*, still, unless knowledge is a sentential state, it does not follow that *m-ii* knows everything—or even anything— known by *m*. Merely in having every absolute property possessed by *m*, *m-ii* does not thereby achieve all the *relational* properties of *m*. He will not, for example, be the husband of *m*'s wife, for though indiscernible from *m*, he never *married* the woman *m* married. So what will have been transferred will have been understanding, including all that *m* knows how to do. But not knowledge. If *m* knows that *s*, then either this is or this presupposes *direct* knowledge; and as the latter presupposes knowing in the relational sense here specified, *m-ii* knows nothing unless he has stood in the required relations. And merely being a duplicate of *m* is insufficient for that. At any rate, all I shall wish for the present to be saying will be indifferent to these large questions, and the skepticisms we shall have to face will likewise be different skepticisms. So let us press on with our analysis.

The class of basic sentences for *m* will be limited by the class of experienda accessible to *m*, so that even if *m*'s mind should be contra-empiricistically stocked with ideas which he ought, according to their theory, to be modally incapable of having, he would still have an exactly comparable problem of *knowing* that *s*, where this requires that he know *a*, and he is modally insensitive to *a*. In general, *a* will be an object of knowledge for him here only under a mode of experience and, if there is no mode under which *m* can experience *a*, then, unless we permit extra-experiential knowing, *m* cannot directly know that *s*. Yet *s* may correspond to *a*, and *m* may in fact experience *a*, and yet *m* not know directly that *s*, because *m* experiences *a* under a mode of experience discrepant with the aspect of *a* which corresponds to *s*. So *m* hears *a*, *a* corresponds to *s*, but *s* is the sentence '*a* is red'. Well, this is taken care of easily enough. In such a case, we withdraw the unqualified claim that *a* corresponds with *s*: rather, we will propose that an *aspect of a* corresponds with *s*. So then: *m* directly knows that *s* when *s* corresponds to an aspect of *a*, and *m* experiences *a* under that aspect. And we may add: something is an object of knowledge only under an aspect, even if (as may be) there are objects which have only one aspect. But we need not consider here whether there are such objects. All the questions of moment to us concern basic sentences of the sort we have characterized here: if we cannot answer these, it is not likely we can answer any.

III

It may be seen that the truth-conditions for '*m* knows that *s* directly' are rather complicated even in this least controversial case, so that though we have a tendency to say that when *m* knows that *s* directly, he *simply* knows it,[1] there is nothing especially simple about direct knowledge. It is simple only in that justification of direct knowledge claims does not require evidence nor, for that matter, vindication of rules which carry us, as it were, from evidence to that which we claim to know. There *could* be evidence, perhaps, in that whatever is a basic sentence for *m* might express theoretical knowledge for someone else, but that is now not in issue. What is in issue is that even claims to direct knowledge may be justified, though the machinery of justification does not consist in the production of evidence. It consists in making plain that the truth-conditions are satisfied, however this is to be done.

---

[1] A similar notion of simplicity is found in Chisholm's formulation: 'What justifies me in counting it as evident that *a* is *F* is simply that fact that *a* is *F*.' Roderick Chisholm, *Theory of Knowledge* (Englewood Cliffs, New Jersey; Prentice-Hall, 1966), p. 26. Chisholm, on the other hand, feels (p. 28) that 'We can state our justification for certain propositions about our *beliefs*, and certain propositions about our thoughts, merely by reiterating those propositions.' I am not sure that the reiteration of a proposition is itself ever a justification: but making plain the circumstance which would, in the relevant case, rule out any *other* proposition as evidential, might count as the justification for claiming to know that proposition. And this circumstance would be, in Chisholm's idiom, when *a*'s being *F* is 'self-presenting'. The issue then would be to determine the limits on self-presentation.

Justification of this sort is not perhaps commonly required, but a dramatic instance of it would be found if *m* should claim directly to know that *s* and *s* were outside the normal repertoire of basic sentences. A man with a sense of smell, for example, could know directly many things which others only knew on the basis of evidence of some sorts, e.g., he knows, standing in the middle of a dark room, that it has been painted freshly. If others were without this 'sixth sense' they could only know this by sight or touch, and his claim to know it directly would strike them as impenetrably mysterious. Strictly speaking, what his sentence corresponds to is an aspect to which they, in consequence of modal deprivation, are insensitive. Whether they will, under those conditions, accept the man's claim to direct knowledge, much less find it intelligible, is perhaps speculative. Perhaps, indeed, he will have to produce evidence for their benefit that he knows directly here, e.g., by showing that he can do all sorts of what to them are things sufficiently remarkable that they only can explain his ability by ascribing direct knowledge to him. In such a case, supposing they finally could know that he had direct knowledge, the aspect of what he experienced would be a matter of theoretical knowledge to them.[1] And the case would be aggravated in case he knew directly certain things which corresponded to entities which would, to them, be theoretical. Indeed, in the imagined case, smells would be theoretical entities for them, no less theoretical than astral fluids, should there be any, would be to us. Abnormal cases, however, must be used merely to illuminate the normal ones. We best appreciate the situation by considering cases of negative abnormality, e.g., cases where we find ourselves having to explain to the modally deprived (e.g., the blind) how we know directly or what we experience, when we do, things merely opaque to them. Asked on what evidence we are able to say that there are birds, for instance, taking worms on the lawn, we have to say in reply that we have no evidence, or that the birds taking worms on the lawn *is* the evidence, which is, in a sense,

---

[1] It is the possibility of aspects of things which are modally inaccessible to us, to which we are 'blind', which makes the limits of direct knowledge so difficult to draw. Imagine that a whole new mode of sense were to open up. And we then could know directly what had before been only theoretical: 'For now we see through a glass, darkly; but then face to face: now I know in part; but then shall I know even as also I am known.' St Paul, 1 Cor. xiii. 12.

to have no evidence at all. Relative to this, our knowledge is simple. Think, for heuristic purposes, of explaining how we lift our arm to the paralytic. We tell him that we *just* do. There is nothing such that we do *it* in order that our arm rise. And this is something extremely difficult for the paralytic to understand. 'I just know it' or 'I just do it' are tormenting claims to those whose repertoires of basic actions or basic sentences fall short of the knowledge or action reported.[1]

In point of fact, the justificatory demand commonly does not arise quite as I have described. It arises, rather, in connection with showing that what I claim to experience is that with which the sentence I claim to know directly is in correspondence with. Thus the sentence 'There are birds on the lawn' corresponds, if to anything, to birds on the lawn. And I may be challenged to show that what I experience really is birds on the lawn, rather than something altogether different or perhaps nothing at all, but an illusion or a delusion of some sort. The justification here may be complex indeed, but it is in the end a justification through a philosophical analysis of knowledge, through a theory of knowledge, without which we may find that we cannot effect a justification. I intend to provide a complex analysis of the prescribed sort, but once again, the complexity of the analysis and of the justificatory procedures leaves the simplicity of the type of knowledge unaffected. What we have to do, in brief, is to vindicate our claims to *just* know certain things, to *simply* know thus and so, and their simplicity does not spare us the task.

IV

Is it not possible, one may ask, that *s* correspond to an aspect of *a* which *m* knows (experiences) and yet *m* not know that *s*? There is, I believe, one such case, but, if it holds, I should say that *m* does not *understand s*. I think, then, that we may formulate a definition on this basis: if *s* corresponds to *a* and *m* knows (experiences) *a*, then *m* knows that *s* unless *m* does not understand *s*. And from this it follows that '*m* understands *s*' is a necessary condition for '*m* knows that *s*'. There may be, as empiricists insist, sentences such that, unless we experience that to which they correspond, we cannot understand them. But once more,

---

[1] These matters are elaborated in my 'Basic Actions', *American Philosophical Quarterly*, II, 2 (1965).

10-2

I am less impressed by this essentially empirical claim than I am by the possibility that I might experience that to which *s* corresponds and yet not understand *s*, something more than mere experience being required for understanding. And I am less impressed even with this than I am by what I take to be non-controversial, that even if experiencing *a* should all by itself cause all the understanding wanted or needed for *s*, so that I *could* not experience that to which *s* corresponds without knowing that *s* since the mere experiencing furnishes me with an understanding of *s*, it still would be true that understanding *s* would be a necessary condition for knowing that *s*.

There may be thought to be an objection against this that it would be well to get out of the way at this point. One may say such things as this: *m* knows that Gödel's Theorem is true, but *m* does not understand Gödel's Theorem. So how does knowledge always presuppose understanding? Well, consider, by comparison, such a common case as this: I know that Gloria is vain, but I do not understand Gloria. It is not plain what 'understanding Gloria' means here. It may mean that I cannot explain why she should be vain. Yet, whether I can explain it or not, that she is vain is something I know. And now return to the original example. The *sentence* which expresses my knowledge is this: 'Gödel's Theorem is true.' And surely I can know this *sentence*, and not understand Gödel's Theorem, without it following that I do not understand the sentence with which I claim to have knowledge. And if we examine the sentence, what we see is that it contains the expression 'Gödel's Theorem' as its *subject*. And surely I understand this expression! All that is required in order for me to do so is that I be able to say which theorem is Gödel's. Similarly, the sentence 'Gloria is vain' contains the name 'Gloria' as its subject, and to understand the expression (name) I need but know to whom it refers. Russell, in his early theory of acquaintance, held that we must be acquainted with every component in a proposition if we are to understand that proposition. But I am insisting upon nothing so radical as this. All I am saying is what is unexceptionable, that understanding the expression 'Gödel's Theorem' does not in general require that I understand Gödel's Theorem (whatever that entails), but only that I be able to say to what specific thing the expression 'Gödel's Theorem' refers. And this may be generalized.

Indeed, I can understand what 'Parsons understands Gödel's Theorem' means without understanding Gödel's Theorem myself, and even can know that 'Parsons understands Gödel's Theorem' without myself knowing Gödel's Theorem. But I am not here undertaking an analysis of understanding so much as I am insisting upon inclusion of 'understands *s*' in the analysis of 'knows that *s*'.

v

If, now, this condition be granted, we are, I believe, in a position to make good a promise made in chapter 4. I shall proceed to demonstrate that '*m* knows that *m* knows that *s*' has a truth-condition in excess of the truth-conditions for '*m* knows that *s*', and in such a way that the full satisfaction of the truth-conditions of the latter leaves indeterminate whether the excess truth-condition of the former is satisfied. In this case, the former could be false though the latter were true and, if this is (as I shall argue it is) true, then we shall have proved not only that we can know without knowing that we know, but that the virtual equivalence claimed by Hintikka as holding between K*ms* and K*m*K*ms* does not go through.

Let *s* be the sentence '*m* knows that *t*', and let us substitute this sentence for the sentence *s* in the schema '*m* knows that *s*'. Then this yields the sentence '*m* knows that *m* knows that *t*'. But now it should be obvious that the latter demands a truth-condition undemanded by '*m* knows that *t*'. The latter requires that *m* understand the sentence *t*. The former requires in addition that *m* understand the sentence '*m* knows that *t*'. And surely it is possible to understand a great many things without understanding what knowledge is, or what 'knows that' means. I discussed in chapter 4, for example, at least three different philosophers whose knowledge and understanding of many matters I completely esteem, but who plainly do not know what 'knows that' means. For otherwise they could not have argued as they have. There would be no disagreements with what knowledge is, but only with whether something is an *instance* of it. And as Prichard saw with a penetration curiously his own, we cannot wonder whether knowledge is an instance of knowledge if we understand what 'knowledge' means.

But since there is controversy over that, *someone* does not understand this. Perhaps it is only *I* who do not, so that *I* at least do not know what 'knows that' means. But then surely no one wants to seriously suppose that I know *nothing*. I surely know a few things. But if I do, *I* then know them without understanding what 'knowledge' means. Hence there are things I know which I do not know that I know—providing that the understanding of *s* is a necessary condition for knowing that *s*. So the very fact that there should be the sorts of disagreements in the theory of knowledge which the polemic parts of this book have addressed serves us in constructing an internal argument in favor of a thesis in the theory of knowledge.

We do not need that theory of transparency which Prichard rather especially proposed. We can be in a condition of knowing something without being in a condition of knowing that we know it. Knowing that one knows could only have arisen as a concept when men came to be self-conscious about knowledge, when they withdrew, as it were, from their primary involvement with the world and became concerned with the involvement which had un-self-consciously absorbed them before. It was this withdrawal from primary involvements which was the achievement of the first epistemologists, whomever they may have been. There is, then, a kind of reflexiveness here. It is, if you wish, a reflection upon our own condition. This would be Prichard's word but not his meaning. For it is not based upon any fact peculiar to philosophical psychology. It is, rather, a further instance of that sort of circumspection and self-consciousness which is the mark of *philosophical* reflection, whatever its subject may be. Men had knowledge all along. They knew many things about the stars and the animals and the processes of the world they lived in. By coming to *reflect* upon knowledge, they did not, as it were, *add* to the knowledge they had! A reflection does not add to the world, it only shows what is there already, reflections enjoying but a secondary status, in that there could be no reflections of things if there were no things. To know about knowledge made, then, no primary contribution to the stock of knowledge in men's possession:[1] it served only to analyze what it was to be

---

[1] This was the deep problem Plato discovered in the *Charmides*. 'I am not certain whether there is such a science of science at all: and even if there be, I should not acknowledge

in possession of it. Until reflection took its rise in philosophical self-consciousness, men did not know that they knew. They merely knew.

There would, indeed, be no place in the language for the word 'knows', as an essentially *reflective term*, as we may call a term which applies only on condition that another apply, and which has no primary application of its own, if men had not established a distance between them and their primary involvement with the world, and begun to analyze the nature of that involvement and its justification. To speak of that involvement as *knowledge* at all involves a degree of self-awareness for again, men might say all that they have to say about the world without having to *say* that they are saying it, or without having even a *word* for saying in their language. That is why such words as 'knows' and 'says' are curiously gratuitous, in that a man does not add anything by saying 'I say' when he says something. But merely to remark that is to acquiesce in a shallow fact, as merely to remark that 'I know' adds nothing to the assertive force of a sentence is to overlook the immense achievement of self-awareness which merely to have the word already implies. But it is one thing to have achieved this distance, and another correctly to have analyzed what we have learned to describe. There cannot be anything much more difficult to analyze than our primary involvement with the world, a difficulty utterly disproportionate to the ease with which we enter the involvement unawares. For the task of clarifying knowledge has been in an unsettled and unresolved state for millennia, and the species would long since have perished were it essential to our involvement that we should be aware of, much less understand it. Nevertheless, it is plainly possible to be successfully involved without understanding the nature of the involvement, and hence again to know without knowing that we do. The tools of analysis are perhaps the most difficult tools to analyze and, happily, the least essential subjects for analysis.

In mitigation, nevertheless, of Hintikka's theory, and that of Schopenhauer whom he cites as a predecessor in upholding it,[1] one might stress

this to be wisdom or temperance, until I can also see whether such a science would or would not do us any good.' *Charmides*, 169. Plato could not see that KmKms yields Kms. But if it did not, what would be its use? And if it did, what would be its difference?
[1] Jaakko Hintikka, *Knowledge and Belief* (Ithaca, New York; Cornell University Press, 1962), pp. 108–10.

that there *is* a virtual equivalence between KmKms and KmKmKms. The reason is this. Once we have mastered the concept of knowledge— the logic of 'knows'—then regarding knowledge—or 'knows'—there is nothing further to understand. So these two expressions would indeed be mere differing forms of words, no interestingly different truth-condition for KmKmKms being plausible. It would, I dare say, be a rare form of words, and the occasions for its special use a matter of not even remotely philosophical interest. Perhaps it would be only used as emphasis, as repetition so often is. It certainly requires, in order to underwrite its use, no fascinating theory of infinitely expanding con- centricities of self-awareness which the literal mind of the metaphysician is only too ready to postulate!

With this, I hope, the question of whether, if we know, we must know that we know, has been dissolved. We have answered it with only so much of psychology as may be required for understanding the concept of understanding sentences (and think how much we under- stand in comparison with how dark the concept of understanding re- mains to this day!). But it cannot but be noted, somewhat smugly, how gratifying this solution must be to philosophers. For it entails that we may have as much knowledge as we please, and yet not know that we have it until we understand what '*m* knows that *s*' means. And this means that we cannot properly claim the knowledge we have as our own until we have a *correct theory of knowledge*. Epistemologists then contribute nothing to the world's stock of knowledge. *Their* enterprise, which is the enterprise of this book, is only internally related to the possibility of our justifiably claiming to have it. Men can assert many things, but they can only assert that what they assert expresses *knowledge* when they know what knowledge is; and they can only justify their claim to know what knowledge is when they have a theory of knowledge.

Here, then, we have a second mode in which the theory of knowledge enters into the justificatory procedures for knowledge claims: for claims not so much to know things as that what we are claiming is in fact *knowledge*. All of that is just obscured by the performative analyses from which we have been to such pains to detach ourselves.

VI

Because a man might know, might even know directly that *s*, and yet not know that he knows that *s*, it seems certainly possible that he might not believe that *s* under these conditions or might even actively *disbelieve s* in case his failure to know that he knows is due to an inadequate or incorrect theory of knowledge. For these reasons, I am inclined to regard '*m* believes that *s*' as not analytically entailed, hence not a necessary condition for '*m* knows that *s*'. He may believe that *s*, when he knows that *s*, but then again he may not, so knowledge and belief are, I should argue, conceptually independent. And this is so even when a man should in fact know that he knows that *s*. He perhaps knows that he *ought* to believe that *s*. But perhaps he does not and cannot believe that *s*. I can imagine, for example, coming to accept as valid and sound the Ontological Argument and yet disbelieving its conclusion. To be sure, I would be irrational, if it is the touchstone of irrationality to reject what follows from unexceptionable premisses with logical rigor. But then presumably men are at times irrational in this way. Knowledge perhaps ought, but does not in fact always cause that sentential modification of individuals in which I have supposed that believing something consists. The fact that we feel justified in saying that a man ought or ought not to believe something is evidence that we do not conceptually require that belief figure in the analysis of knowledge. That we apply at all the notions of *ought* and *ought not* to believing, however, is also evidence that we have room in our concept of belief for the exercise of a measure of control, so that man is not *ipso facto* justified in holding a belief through the *mere* fact that he holds it. Some exceptions to this perhaps exist. It is conceivable that with *faith*, for example, the mere fact that a man should have it may for him be a sufficient justification for his having it, and at any rate, if it is faith, the likely thing is that he *cannot help* having it, is impotent to believe otherwise. But this is not regarded as typical of our beliefs and, in the typical case, we *are* credited with being able to help what we believe. And indeed, the justification of beliefs, like the justification of actions, may be made the subject of a normative investigation.

There can be an ethics of belief, as Professor Chisholm has especially pointed out, and this will be because the reasons for holding a belief are not always congruent with the causes of our having the beliefs we have. We should be purely rational mechanisms if it were otherwise, the strength of our beliefs and commitments varying purely as functions of the evidence in our possession. Now the evidence available to, or in the possession of m at time t may occur in any of the rows in the following rough matrix: It will be convenient to suppose that any positive evidence for not-s will count as negative evidence against s. I shall let $+$ merely mean that there is favorable evidence, and o that there is no evidence at all. Then the following array, though artificial, is exhaustive:

	s	not-s
(1)	o	o
(2)	o	$+$
(3)	$+$	o
(4)	$+$	$+$

The artificiality here is due to the underdetermination of not-s: in general we will count evidence as favoring not-s when there is evidence favoring any sentence incompatible with s. It is to be understood, however, that the evidence in question is only what is in the possession of m at time t. Then, with (1), m has no basis for believing or doubting s or not-s, and his permissible attitude is merely the judicious one. He may indulge a propensity either to believe or doubt, but there is in so far no justification for either. His attitude in (2) and (3) must be obvious: doubt that s in (3), and belief that s in (2), are respectively groundless. Fundamentally, s ought to be believed in (3) and disbelieved in (2). In (4), which is the interesting and the typical case, it seems only natural to suppose that justified disbelief and belief will vary simply as a function of the differential strength of evidence pro and contra s. But I have no intention of pursuing here a subject which belongs to a deep and useful study, concerned with the logic of rational decisions. Choosing a course of action cannot much differ from choosing a set of beliefs on the basis of partial information. And in a responsible analysis, it is unlikely that sentences would be considered in isolation from one another, and hence considerations other than mere differences in evidential strength might preponderate, e.g., the degree of gained or lost coherency as the price for admitting *s* into a system of sentences, or rejecting it from a system. But none of this is of immediate concern in this investigation.

Given that causes may diverge from reasons, belief is too idiosyncratic a matter for us to suppose that a man will believe what he ought to, given the evidence which he has. At best we can say that were he to believe *s*, he would be justified in doing so. In any event, it is not plain that there is room for belief in the case of direct knowledge. For strictly speaking, there is no evidence for *s* when *m* knows directly that *s*. Nor, for that matter, is there room for doubt, at least not doubt of the sort which naturally alternates with belief, as when a man doubts because the evidence for a sentence is insufficiently strong, or when the evidence for a contrary sentence is stronger than the evidence for *s*. In such a case, where there is no evidence, doubts which may be entertained must be of a different sort altogether. For if a man doubts what he experiences, or doubts that the experience relation is satisfied, how shall we equip him with evidence to remove it? His is a doubt which logically diverts the stream of evidence into unhelpful channels. This is a *skeptical* doubt, which is not the ordinary justified doubt since it calls in question the entire mechanism of justification. It is for this reason that such doubts belong to the philosophical theory of knowledge rather than the normative study of belief. They concern the space *between* us and the world, rather than a space *within* the world itself.

VII

Let us, for a moment, relax our analytical watchfulness and take a synoptic view. The insertion of a distance between our primary involvement with the world, which created logical space in language for such *words* as 'knowledge' and for such a concept as 'knowing that we know', revealed, at the same time, a distance between ourselves and the world with which we were primarily involved. Consciousness is in general an alienating mechanism, in that to be conscious of something is at once to be conscious of a separation of consciousness from that thing *and* to be conscious of the separation; so that when knowledge became self-conscious, as it were, two gaps simultaneously appeared: a gap first between knowledge and its object, and then the gap between this relationship and our knowledge of it, which would be knowledge of *knowledge*. A frantic, self-indulgent metaphysical redescription of this would be perhaps, that with consciousness a wound opened in the oneness of Being.[1] It is at any rate a wound which philosophers have sought, with results almost exponentially disastrous in proportion to the intensity of their efforts, to staunch. For as a space between man and the world was disclosed (a space which, incidentally, reappears within man himself, alienating himself no less from himself than from the world), it became a problem of increasing perplexity as to how this space might be traversed. Hence Prichard's ingenious thought that if we knew what knowledge is, we have an instance of it, and so, having traversed one gap, we had logically traversed the other. But this was ingenuity misspent.

It may be surmised that the gap between us and our involvement, and the gap within that involvement, first emerged in consciousness when something *went wrong*, when it was recognized that a mistake had been made, or an error committed. As always, it is the indispensable function of *Le Néant* to reveal *l'Être* to itself, a revelation which trails an attendant despair when *l'Être* finds that it is separated from itself by the awakening *Néant*. Its spontaneous response is to endeavor to annihilate *le Néant* to so regain integrity within itself, not realizing, if we may continue this fanciful but useful poetic *façon de parler* that it itself is now *constituted* by the *Néant* which it endeavors to eject. Epistemology has often expressed the view, which is only a reflection of the metaphysical horror which the existence of this gap has provoked, that there only can be knowledge when there *is* no gap, demanding as the condition for knowledge that there be a perfect congruence between he who pretends to knowledge and the purported object of the knowledge: a mystical collapse of knower into known which is cele-

---

[1] 'What if it were possible that man, that nations in their greatest movements and traditions, are linked to being and yet had long fallen out of being, without knowing it, and that this was the most powerful and most central cause of their decline?' Martin Heidegger, *What is Metaphysics?* (trans. Ralph Mannheim) (New Haven; Yale University Press, 1959), p. 37. But of course Heidegger is not encouraging, so far as I can tell in his books, a collapse of beings into Being: he is concerned rather to return us to the view that there is Being to which we beings are related, and which we have forgotten. I could accept that.

brated, amongst others, by Bergson. This leads to the pathetically mis-created view that since we only are perfectly congruent with ourselves, ourselves is all we finally can know. As though there were not within ourselves exactly the sort of consciousness-created gap which characterizes *l'Être* as a whole and which the turning inward of the self upon the self was meant to avoid!

There is an essential stupidity in these manoeuvers, which pivot on the theory that any discrepancy whatever, in nature of existence, between the would-be knower and the object of his cognitive ambitions, is fatal to the fulfilment of these ambitions. It is this. Precisely the sort of discrepancy which is lamented is what makes knowledge possible or needed.[1] And far from rendering knowledge—much less knowledge of knowledge—impossible, it is analytic to the concept of knowledge that there be this discrepancy. So much is reflected in the stubborn resistance of 'knows that *s*' to be absorbed into the class of sentential predicates, meaningfully predicable absolutely of a subject. As a concept it is *irremediably* relational.

The avoidance of error is a legitimate human and scientific preoccupation, and it is the subject-matter of the theory of rational decisions, the aim of which is the minimization of risk and the maximizing of cognitive utility. But the manner in which philosophers have been concerned with the avoidance of error has been none of this. They have sought for a shelter which is logically impervious to the intrusion of error, a bedrock of certitude upon which finally to erect all that we may salvage from the skeptic. Quests for certainty, which are the characteristic enterprise of epistemologists, may, to revert to the poetic diction of our recent paragraphs, have been essentially involved with the effort to cope with gaps they despaired of traversing by restricting knowledge to just one side of it, rejecting, unfortunately, the world along with the gap between themselves and it. But the irony lies in the fact that nothing recognizably knowledge can logically be achieved by these means. The metaphysician, who makes it his prophetic labor to 'recall us to Being', to demand that we overcome the nothingness which sunders *Sein*

---

[1] 'Only where there is language, is there world.' Martin Heidegger, 'Hölderlin and the Essence of Poetry', in *Existence and Being* (Chicago; Henry Regnery, 1949), p. 300.

within itself, is in fact demanding that we repudiate our humanity, for it is precisely that sundering which defines us as conscious, hence metaphysical entities. The call is therefore pernicious. The epistemological counterpart to the Prophet of Being is he who quests for certainty. And it is to an examination of the logic, and then to the repudiation altogether of Quests for Certainty, that I now must turn.

7

QUESTS FOR CERTAINTY

I

What I shall refer to as *quests for certainty*[1] constitute a family of philo-sophical disorders with a symptomology almost as rich as philosophy itself. By this I mean to suggest that much of philosophy, including some of its most famous monuments, is nothing other than the quest for certainty in disguise, sharing a logical characteristic which is tire-lessly varied but essentially of a piece throughout the entire *bal masqué*. All of these endeavors, even those which take their mask for their true face, having forgotten or perhaps never realized that they go *en travestie*, rest upon the one essential misconception; each is exultant in supposing itself possessed of the answer to a prayer for a *logical miracle*. The miracle is this. A concept has been discovered, or a class of concepts has been identified, whose semantical value is uniquely determined by some in-ternal feature of itself, whose contact with reality is guaranteed by some internal mark which, having once been discovered, renders us both in touch with reality and immune for ever to mistake. We need not traverse that horrendous gap between concept and reality since the concept itself gives us all of reality we require. Philosophers, however otherwise ingenious and astute, are often almost neurotically oblivious to the fact that their projects fit this unfulfillable characterization to perfection. The mistake upon which they all rest is the blind confusion of *semantical* and *descriptive* notions.

[1] The term is of course taken from John Dewey. Dewey describes the motivation for undertaking quests for certainty with a nice exactitude: 'Men have longed to find a realm in which there is an activity which is not overt and has no external consequences.' *The Quest for Certainty: A Study of the Relation of Thought and Action* (New York; Minto, Balch, 1929), p. 7. Again: 'rational activity is [taken to be] complete within itself and needs no external manifestation'. *Ibid.* p. 8. I am not convinced Dewey would count me an ally, however, inasmuch as the theory of truth I develop here is at odds with Dewey's. But this is because he must have felt that any comparable theory of truth must have consequences of a sort I think I am able to show they need not have. And the consideration which Dewey felt essential, *viz.*, practical manipulation of the world, is irrelevant to an analysis of truth, however indispensable it may be for *determining* the truth.

II

A *semantical vehicle* is anything whatever which bears, or which can be made to bear a semantical value; but it is extremely difficult to specify, in a way which does not beg all the crucial questions, what conditions a semantical vehicle *v* must satisfy in order that *v* bear a semantical value. I shall just begin by giving some examples of what I mean by semantical vehicles, and let general characterizations emerge more or less inductively as we proceed. Philosophically important instances of semantical vehicles have been *sentences* [*propositions*], *ideas, concepts, terms,* and *pictures.* Various attempts have been made, in the past, to reduce one or another of these to some favored or tractable type. Thus Hume took ideas to be copies, hence *pictures,* of impressions;[1] Berkeley took ideas to be pictures *überhaupt,*[2] which was why he took abstract general ideas to be essentially unintelligible; Wittgenstein thought that in at least an ideal language (and its ideality would perhaps lie in this fact), sentences would be *pictures* of facts, and would *show* rather than say;[3] Geach more or less equates mastery of a *concept* with the intelligent use of *terms* (contending that brutes thus are not masters of concepts);[4] and so forth. I have no interest here in these reductive strategies save in underscoring the fact that since serious philosophers have felt no difficulty in assimilating one class of semantical vehicles to another, there is some support for my own enterprise of treating semantical vehicles *en bloc,* whatever important differentiating features may be blurred in doing so. We may thus use now one, now another type of semantical vehicle illustratively, in case the feature we are interested in is exhibited there with any exceptional perspicuity. But the illustration will be meant to diffuse a uniform illumination over the entire class.

[1] David Hume, *A Treatise of Human Nature,* Book I, Part I, section I; and *An Inquiry Concerning Human Understanding,* section ii.
[2] George Berkeley, *The Principles of Human Nature,* Introduction. In regard to the imagistic theory of thinking in Berkeley and Hume, see the critical account in H. H. Price, *Thinking and Experience* (Cambridge, Mass.; Harvard University Press, 1953), pp. 234–63.
[3] Ludwig Wittgenstein, *Tractatus Logico-Philosophicus* (London; Routledge and Kegan Paul, 1961), 4.03 and *passim.*
[4] Peter Geach, *Mental Acts* (London; Routledge and Kegan Paul, 1957), pp. 11–17.

Examples of semantical values are these: sentences may be *true* or *false*; ideas may have (in medieval jargon) *formal* (and not just objective) *reality* or not; concepts may be *instantiated* or *uninstantiated*; terms may *refer* (denote) or *fail to refer*; pictures may *represent* or *fail to represent*. A picture which does not, in this sense, represent, is not abstract but (rather) imaginary: an imaginary landscape is the picture of a landscape which does not exist in reality, but is pictorially indiscernible from a picture of a landscape which does exist in reality.[1] Semantical values come in *pairs*, and the identical semantical vehicle *v* may typically be thought of as taking either of the appropriate semantical values, indifferently as to its structure. I shall speak of the (+) and the (−) semantical values. Examples of the (+) semantical value are *true*, in the case of sentences; *instantiated*, in the case of concepts; *represents*, in the case of pictures, and so forth. It would only be a violation of surface grammar to employ *true* in connection with *any* semantical vehicle, but we may lose an essential bit of fine structure in this way, and so we shall let *true* be only an *instance* of the (+) semantical values.

In order to take semantical values, hence in order to qualify as a semantical vehicle, *v* must have *meaning*, and we constitute anything whatever as a semantical vehicle by giving it meaning. Now the notion of meaning is immensely ramified, and there are all manner of types of meaning which things have or are said to have; but it is not relevant to our inquiry to sort out and classify the modes of meaning. I shall single out just one species, which is crucial, and make no effort to let this usurp the entire notion of *meaningfulness*. There have been dismal episodes in recent philosophical iconoclasm where meaningfulness was narrowly identified with a certain sort of *meaning*, so that whatever lacked that sort of meaning was automatically *nonsense*, as adherents of this view enjoyed abusively phrasing it. I wish it to be perfectly plain that it does not follow from the fact that something lacks *descriptive meaning*—which is the sort of meaning I wish to single out—that it is nonsense, or meaningless, or anything of that sort. I characterize descriptive meaning as follows: the *descriptive meaning* of a semantical vehicle *v* is given by a rule specifying the set [*k*] of conditions to be

---

[1] See my 'Imagination, Reality, and Art', in Sidney Hook (ed.), *Art and Philosophy* (New York; New York University Press, 1966), pp. 220–35.

satisfied if v is to take the $(+)$ semantical value. In general, a rule of descriptive meaning r has the form: $v(+)$ if and only if $[k]$. It will be remarked that when v is a sentence, r is a definition of truth. When v is a term, r gives its definition, etc. Henceforward, when I speak of *meaning*, I shall be taken to be talking about descriptive meaning, and I shall concern myself with no other kind.

Since explicit reference is made in this characterization to the $(+)$ semantical value, it should be plain that the meaning of a sentence, say, is defined in terms of the conditions under which it is *true*. But a sentence retains its meaning independently of whether those conditions are satisfied, and hence even when its semantical value is the $(-)$ one. It ought in principle therefore to be possible, and it is in fact utterly indispensable, to keep the notions of meaning and truth from collapsing into one another. In general, the rule of meaning for a semantical vehicle v only specifies what conditions v must satisfy in order to take the $(+)$ semantical value. It does not say whether these are satisfied. Again, it is generally such that v has just the same meaning whether or not $[k]$ is satisfied, and hence whether its value is the $(+)$ or the $(-)$ one. These characterizations are for the entire class of semantical vehicles, those I have mentioned and any others. Thus, the descriptive meaning of a *concept*, for example, would be the set of conditions $[k]$ which anything must satisfy in order to be an *instance* under that concept. Here $[k]$ expresses what the medievals would have termed the *essence* of the concept, and what moderns perhaps would term the set of conditions necessary and sufficient for something to be an instance of the concept. *Anything* may be constituted a semantical vehicle, providing only that there is a way of bringing it under a rule of meaning, and if there is some way in which it may be determined, in principle at least, which semantical value it takes. A mountain, a cloud, a noise could be incorporated into a system of semantical vehicles if there were any point in doing so. If noises are in fact the typical semantical vehicles, this is in large measure due to the fact that we can *perform* with them rather more easily than with mountains.

Philosophers have made a number of surprisingly hard-won distinctions along the lines I have been laying out: examples are such distinctions as meaning and truth; sense (*Sinn*) and reference (*Bedeutung*);

connotation and denotation; essence and existence. In each of these pairs, the right-hand member specifies the name of the (+) semantical value for the *type* of semantical *vehicle* to which the left-hand member most naturally applies. Frege, whose perspicacity in such matters has perhaps no precedent since the great days of scholasticism, sought to work out the sense–reference distinction for the main classes of semantical vehicles, though when he had to find referenda for sentences, he manufactured two curious entities, the True and the False, for sentences which respectively are true or false to denote.[1] In this he was excessive since after all there is no need for semantical vehicles to refer: they need refer only when they are taken as bearing semantical values, and then, even supposing we were to follow Frege, there would be need at best for the True: a false sentence would be so in virtue of failing to denote the True, rather than through succeeding in denoting the False: so we could effect, even within Fregean ontology, a degree of economy. That it should, meanwhile, be always the (+) semantical value which is mentioned in our characterization of descriptive meaning, ought not to obscure the fact that it is but one of a pair of possible semantical values, and that considerations of meaning remaining constant, the same semantical vehicle may take either. I mention the (+) semantical value on the grounds that to understand, say, a sentence is to understand under what conditions that sentence is true. And so for the other semantical values. Truth, as they used to say in the seventeenth century, illuminated itself as well as falsehood.[2]

III

All along I have been saying that variations in semantical value are determined independently of the meaning of the semantical vehicle which bears them, so that meaning remaining constant, either member

[1] 'Every declarative sentence, in which what matters are the nominata of the words, is therefore to be considered as a proper name; and its nominatum, if there is any, is either the True or the False.' Gottlob Frege, *On Sense and Nominatum*, in N. Feigl and W. Sellars (eds.), *Readings in Philosophical Analysis* (New York; Appleton, Century, Crofts; 1949), p. 91. In this Frege is followed by Alonzo Church in *Introduction to Mathematical Logic*, I (Princeton; Princeton University Press, 1956), p. 25. Church postulates less conditionally than Frege. Frege is not certain that sentences have nominata, but only that, if they *do* have nominata, what the latter are.

[2] 'Just as light reveals both itself and the darkness, so truth is the standard of itself and of the false.' Benedict Spinoza, *Ethics*, Part II, prop. XLIII, note.

of the pair may be borne. So the meaning of the semantical vehicle v will not commonly determine which semantical value applies. In saying this, however, I am taking a stand against the entire enterprise of philosophical quests for certainty, whose character is defined through the fact that they seek to make the $(+)$ semantical value a uniquely determined function of the meaning of the semantical vehicles which concern them. Or, to put it somewhat allegorically, since Understanding is concerned with Meaning and Knowledge with Truth, it is the aspiration of those who quest for certainty to make Knowledge an adjunct of Understanding, so that through, say, the correct understanding of a concept, we will, in the very nature of the understanding, achieve knowledge, namely, whether or not the concept is instantiated. Then cognitive failures may be regarded as failures of understanding.

We have already seen an example of this in Prichard's argument that to understand what knowledge is, is in effect to have an instance of it. But the paradigm for all quests for certainty is the celebrated Ontological Argument of St Anselm, according to which the existence of God was to be entailed by the very idea or concept of God. A few words on this would not be counted digression, perhaps, in view of the general trajectory of our argument. In medieval terms, the essence of a concept c would be the set $[k]$ of necessary and sufficient conditions for any individual i to be an instance of c, and to understand a concept required that one understand what conditions something must satisfy to be an instance of it. It was in general regarded not part of understanding a concept that one know whether, in fact, anything did satisfy what we might term the *existence-conditions* for c. If anything did satisfy these, then c would take the $(+)$ semantical value appropriate to concepts, otherwise the $(-)$ one. We would speak of the $(+)$ semantical value here as *existence*.[1] It is absolutely crucial that we stress that *existence* is a

---

[1] The semantical character of 'exists' is, in modern times, chiefly the teaching of Russell. Thus: 'There is a vast amount of philosophy that rests upon the notion that existence is, so to speak, a property that you can attribute to things, and that the things that exist have the property of existence and the things that do not exist do not. That is rubbish...It is only where propositional functions come in that existence may be significantly asserted...' 'Lectures on Logical Atomism', in R. Marsh (ed.), *Logic and Knowledge* (London; Allen and Unwin, 1956), p.252. 'We say that "men exist" or "man exists" if the propositional function "x is human" is sometimes true; and generally,

semantical term, that it says nothing about things but only about concepts, about which it says they are instantiated. It would be less misleading to speak of the *existence-value* of a concept: (+) if instantiated, (−) if not. It was widely held (and correctly so) that the existence [-value] of a concept *c* was not part of its essence [= its meaning], and Kant, in contending that 'existence is not a real predicate' was merely echoing a truism of medieval analysis.[1] It was then generally held as possible, and widely held as typical by the schoolmen, that one could be complete master of a concept without knowing whether it was instantiated and, more importantly, knowing whether or not it were instantiated would not in the least affect the meaning of that concept. This again is what is meant by Kant in his apparently somewhat unfortunate example of the hundred thalers: the concept of a hundred thalers is invariant as to whether or not it is instantiated; *ergo*, that it *should* be instantiated adds nothing to the concept, for otherwise it would not be *that* concept but another. If instantiated, this would be by the hundred thalers, but to say a hundred thalers exists is not to say anything about the hundred thalers which instantiates the concept: it is to say about the concept that it is instantiated by the hundred thalers. Hence 'exists' is not predicated of the hundred thalers but of the concept, and then not

"a so-and-so" exists if "*x* is so and so" is sometimes true.' *Introduction to Mathematical Philosophy* (London; Allen and Unwin, 1919), pp. 171–2. Russell was characteristically incapable of resisting such claims as 'The individuals that are in the world do not exist'—which he then responsibly qualified by adding: 'rather, it is nonsense to say that they exist and nonsense to say that they do not exist'. *Logic and Knowledge*, p. 252. I analyze this as meaning that a word whose role it is to express the fact that a relation is satisfied is *not* necessarily, and perhaps not at all descriptive of the things which satisfy that relationship. Russell brings this out by saying that '"Humans exist" means "Human" applies to something.' *Ibid.* This is apparently a difficult teaching, for otherwise it would be the philosophical commonplace it should be.

[1] Immanuel Kant, *Critique of Pure Reason*, A 592–603; B 620–631. Hume held a nearly similar but characteristically shallower view. 'The idea of existence is the very same with the idea of what we conceive to be existent.' *Treatise of Human Nature*, II, 6, 4. Paraphrasing this, we might say that to conceive of *a* is to have the idea of *a*, and to conceive of *a* existing is just the same as to have the idea of *a* all over again. But surely Hume will not wish to say that to have the idea of *a* as not existing is the same as *not* to have the idea of *a*. For then this yields a curiously Parmenidian theory to the effect that we cannot think what is *not*. But surely we can think that something does not exist, and how is Hume to explain this? As we shall argue, when we think of *a* existing, the idea of *a* is the same as it would be were we to have thought of *a* as not existing. The difference lies in thinking of the idea as instantiated, or as not instantiated.

absolutely, but only as a value which the concept bears in virtue of a satisfied semantical relationship.

This must be the background against which to appreciate Anselm's argument, in view of the fact that, in certain versions of Anselm's thesis, as well as in the famous version of Descartes' *Fifth Meditation*, the instantiation of 'God' follows from, or was in fact part of the essence of, the concept of God: *suum esse est sua essentia*. Accordingly, to suppose there were logical room for 'God' to take the (−) semantical value—or to suppose, agnostically, that there should be room for doubt as to which semantical value might be taken—is merely to betray ignorance of the meaning of 'God'. Descartes wrote: '*Je trouve manifestement que l'existence ne peut non plus être séparée de l'essence de Dieu, que de l'essence d'un triangle rectiligne la grandeur de ses trois angles égaux deux droits, ou bien de l'idée d'une montagne l'idée d'une vallée.*'[1] So 'God' would be the unique exception to the logical independence of essence (meaning) and existence (reference). But this is too abrupt. Since, after all, the whole usage of 'existence' is taught as in explicit contrast with 'essence', it is not as though there could meaningfully be supposed an exception to the rule that existence is distinct from essence: it is not that 'God' is an exception to the rule, but that the word 'exists' as used in connection with that concept is deviant from standard scholastic usage. So let us augment the concept of God by this predicate, now incorporated as part of the essence of the concept, and part of the essence of *God* in case that concept is *instantiated*. But this cannot be determined from the meaning of the concept, even thus augmented. For the word 'exists' which appears now in the essence is not the word which signifies the (+) semantical value for concepts. To insist that 'exists' is part of the meaning of 'God' simply by-passes the issue. For the proper use of the word 'exists' is such that *it* does not enter into the meaning of any concept. The Ontological Argument traffics on a homonymic pun, hoping thus to trick Reason into affirmation of Faith. Or, to put it more analytically, it hopes through taking a *semantical* term descriptively, to collapse *Sinn* and *Bedeutung* into one.

The Ontological Argument has, of course, many versions, and is a deep achievement, for through it, as through a ring, the whole of

[1] René Descartes, *Méditation Cinquième*.

philosophy may be drawn. Yet this is a version which Anselm himself fell back upon in countering the brilliant parry of the monk Gaunilon,[1] who made it plain that unless some such move were made, an infinity of necessarily existent things could be argued for in perfect analogy with the 'proof' of God. But Gaunilon did not himself realize that to talk about existent entities, no less than *necessarily* existent entities, was already to traduce a rule of meaning of scholastic usage, which withheld the *word* 'exists' from proper application to things. It does not denote, as it were, a property which things have, and which some have necessarily, but has application solely as a value of concepts. Strictly speaking, as Russell relished putting it, things do not exist at all. But to say this, far from advancing a bold metaphysical nihilism,[2] is only to draw attention to a banal fact of language, namely, that 'exists'— like the other semantical values, merely expresses the scoring of a semantical success, it does not as it were enter in as one of the conditions for that success. That there are descriptive or predicative uses of 'exists' is totally irrelevant to the Ontological Argument and Kant's criticism of it.

The Ontological Argument is a paradigm for the quest for certainty, since it hopes—in at least one crucial case—to lay the possibility of doubt for ever aside, once understanding has been achieved. In brief, it makes it unnecessary to go outside a concept in order to determine whether or not that concept is instantiated, so that, come what may elsewhere, the world must underwrite our understanding. And hence, having understood, we have attained knowledge as well, and to suppose we have understanding without knowledge is not to have understood at all. It is this singular fantasy which I propose systematically to dispel.

IV

A chief immediate frustration for those who quest for certainty is, as I have construed such projects, that semantical successes and failures appear so blankly indiscernible at the surface level of the semantical

---

[1] See Norman Malcolm, 'Anselm's Ontological Arguments', *Philosophical Review*, LXIX, I (1960), 41–62.

[2] Nietzsche held a deep view on the thesis that things do not exist: his view was that things are fictions, the world not consisting of things. See Karl Schlechta (ed.), *Nietzsche Werke in Drei Bände* (Munich; Carl Hanser Verlag, 1960), III, 776. Also my *Nietzsche as Philosopher* (New York; Macmillan, 1965), pp. 86–93.

vehicles themselves. Those with the (+) seem so very like those with the (−) semantical value. Consider, for a more apposite example, pictures. In the period in which philosophers took thinking to consist in the shuffling and contemplation of mental images, pictures would have been the standard candidate for the paradigm semantical vehicles. Think, now, of what I have termed 'real' in contrast with 'imaginary' landscape paintings, e.g., one of Monet's paintings of the Japanese bridge at Giverny in contrast with one of Paul Brill's fantastic landscapes. There need be no way of telling these two sorts of pictures apart from any examination, however minute, of their pictorial content alone. To one who did not know the Grand Canyon, for example, a painting of the Grand Canyon would look merely fantastic. A skilled miniaturist can paint a woman's head down to the least mole, although there is no actual woman who stood as model for him; while an uncouth wandering portraitist in Colonial New York will have produced woodenly abstracted likenesses of real patrons. The distinction between real and imaginary has nothing to do either with the delineative skill of the artist (i.e., the picture's 'realism') nor, for that matter, with the content of the work (what it is a 'picture of') but only with whether there is a relationship of representation between the picture and something in the world which resembles it. Since this relationship may be satisfied or not, and yet the vehicle here still be a 'picture of x', it is proper to regard 'picture of x' as a one-place predicate true or false absolutely of a picture, invariantly as to whether there are x's which it in fact does represent. Hence being a picture of x may be true indifferently as to whether the picture itself is imaginary or real. Were it a two-place predicate, you could find proof of the existence of God the Father in the *Santa Trinità* of Masaccio in Santa Maria Novella. So x in the predicate 'picture of x', will have reference to the *content* or *genre* (or bluntly, the *Sinn*) of a picture, or what the picture is 'about'.[1] Let us then say that p is a *real picture of x* if, and only if, p is a picture of x and x exists. It is an imaginary picture of x if the first but not the second condition is satisfied. We may now speak of pictures as taking

---

[1] Hence 'about' is not, in this sense, a semantical term: it pertains to *Sinn* rather than *Bedeutung*. Thus a children's book will be 'about a rabbit' without there having to exist a rabbit which it is about.

the $(+)$ or $(-)$ semantical values strictly depending upon whether they are real or imaginary. Since it is by no *absolute* characteristic of a picture (not even by the fact that it is a picture *of x*) that its realness or imaginariness may be ascertained, pictures as such are semantically neutral with regard to the $(+)$ or $(-)$ semantical values, and differences in their semantical value are due to external correspondence.

Such considerations tormented Descartes. Dreaming, he argued, is very like gazing at painted pictures, though in the solitary gallery of the soul.[1] But if, as he also seriously argued, there is no *internal* criterion for distinguishing waking life from dreaming life, we might take waking life itself to consist in contemplating those things of which, in dreams, we contemplate pictures. Since, however, there is to be no way of distinguishing internally between dream and waking, there is no way either of internally distinguishing whether I contemplate pictures of things or things themselves: no way of discriminating internally between contemplating *x* and simulacra of *x*. So the content of experience must be indiscernible as between dream and waking life, for otherwise there *would* be an internal criterion on the basis of which we could so discriminate. Hence the content of experience must be *neutral* with respect to the difference between dreaming and waking. And this entails that the difference between dreaming and waking is *externally* determined, the identical neutral content being dream-content or waking-content strictly depending upon factors which, external to the content, confer upon it the $(+)$ or the $(-)$ semantical values. Nor is there any way of bringing these external factors *into* the content of experience, for again, there would, contrary to Descartes' claim, then be an internal criterion for distinguishing dream from waking life.

Descartes' Dream Argument has borne the disgruntled criticism of a good many recent philosophers, who find in it traces of nonsense, and the literature abounds by now in subtle refutations of the claim that I

---

[1] '*Toutefois il faut au moins avouer que les choses qui nous sont representées dans le sommeil sont comme des tableaux et des peintures.*' René Descartes, *Méditation Première*. It may be argued that Descartes' point is different, i.e., that, as he goes on to say, the elements of a picture cannot be imagined, though the arrangements of these can be. But the fact is that for Descartes, who is a thoroughgoing Representationalist, *all* perception, dreamful or otherwise, is like contemplating pictures, some more vivid than others. Cf. his *Dioptrique*, IV and *passim*.

may always be, or I may now be dreaming.[1] And it is, in fact, easy to produce such arguments oneself. Here, for example, is one which I have not seen in the literature. Descartes moves to the Dream Argument after having discussed the senses, which he claims can always deceive him. But we might ask how, save on the basis of the senses themselves, one knows the senses may always deceive? For surely it is closer looks, observations under optimal viewing conditions, and the like, on the basis of which I am able to say that the senses deceive me. If, as Descartes recommends, I am to reject all sentences 'based upon the evidence of the senses', it follows that I must also reject the sentence that the senses deceive me, since this could have been discovered in no other way. This is a paradoxical consequence, of course, and Descartes perhaps intuited as much, for his next point in the great *First Meditation* is not so much that the *senses* deceive me, as that *I* may be deceived in supposing myself to be *sensing*! If I were sure I *were* sensing, then I could in special cases trust my senses: but I have no way of knowing whether I am sensing or not, and certainly the *senses* cannot tell me whether or not I am. It is at this point that the *Dream* Argument enters, for in a dream I seem to be sensing but am not, and there is no internal way of deciding which is the case without begging the question. Here, now, is a refutation of the Dream Argument. One must be awake no less to argue than to sense. So, if the argument is to be taken seriously, it must be presupposed that he who offers it is awake. Or else he is not arguing but only talking in his sleep. If he is really arguing, he is awake, and if he is awake, he is sensing and not seeming to sense, and so the Dream Argument cannot be sound. But if he is not awake, he is not really arguing, and since there is no argument, there is nothing to refute! So either there is no Dream Argument, or else the Dream Argument is refuted through its very presuppositions.

But like all attempted refutations of the Dream Argument, this one takes literally considerations concerning dreams which are only in fact heuristic in Descartes' thought. That thought, stripped of ornament, presents a theory of perception which is essentially as I have characterized it, namely that experience consists in contemplating certain con-

[1] See particularly Frank Ebersole, '*De Somnis*', *Mind*, LXVIII, 271 (1959), 336–49; and Norman Malcolm, *Dreaming* (London; Routledge and Kegan Paul, 1959).

tents [= pictures], from the minutest examination of which we cannot determine whether they represent anything in the world or not, hence whether they sustain the $(+)$ or the $(-)$ semantical value. Nor, to revert to Descartes' metaphor, would there be any way of telling save by exiting from the gallery. But this would mean going outside experience, for whatever our experience may be in 'exiting from the gallery' it will consist in *some* content, and with this exactly the same question arises as to whether *it* takes the $(+)$ or the $(-)$ semantical value. So we have in the end no way of comparing the contents of experience with their counterparts in the real world, or even knowing whether they have counterparts in the real world or, in the extreme agony, whether there is a real world for them to have counterparts *in*. So whether the pictures are imaginary or real we have no way of telling, and hence the semantical value which they bear remains radically indeterminate within experience. We only can compare pictures with pictures—a consequence which Berkeley was later to seize upon when he sought to collapse the distinction between the real world and our ideas—and hope to eke a coherent set out of these which we might, hopefully, now suppose 'real'. Any vagrant idea, i.e., any idea incoherent with some body of ideas taken as canonical, will henceforward, and in virtue of just this fact, be counted illusory. But even in *this* strategy, let it be noted, nothing *intrinsic* about our ideas tells us whether they are illusory or not. This, again, is a matter of their *external* congruity with other ideas. So coherency, like correspondence, makes the semantical value borne by an idea a matter externally determined.

The Dream Argument, however, is but a picturesque way of expressing what is known in the textbooks as a Representational Theory of Experience. According to this theory, to experience, say, Shelley, is to stand in some direct relationship with a representation-of-Shelley, when the latter stands in a relationship, largely semantical, with Shelley himself. There is no such thing as seeing Shelley plain. The crucial factor, for our purposes, is that the former relationship, between an experient and a representation-of-*a*, may be satisfied even if the *latter* relationship, between the representation-of-*a* and *a*, should fail. So the experient himself has no way of telling, internally to his experience, whether the relationship holds between the immediate content of his experience and what it represents. This makes acute the so-called problem of the External World, since our experience would be the same whether it correctly represents the External World or not, or even whether there is an External World for it to represent. Our representations, then, operate fundamentally as semantical vehicles, taking the (+) or the (−) semantical values as a function of the satisfaction of an external correspondence between them and their 'representation-conditions', if we may put it so.

Representationalism must sound curious, as perhaps it should, to the non-philosopher. But the non-philosopher would have no hesitation in accepting an exactly analogous account of what it is to understand a *sentence* which describes Shelley truly. This would be to stand in a certain relation to a description-of-Shelley which, in turn, stands in a satisfactory relationship, largely semantical, with Shelley himself. Since the description-of-Shelley will be the same, and our understanding of it as well, invariantly as to whether the latter relationship between it and Shelley is satisfied, the distinction between a true and a false description is a matter of external correspondences. So we are all more or less Representationalists in our spontaneous theories of sentential understanding. Descriptions-of-*a* are, thus, commonly recognized as semantically neutral, i.e., neutral as between semantical values they may in fact bear; and Representationalists have evolved a theory of *representations* which likewise are neutral. Hence they have, in effect, inserted between the world and we experients, an intermediating membrane of semantical vehicles, which happen also to be the immediate objects of experience. The *motive* for this curious manoeuver is to cope with the facts of illusion. So let us return, for a moment, to Descartes and his quandaries.

Descartes was obliged, in logical consequence of the structure of his doubts, to conclude that all he ever had or could have direct access to were 'ideas', except, perhaps, in the case of his *self*, which we shall not concern ourselves with here. He was driven to this in virtue of his demand that there be no internal manner of distinguishing between a state of sensing and *seeming* to sense. He responded to this by neutralizing the content of experience, by supposing his relation with this would be the same indifferently as to the two cases, and then by letting the difference be a matter of external correspondences. The neutralized entity, between which and himself the same relation would hold whether or not the *external* relation between it and the External World held in turn, he labelled an 'idea'. His ideas were thus the forerunners of a dismal philosophical progeny, petering out in the sense-data of recent epistemological infamy. We see exactly the structure of cartesian thought in the work, for example, of C. I. Lewis,[1] who refers to that which Descartes spoke of as ideas, as 'hard kernel(s) of experience —e.g., what we *see* when we think we see a deer but there is no deer'. Lewis adds that 'if there were no such hard kernel', then 'the word "experience" would have nothing to refer to'. And it is symptomatic of philosophical prodigality in such matters that, in order to have a referendum for 'experience' in the case of illusion, what we *see* is prized off the surface of the world, neutralized, and then made to bear the (+) or (−) semantical value in virtue of external connections—connections, that is to say, external to experience. We shall later explore the explicit neutrality of sense-data and phenomenalistic philosophy, but our concern now is with Descartes who, having neutralized his ideas and, at the same time, made these ideas the sole objects of experience, found to his dismay that the External World had fallen away irrecoverably. Or it had done so unless, by some logical miracle, there should be some idea which bore the internal mark of the (+) semantical value.

In Descartes' case, this took the form of a search for an ontological argument. And indeed, there is no alternative. *Experience* would certainly not carry him beyond his ideas. So it is ontological arguments or nothing. Quests for certainty are in the end quests for ontological argument: arguments which exhibit the semantical value of a vehicle as entailed by the rule of descriptive meaning for that vehicle, and hence yield a piece of knowledge as the cognitive dividend of adequate understanding. This then makes satisfaction of the representation-conditions of an idea—or satisfaction of the truth-conditions of a sentence—a further *part* of the representation—(or truth)—conditions which have to be satisfied. And it is thus a futile, pointless conceit. If *it* is the only alternative to skepticism, skepticism must be endured. If

[1] C. I. Lewis, *An Analysis of Knowledge and Valuation* (Lasalle, Illinois; Open Court, 1946), p. 183.

we only can escape irresoluble doubt by means of a logical miracle, we had better learn to live with irresoluble doubt. *I* have, however, only tried to explain the inevitable appeal which ontological arguments conspicuously held for Descartes once he had walled off the world by his semantically neutral ideas-of-the-world.

What I have said regarding Descartes holds for Representationalists generally, whose curious theory demands that the immediate objects of experience be semantical vehicles in search of the (+) semantical value. It holds, as well, for some of the rivals of Representationalism. Berkeley, who pointed out the hopelessness of Representationalism, persisted in treating ideas as semantical vehicles, and so must every philosopher who regards the objects of experience as neutral in this specific way. That is, sentences and stones are semantically neutral, but in different senses—sentences because they do not determine their semantical values, stones because they are not semantical vehicles to begin with.

v

'Exists', like 'is true', is a semantical, not a descriptive expression. Much as 'exists' adds nothing to the concept of a hundred thalers, but only expresses the fact that that concept is instantiated and so bears the (+) value appropriate to concepts, so 'is true' adds nothing to the meaning of a sentence it is attached to, but expresses that the truth-conditions for that sentence are *satisfied*. If 'exists' or 'is true' augmented the concept or the sentence to which they are respectively attached, to make a new concept, or to make a *new* sentence with a *different* descriptive meaning, then the question of the instantiation of this augmented concept, or the satisfaction of the newly augmented truth-conditions would arise. But exercising the same prerogatives which motivated us to flatten existence into a conceptual feature, or truth into a further truth-condition, nothing would prevent us from similarly flattening 'instantiation' or 'satisfaction' into yet further conceptual features or further truth-conditions. And this process could go on for ever. It is a process which consists in the endeavor to make the connection between language and the world a further part of language, or a further part of the world. But having effected this marvelous feat,

174

we are left still with the problem of how language and reality are connected. And so we have to retreat, de-predicating 'exists', and withdrawing 'is true' from just being another truth-condition to expressing the fact that truth-conditions are satisfied, where the satisfaction of truth-conditions is not just another truth-condition to be satisfied.

It is then correct, in a way, to say that '*s* is true' adds nothing to the descriptive meaning of *s*, and philosophers have drawn the conclusion that '*s* is true' is therefore redundant upon *s*, saying nothing over and above what *s* itself says. By parity of reasoning, I should suppose, '*a* exists' should say nothing over and above what *a* itself says. But the latter is less persuasive, if only because '*a* exists' appears to be a sentence while *a* would be just a word, so that '"*a* exists" is true' makes sense, while '"*a*" is true' does not. The analogy is only re-enforced by drawing attention to this, however, for there is no discrepancy at all. In '*s* is true', '*s*' is a name. It names a sentence which it resembles. There is a theory which makes '*s* is true' equivalent to *s*. But they have different meanings, as do '*a* exists' and *a*: '*a* exists' says something in excess of *a* alone. It says, in effect, that '*a*' is instantiated, and '*a*' neither says, nor means, that. But there is a sense in which one can *use* the expression '*a*' in a kind of act of demonstration, e.g., one may say '*a*' with the force of '*Voilà! a!*' using *a* demonstratively. But since the *use* of *a* in a demonstrative act does not appear as part of the surface of *a*, that use could be reflected in the word 'exists': to say that *a* exists, or to make a demonstrative use of *a*, would come to perhaps the same thing. Comparably, to say that *s* is true comes to the same thing as *using s* to make an assertion. So that while it is indeed true that 'is true' adds nothing to *s*, it does not *reduce* to *s*: it is equivalent, on this analysis, to *s* embedded in an assertion. Comparably, 'exists' adds nothing to *a* while not reducing to *a* since it is equivalent to *a* as embedded in an act of demonstration. With this analysis I have, as it happens, both sympathy and reservations, as should be obvious from earlier encounters with a pretty analogous interpretation of 'I know'. I shall, in my final chapter, come to terms with these analyses as a class, but for the present I wish to register my agreement with at least one *consequence* of them, namely, that such words as 'exists' and 'is true' do not—in this they have in common with the entire class of semantical words—belong to the descriptive surface of language. But neither are they simply syn-categorematic, belonging, as it were, to the structural part of language, like the copulative 'is' or the truth-functional connectives. Rather, these words concern the *connection between language and whatever confers upon units of it semantical values*. For the present I shall designate this as the *applicative* part of language, its function being to make application of language to the world in the hope of achieving semantical values of the favored kind.

With applicative words, we shift direction in speech, not augmenting our descriptions but *applying* them, so making a plunge in the direction of the source of semantical values. But as 'exists' and 'is true' are not further descriptive predicates, neither are truth and existence further describable features of the world. To scrutinize the surface of the world for truth is like examining the sides of horses for their existence: they are not mysterious, recondite properties, but no properties at all. If, thus, language *were* a picture of the world, it would, let us suppose, represent the world in its entirety without, in one special corner of itself, representing this further fact. This further fact is not a fact either of the world nor of language, but belongs to the interspace between the two; and language, now taken as a semantical vehicle (or as a set of semantical vehicles), could not express, if it were *only* a picture, the fact that it bears the semantical value which belongs to it in virtue of being a *correct* picture. This I take to have been the closing message of the *Tractatus*, expressed in those mystical sentences[1] which must for ever be excluded from the ideal language.

If this is correct, as I am convinced it is, then it is also correct, if somewhat misleading, to say that these relationships cannot be described. They cannot be described because, if I may be forgiven an image, they are constantly at right angles to the surface of language: to effect a description would require a rotation of language through ninety degrees, but then it would succeed in achieving description only if there were a fresh connection, intersecting it and the plane which has become the source of semantical values, and which cannot itself now be described. So it is not as though there were here the sort of linguistic poverty which

---

[1] Ludwig Wittgenstein, *Tractatus Logico-Philosophicus* (London; Routledge and Kegan Paul, 1961), 6.53–54; 7.

could be remedied or mitigated by absorbing 'exists' or 'true' into the descriptive resources available to us. We would defeat our entire purpose in this, having lost the use of one set of applicatives and placing ourselves under the obligation of finding a new one.

Whatever is at right angles to language is at right angles to the world, so that Wittgenstein was entitled to his view that the world and language must be parallel planes, having no common line of intersection. It is the mark of quests for certainty that they set out treating semantical vehicles as parallel to the world and then look in hopeful forgetfulness for that line on the surface of language where the plane of the world passes through it. This account is intolerably metaphorical. But one falls back on pictorial imagery inevitably but again misleadingly, as we must recognize if our own account is correct: no picture could significantly *show forth* the relationship we wish to have in such a way as not to show it descriptively and hence misleadingly. To paraphrase a brilliant, bitter remark of Ramsay's, if we cannot say it neither can we draw it.[1]

Yet what are we to do? For we want to talk about this relationship if we wish to do philosophy—which incidentally could not be done in the ideal language of the *Tractatus*. Since philosophy is concerned with the interspace between the world and language, it is correct to say that philosophy describes no features of the *world*. Nor is it possible to translate philosophical sentences into sentences which use the descriptive resources of language conformably with the rules of descriptivity. Relative to *all* such rules, philosophy must be nonsense, as, relative to all facts, philosophy must be empty. Philosophy is at right angles to every discipline in so far as it is the task of every discipline which is not philosophy to describe the world. To our knowledge of the world, philosophy contributes nothing.

All of this can be made to sound dismal, to knell the death of philosophy, when all I mean to do is to state the curious conditions under which philosophy is possible. The singular miracle is that philosophy should be understood or practiced at all! For men might

[1] 'What we can't say, we can't say, and we can't whistle it either.' Frank Ramsay, 'General Propositions and Causality', in his *Foundations of Mathematics* (London; Routledge and Kegan Paul, 1931), p. 238.

have gone on describing the world (or imagining it, or conceptualizing it, or acting in a primary way with whatever chosen semantical vehicles may have been opportune) without seeing that crucial distance between vehicles and world in the emptiness of which philosophy belongs. Philosophy begins when one becomes conscious not of some new fact in the world, but of the space between the world and ourselves as manipulators of semantical vehicles. And it is through the phobia aroused by that emptiness that quests for certainty take their rise. So long as there is that gap, the neutrality of semantical vehicles and their dependence for their values on factors outside their scope become revealed. And thus exposed perpetually to external fortune, one never is sure unless, as Descartes and Anselm hoped, the prayer for a logical miracle were answered.

VI

It will be argued that there is at least one class of sentences in connection with which the quest for certainty must be unexceptionable. These are analytical sentences, sentences whose truth-value *is* a uniquely determined function of the meaning of their terms or of the 'sign design' which they exhibit. Hence merely to have grasped the meaning or structure of such sentences is to know that they are true or false, and with these, accordingly, Knowledge *is* logically consequent upon Understanding. But I want to ask, for once, what can be *meant* by the notion of *truth* in connection with analytical sentences? The topic of analyticity is, of course, too ramified a philosophical one for justice to be done it in the following schematic remarks but, in outline, I propose them as a largely adequate account of the matter, recalling that *le bon Dieu est dans les détails.*

(1) So far in our discussion, to understand a sentence s with descriptive meaning is to have mastered a rule r which specifies a set $[k]$ of conditions under which s is true. In general, s is true if, and only if, $[k]$ is satisfied. Let m now understand s. In the ordinary case, a further thing is required if he is to *know* that s: he must know that $[k]$ is satisfied. For in these cases, truth is not entailed by descriptive meaning, nor is knowledge caused by understanding alone. In this regard, then, m can only know that s through understanding s if the satisfaction of

178

[*k*] is part of [*k*]. But surely it is not *part* of the *meaning* of an analytical sentence that it is true! We then should have ontological arguments for the existence of bachelors and unicorns if we have any analytical sentences in which 'bachelors' and 'unicorns' figure as subjects! For it is bachelors and unicorns which satisfy the truth-conditions for sentences about bachelors and about unicorns. So the question becomes intense what can be meant by 'is true' in connection with these sentences if we mean by it, roughly, that the truth-conditions for the sentences it is applied to are satisfied. Granted, if there are any bachelors or unicorns at all, then the truth-conditions of these sentences must be *fully* satisfied. For they specify what properties something must have if it is of a certain sort. But they do not, for they cannot, guarantee that there *are* things of that sort, and hence that their truth-conditions are satisfied.

(2) But I hesitate to say that analytical sentences have truth-conditions at all. Rather, I suggest that they do not *have*, but rather that they *provide*, descriptive meaning for semantical vehicles. Thus, 'Bachelors are adult unmarried males', to take a standard candidate, specifies the conditions under which '*m* is a bachelor' is true. So in general, to be master of an analytical sentence *r* is merely to understand whatever semantical vehicle it is for which *r* specifies the conditions under which it bears the (+) semantical value. Since they primarily *give* descriptive meaning, I shall radically suggest that they *have* no descriptive meaning of their own. If this is accepted, then '*m* knows that *r*' is nonsense where *r* is analytical. For the former is to entail that *r* is true. But to be true requires that *r* have descriptive meaning, which analytical sentences lack. So they express not knowledge but understanding only. This has some importance in view of an earlier discussion. Let *A* be an analysis of the expression '...knows that...' and let *A*, accordingly, express a set of conditions under which '*m* knows that *s*' is true. To know what knowledge is, is then only to understand *A*, i.e., what '...knows that...' means. But it is consonant with this that one *know* nothing at all. Understanding what knowledge is, is *not*, contrary to Prichard, to have an instance of knowledge, but only an instance of understanding. Here, as elsewhere, understanding, even understanding 'knowledge', does not entail having knowledge. Prichard at best can suppose that if we understand 'understanding' we have an instance of understanding.

(3) A sentence r, if analytical, specifies a set $[k]$ of conditions under which some semantical vehicle v bears the $(+)$ semantical value. Let s now be the vehicle v. Then $[k]$ expresses *adequate evidence* for s. For if $[k]$ is satisfied, s is true, given our conception of descriptive meaning. It follows that analytical sentences are implicitly universal, in that they allow no exceptions, i.e., no cases under which $[k]$ is satisfied and s false. So to know $[k]$ to be satisfied, and to have doubts on s, either is to have failed to understand s or else to have some sort of *philosophical* difficulty. Meanwhile, to the degree that it is an inaccessible ideal that there should be analytical sentences, i.e., to the degree to which analyticity is in doubt, to precisely that degree is adequate evidence an inaccessible ideal. To the degree that s can be true and $[k]$ not satisfied, or $[k]$ satisfied and s be false, to that degree is the descriptive meaning of s itself indeterminate. Only by tightening meaning can we hope to have knowledge of the mooted sort. But so far as we keep it loose, so far is the application of semantical values pointless. It is no accident that attacks on analyticity have been launched by Naturalists in recent years, who hold in suspicion the conception of truth as a semantical value, i.e., they suppose it is a 'natural' trait.

(4) The distinction between, or better, whether there is in fact a distinction between analytical and synthetical sentences, has been a matter of recent philosophical dispute. However, not all sentences could be analytical, since not every sentence could be a rule of descriptive meaning: if there are rules of descriptive meaning, some sentences have to have descriptive meaning, and hence to be non-analytical. So if there are any analytical sentences, there are synthetic ones. The reverse argument is perhaps less obvious. It merely seems to me unlikely that we could speak of sentences as having descriptive meaning unless there were rules in terms of which they hold what descriptive meaning they do. Here, again, there is a radical Instrumentalist suggestion that we are to give up descriptive meaning altogether in favor of speaking of *uses*. This might perhaps help, but we should still have to distinguish instruments from the rules of their use, even if we also speak of *using* rules. For rules and what they apply to belong on different levels of language, and the gist, perhaps, of the controversy is that there is no distinction, on the level occupied by synthetic sentences, between these

and analytical sentences. And here I would agree. For on this level there are only synthetic sentences. Whether, amongst synthetic sentences, distinctions may be interestingly drawn, e.g., between synthetic *a priori*, or *a posteriori* sentences; or whether the sentences of mathematics belong here or with rules, are questions which lie beyond my scope, and belong to a different study.

VII

Quests for certainty are attempts to rise to the challenge of skepticism, and skepticism is essentially the view that everything could remain the same with regard to our semantical vehicles and yet they all bear the (−) semantical values. This is more frightening, perhaps, when we take the *objects* of experience, as Descartes and others have taken them, to be coincident with our semantical vehicles, for then the claim of the skeptic is that *experience* could be just as it is and yet correspond to nothing and hence everywhere bear the (−) semantical value. But I am stating this in a more general way, as having application to semantical vehicles generally. Quests for certainty rise to this challenge by seeking to find semantical vehicles the (+) semantical value of which will be determined internally. Metaphorically, they endeavor to assimilate the space between language and the world into a further reach of language. But through whatever success they might achieve along these lines lies their failure, for the extended language must needs now be applied to be true: and so there would be a space to traverse, and so the skeptic would once more emerge. But if we see these matters in this way, we realize that the skeptic merely is describing the conditions which make knowledge possible, since there is no knowledge without truth, and no truth without successful crossing of the space between semantical vehicle and whatever confers semantical value. Skepticism, thus described, is only a disguise for the description of the conditions of knowledge. There is knowledge only if, after having attained understanding, it is open whether what we understand is true or false. That means that there is knowledge only once we have turned at right angles away from the level of our semantical vehicles. Quests for certainty, in attempting to avoid that turn, forfeit, at once, the possibility of attaining knowledge. It is always doubtful, given the meaning of semantical vehicles, that they in fact do bear the (+) semantical value. This doubtfulness is irremediable. It follows, indeed, from the very concept of semantical vehicles. But it is not a doubtfulness we should want to have remedied. For it is not some fatal impediment to the possibility of knowledge. It is, rather, the very character we are obliged to ascribe to the structure of knowledge itself! And the comic ministrations of the quest for certainty would be parallel to an endeavor to avoid death by attaining some station beyond life-and-death without realizing that, if it is *life* one happens to prize, that station sought beyond life-and-death will be quite as fatal as death itself. Truth does not lie *beyond* truth-and-falsity.

Consider, in the context of these considerations, that cliché of contemporary philosophy that, in order for a man to be significantly right, there must (in Miss Anscombe's terms) be room for his only thinking he is right: that for him to be significantly right, it must be possible for him to be *wrong*. This is a claim I wish to endorse myself. Yet I believe it has been seriously misapplied by the philosophers who advance it, for they wish to rule out as an instance of knowledge any situation where it seems impossible that, in that situation, a man might be wrong. But I wish to say that any semantical vehicle is *always* indifferent to the value it bears. The possibility of being false is *always* the logical shadow of the possibility of being right. But this is never a reason for denying that we have knowledge in case (as the skeptics argue) we might be wrong or (as these philosophers argue) we *cannot* be wrong. Any sentence *s* such that I claim that *m* knows that *s* is, *just in virtue of being a sentence*, capable of sustaining either semantical value. So the conditions demanded by these philosophers are *always* satisfied, just as the conditions mockingly deplored by the skeptic are always ineradicable. But since these are necessary conditions for the possibility of knowledge, either position is compatible with the justified claim that *m* knows that *s*. When a man knows, of course, he cannot be wrong, even if it is in principle always possible that the semantical vehicle with which his knowledge is expressed can bear the (−) semantical value and so, on cartesian grounds, be subject to doubt. Again, its dubitability follows from its being a semantical vehicle, but in recognizing this, we remove once and for all the seriousness of such doubts, and remove, along with

them, the serious pretension of general skepticism. We have not removed the possibility of horizontal doubts, of course, but only unmasked the characteristics of generalized or *vertical* doubt.

VIII

Something must be assigned the role of intermediating between the
the world and semantical vehicles in order to determine which semantical value these bear. I have assigned this role to experience, and have
defined experience through its role, and I have left a space in which
experience can function: a space which skepticism misdescribes and
which quests for certainty abhor. Cartesians, and Representationalists
generally, believe experience to be prohibited from mediating between
the contents of experience, which they have neutralized, and the world,
which they have separated from the contents of experience. So the
'contents of experience' will then constitute one class of semantical
vehicle which experience is impotent to mediate, and with *these* the
issue of skepticism seems acute. For we are dealing with a class of
semantical vehicles which we cannot significantly apply. Let us, then,
suppose for a moment that the Problem of the External World is as
cartesians characterize it.

We now must ask what it is to understand an idea, or a content of
experience, or whatever it is to which we are related when it is true
that we experience a, even if it is false that a exists. For, if these are
semantical vehicles, it is essential that we understand what they *mean*,
which is, presumably, independent of questions of their reference, and
hence of their semantical values. To understand an idea i, then, is to
bring i under a rule of descriptive meaning. This assigns a set of conditions $[k]$ to i such that, if these conditions are satisfied then and only
then does i bear the $(+)$ semantical value. It is the *world* which satisfies
these conditions, if anything does, but the world is what the cartesian
complains he cannot, short of ontological argumentation, know. Hence
he cannot know whether, nor when $[k]$ is satisfied, nor whether, nor
when if ever, i bears the favored semantical value. My 'experience' will
be the same in either case. I shall in a moment inquire whether, under
those conditions, a man can be said to understand i. If he cannot, then

183

one might propose that the conditions demanded by the quest for certainty are curiously near to satisfaction after all. For it may then appear that, without the possibility of knowledge, there is no understanding, hence if there *is* understanding, the possibility of knowledge is entailed. This would be so. But while it may bring a measure of comfort to him who quests for certainty, it is important that we mark the fact that it rules out the situation which he presupposes: the situation where everything would be the same and I should have no way of knowing, save by an internal mark on my semantical vehicle, which of them is $(+)$.

It is a curious fact that quests for certainty resemble some famous philosophical quests for happiness, *viz.*, to seek a location outside the vagaries of the order of the world in such a fashion as never to be harassed by them. *Our* happiness, I should argue, must consist in a satisfactory relation to the world, rather than in some station external to it. The temptation to elaborate at this point a Correspondence theory of happiness is strong, but I resist it, and turn instead to the removal of some of the impediments to cognitive infelicity: for we are in position, I believe, to disarm the skeptic.

8

THE REFUTATION OF SKEPTICISM

I

To understand a sentence *s* is to understand a *rule of meaning* for *s*. To understand a rule is in principle to be able to apply that rule. To understand a rule of descriptive meaning for a sentence *s* is to be able to tell when *s* is true. The rule of descriptive meaning for *s* specifies a set [*k*] of conditions under which *s* is true. If, for any reason, a man is in principle incapable of telling when these conditions hold, then it is not *merely* the case that he does not and cannot know when *s* is true. Rather, he is in so far incapable of applying the rule of meaning for *s*. But since to be incapable of applying a rule is not to understand that rule, it follows that, if the man is in principle incapable of applying the rule of meaning for *s*, then he does not understand *s*. Any theory of knowledge, then, according to which one is precluded from applying the rule of descriptive meaning for a class of sentences consigns that class of sentences to *unintelligibility* for the class of individuals held incapable of applying those rules. This goes considerably beyond skepticism. But as we shall see, just these considerations rule skepticism out as untenable when it does more than redescribe the conditions of knowledge.

The rules of meaning for *s* are part of the language *l* in which *s* is a sentence. It is difficult to suppose that the meaning of *s* (or in general the language *l*) could in any philosophically interesting respect be private to a speaker, that is, private not in the sense of being arbitrary or idiosyncratic or hermetic but in the sense of being, for whatever reason, logically incommunicable to another speaker. I *need* not divulge my meaning to another, and another may find it difficult to decode my sentences, but these are mere *de facto* blocks to understanding, and have no philosophical, and certainly no skeptical interests. For imagine a skeptic sufficiently ill-advised to make the understanding of a sentence rather than the knowledge of a sentence the fulcrum of his doubts.[1]

[1] The skeptic manufactured by Friedrich Waismann, *The Principles of Linguistic Philosophy* (London; Macmillan, 1965), pp. 15 ff., is of this type: he is not sure his words mean

He would be ill-advised because that form of skepticism turns back against itself in internal defeat. Suppose, for example, that the skeptic were to insinuate that we might each be using words in conformity with idiosyncratic rules, so that, for all we knew, we each spoke a language peculiar to ourselves. Those who quest for certainty might rise to this bait, of course, and retreat before the danger by saying that while they are not certain that their meaning is *the* meaning of a sentence *s*, they at least know what *they* mean by *s*, so whether they understand another, they at least understand themselves. How then, the skeptic argues, will you ever find your way back to the common tongue? This is like Representationalism all over again, like saying that at least I know what I experience, it being an external matter whether what I experience corresponds or not to reality. How should I ever insert myself in the space between my meaning and the factors which confer upon my meaning the status of being *correct*—*viz.*, *the* meaning, according to *l*, of *s*? But in fact the question is not interesting and the retreat to '*my* meaning' merely comical, the habitual backspring of a philosophical clown. To the skeptic here we reply as follows. Either I do not understand what the skeptic means by his insinuations, and he has not really communicated an argument to which I am under obligation to reply, or else he has communicated, in which case I am under no obligation to reply since he has communicated something *false*. Either he is incoherent or wrong.

   This 'short way' with the skeptic, of course, is altogether for his benefit. For it is essential to philosophical skepticism that general questions of meaning should never arise, that sentences or semantical vehicles in general should have what meaning they have, that we should understand them just as we do, that the surface of things should remain unsullied and undisturbed, so that, for all we can tell by understanding alone, our sentences might be false, our semantical vehicles bear universally the (−) semantical value. Meaning must remain invariant under changes in semantical value; and skepticism must leave everything exactly as it is, or it will not work. Thus the dream must be *indis-*

what they should because he cannot remember whether their meaning is constant over time. Well, he had better make his mind up, or we cannot pretend to understand him. And when he *does* make his mind up, his skepticism cannot any longer be advanced by him: for he will have traduced it.

tinguishable from waking experience, or there would be a way to tell by internal criteria. The present must be just as it is, even if the world were only five minutes old, otherwise there would be an internal way of telling. It is *indispensable to its enterprise* that skepticism never disturb the surface. That is why the quester for certainty is helpless against the skeptic. He looks for a mark *internal* to the surface which certifies external reference, hoping to find in meaning the guarantee of truth. But the skeptic need but insist that whatever pertains to the surface can be incorporated into the surface, the test for whether one is dreaming can always be dreamt itself, and so forth. Against this strategy there is no recourse.

But I have raised an argument which goes rather further against the skeptic than the short way with him will take us. Let us take the entire class of sentences with descriptive meaning in *l*, which may as well be our language. Suppose the skeptic is right, whatever his argument. We in principle can never tell whether a single such sentence is true ! Good. But this means that we can in principle never apply the rules of meaning for these sentences, which means we do not understand these rules, which means we do not understand those sentences. So I am asking whether the skeptic can suppose that we do understand sentences (as he must hold, given the nature of skeptical argument) and at the same time suppose there are logically insurmountable barriers against knowledge. I wish to say that if it is impossible to have knowledge—as it would be on the skeptic's theory since knowledge is expressed by specifically those sentences of our language which we have isolated— then it is impossible to have understanding. But it cannot be to the skeptic's interest to deny that we have understanding of the sentences with descriptive meaning, since he could not then state his position. But my argument is that if he can state his position, his position is untenable. This is not to say that knowledge is entailed by understanding, as the quests for certainty require, but only that the impossibility of knowledge entails the impossibility of understanding. Skepticism, accordingly, is an impossible position, for the moment a condition necessary for its tenability holds, so does a condition sufficient for its falsehood. Knowledge has to be possible if there is such a thing as understanding, at least of descriptive meaning, which is alone relevant here.

II

To understand the rules of descriptive meaning for the sentences of *l* does not really require that we in fact know which of these sentences is true, nor that we in fact have any knowledge at all. It only means that we must in principle be able to tell when they are true, and that such obstacles as there may be to this are not of a philosophical nature, nor provide the slightest evidence for a truly philosophical skepticism. And this is so for all speakers of the language except those for whom it *is* in principle impossible to tell whether a given sentence or class of sentences in *l* is true. But for such people the sentences in question cannot be understood. The Empiricist theory of Learning, to which we alluded, holds that a man *m* is incapable of telling whether a given basic sentence *s* is true if he has not *already* told when *s* was true, that is, if he has not in fact experienced the conditions which make *s* true and hence learned through that experience the meaning of *s*. Hence *nihil est in intellectu quod prius non fuerit in sensu*. It follows from this theory that, if the only way in which what makes for *s*'s truth can be experienced is by means of *sight*, then a congenitally blind man cannot have understood and hence cannot ever, supposing the affliction to continue, understand *s*. This theory of learning hence is committed to the truth of some *historical* sentence in connection with every basic sentence we in fact understand, and since this historical sentence must be false for *s* when *m* is congenitally blind, *m* cannot now understand *s*. I do not regard this theory of learning as necessarily true, and I do not believe it really is true in general at all. But I am far from convinced that the theory of learning here could be generally *false*, that it is possible in principle to understand all the sentences we do understand if *none* of their meanings had been learned through experiencing the conditions which render them true. But it is not important either to my present argument, nor to the argument of this book, that a qualified Empiricist theory of Learning should be true.

A rule of meaning for *s* specifies how the world must be if *s* is true, since, by our characterization of rules of meaning, these specify the conditions which, when satisfied, confer the (+) semantical value upon a semantical vehicle. There is, however, no logical determinism implicit in this claim, in the sense that how the world is cannot be deduced from, nor is it entailed by any feature of language. It is only entailed by the sentences of a language being true: and their being true is not a feature of language, as I have argued. Now, unless the speakers of the language *l* are in principle able to tell how the *world* is, they are in principle incapable of applying the rules of meaning for *l*, and so the descriptive sentences of their language must be supposed unintelligible to them. Speakers tell how the world is by knowing, and typically by experiencing it under descriptions to which it corresponds. If they cannot experience the world, they cannot apply the rules of meaning for *l* and hence cannot be speakers of *l*. So I argue that, the entire skeptical tradition in philosophy notwithstanding, we cannot seriously doubt whether the world can be experienced, nor can we seriously doubt our ability to be able to tell whether it is the world which we are experiencing or not. For if it were in principle impossible to do this, we could not tell when sentences whose truth-value is conferred by the world are true, and in our incapacity to apply the rule, we cannot be said to understand the sentences whose meaning is given by it.

III

It is commonly conceded that a large portion of our language is composed of terms which can only be seen correctly to apply, and of sentences which can only be known to be true, by means, or on the basis of *experience*. So far as there should be doubts and reservations regarding our ability to apply this crucial portion of language, there must, on the argument just presented, be corresponding doubts regarding the intelligibility of these terms and those sentences. And the difficulties are compounded when we consider the remainder of language, the correct application of which is held to be largely dependent upon that portion of language the applicability of which requires experience. Now none of the instability of meaning, which doubts concerning applicability entail, would arise if we could suppose that the critical portion of language need not, in order that it be applied, presuppose that we experience the *world*. If only our experience might be just as it is, whether there were a world or not, then the alleged existence of the world would not be a precondition for the intelligibility of language. There thus arises a massive philosophical effort, ostensibly as a quest for certainty, to redirect the purported reference of the components of this portion of language away from the world to something else, and hence to redescribe experience in such a manner as not to require the world as one term of the experience-relation.

Here there are two main types of theory. First, there is a non-relational view of experience. According to this, 'experiences-*a*' will be a one-place predicate, true absolutely of *m* when '*m* experiences *a*' is true. The latter sentence ascribes to *m* some absolute condition, and such that *m* can, perhaps by introspection, determine that he is *experiencing-a*, and it is not required, in order that he be in this condition, that *a* itself exist. Formally, '*a*' does not have a primary occurrence, as a name, in the sentence '*m* experiences-*a*'. It occurs, rather, as a fragment of a predicate which has many features in common with the sentential predicates of earlier chapters. An example of this type of theory is this: '*m* experiences *a*' is to be understood as '*m* is appeared to *a*-ly'. From which it does not follow, since it is not presupposed, that there *is* an *a* which appears to *m*. The *second* type of theory preserves the relational interpretation of 'experiences', but in such a way that, when '*m* experiences *a*' is true, there is a relation between *m* and an experiendum of a special sort, such as a sense-datum, where sense-data are entities not really part of the world, though they may be related to the world in some philosophically complicated manner. In general, again, it does not really follow that *a* itself should exist, given that '*m* experiences *a*' is true: what follows only is that some sense-datum, some *neutral* entity, exists, and we should make reference to this neutral entity, instead of to *a*, when we speak of *m* as experiencing *a*. I shall not bother to differentiate these theories further here, since from my point of view they amount to much the same thing. Henceforward, when I speak of the 'content of experience' as understood by these theories, the concerned reader may interpret this in terms of whichever type of theory he may prefer. What both theories have in common, of course, is the desire that our experience should remain stable whether *a*, as a genuine portion of the *world*, exists or not. So, if I restrict my experiential language to experience so understood, I have immunized meaning from the depredations of doubt.

Both types of theory arise in response to, and in the hope of voiding the skeptical consequences of the celebrated Argument from Illusion. According to this argument, in *any given instance* our experience might be just as it is, the content of experience be exactly as it is, though we are sustaining illusion and not having, in fact, a *veridical* experience. Both theories respond to this by *neutralizing* the content of experience in such a manner that '*m* experiences *a*' may be true *independently of whether* there is in fact a (real) *a* for *m* to experience[1] or not, and hence independently of whether *m* sustains illusion, when it is true that *m* experiences *a*. Since *m*'s experience is then invariant as to the two cases, the radical instability of meaning threatened by incertitudes concerning the *objects* of experience, when these are understood realistically, is for ever forestalled.

The question only arises as to what meaning we are henceforth to give to the notion of an illusion. Since, according to the very statement of the problem, our experience would be the same *whether we were under illusion or not*, the latter difference cannot be reflected as an internal feature of an experience. It follows, then, that 'is illusory' and 'is veridical' are predicates, whose application to the *contents of experience* is *externally* determined. A veridical experience, as it were, is a content of experience with a (+) semantical value, while an illusory experience is that same content with a (−) one. Notice what has happened. The contents of experience—which had been neutralized in order to accommodate the skeptical irritant of the Argument from Illusion—*have been converted in the process into semantical vehicles*, between which, as such, and whatever it may be to which they are to be related in order that a positive semantical value be attached to them, a gap has been opened up. Almost by definition, the world is what confers semantical values. So what we have done has been to open up a semantical gap between experiences, taken now as semantical vehicles, and the world. The neutralization of experience is like the neutrality which in general characterizes semantical vehicles, where meaning is unaltered by the precarious and externally determined variations in semantical value, and the neutralized contents of experience are made to play two roles at

[1] C. I. Lewis, *An Analysis of Knowledge and Valuation* (Lasalle, Illinois; Open Court, 1946), p. 183.

once. They are (1) objects of immediate experience but (2) also semantical vehicles, land reate to the world in exactly the same relation that language does. In the process of neutralization, the content of experience is *converted* into language.

It is crucial that we note the fact that these theories of experience must, as it were, go outside experience in order to define that which they arise in response to, namely illusion. This is so whether one is a Representationalist, such as Locke, believing our experience non-illusory in case there is an external relation of representation which is satisfied by our experience and some external object which corresponds with the content of experience; or if we regard a sense-datum as non-illusory in case it should be part of the physical surface of a material object. Or in case, as with Berkeley, though we refuse to countenance an ultimate distinction between what we experience and the world, we must nevertheless count an experience as illusory in case it does not cohere with a large body of self-coherent experience-contents which are taken as *ipso facto* real. In every case, the status of illusoriness accorded to a content of experience is externally conferred, and the problem of *defining* illusion remains, even if the theory of experience in question removes us from the threat of suffering illusion.

Once neutralized, contents of experience are not open to doubt. But what does this now mean? It means as much as it would were we to say, regarding a sentence, that, just as a sentence, it is not open to doubt. Or, as Descartes said, ideas, just as such, are never false.[1] He ought rather to have said: ideas, just as such, are neither true nor false, are mere modifications of the mind—just as sentences, as such, are modifications of paper. But of course all this is so. It is only that, in semanticizing the contents of experience, we escape illusion only in so far as we refrain from using them to *assert* anything. What then *can* we do with them? Well, we can *describe* them. This would be like refusing to use

---

[1] René Descartes, *Méditation Troisième*. 'Maintenant, pour ce qui concerne les idées, si on les considère seulement en elles-mêmes, et qu'on ne les rapporte point à quelque autre chose, elles ne peuvent, à proprement parler, être fausses; car soit que j'imagine une chèvre ou un chimère, il n'est pas moins vrai que j'imagine l'une que l'autre.

Ryle notes that sensations cannot be mistaken: 'But not because it is a mistake-proof observing, but because it is not an observing at all. It is as absurd to call a sensation "veridical" as to call it "mistaken". The senses are neither honest nor deceitful.' *The Concept of Mind* (New York; Barnes and Noble, 1949), p. 237.

language to describe the world, since false statements are always possible, and restricting ourselves henceforward to merely the description of language! But the moment we do *this*, we subtly shift the status of the contents of experience from semantical vehicles to something which, external to the descriptions or reports we give of them, confer semantical values upon the latter. And once again, we open a semantical gap.

Masters of Misplaced Slyness are quick to enter when room has been opened up as, after all, room must be opened up if we are to say anything or make any assertions or, for that matter, have any knowledge. Those who have retreated behind contents of experience are challenged on their ability to give correct descriptions of the latter. And indeed the critics are right. There is no guarantee that merely because experiences-*a* should be an absolute condition of *m*, so that *m* need not go outside himself in order to determine whether or not he is experiencing-*a*, that he is immune to error either in saying whether he experiences-*a*, or in describing what experiencing-*a* is like. So perhaps there is no certainty here! We all know the tiresome retreats which philosophers mechanically trace, from assertions of what *is* to assertions of what *seems*, and from assertions of what *really seems* to assertions of what *apparently seems* (to me), etc. And at each stage of the retreat, the same criticism awaits. It does so because each stage commits the same folly as before. We set out to describe the world. Between our descriptive apparatus and the world there is a gap. No unit of the descriptive apparatus guarantees its own semantical value. Doubts are thus always possible. So one sets about describing the descriptive apparatus. But then a gap of exactly the same sort arises, for our erstwhile descriptive apparatus has become a *world* relative to that with which we propose to describe it, and the latter derives its semantical value from the former. Pursuer and retreater are locked, like martyr and tormenter, in some logical and hopeless embrace. And this has been the entire tragi-comedy of post-cartesian epistemology. What has prevented it from being conspicuously absurd has been the insidious conflation of two roles, the role of semantical vehicle *and* the role of object of experience. And so psychological and epistemological questions have drawn illicit support from one another, when the relation between the objects of experience and the world is the same, but not recognized to *be* the same, as the relation between semantical vehicles and the world. But in fact the two sorts of question are utterly independent. The epistemological questions of perception and the psychological questions of perception are all but irrelevant to one another's solution. And this is nowhere more emphatically the case than with the Argument from Illusion.

The Argument from Illusion has used 'illusion' in a way which has nothing to do with optics or the psychology of vision or even mirages. It has used 'illusion' rather as designating a *semantical failure*. It is for this reason that the responses to the Argument from Illusion have consisted in essentially *semantical* adjustments. Once we have penetrated this disguise, we must see that all questions regarding certainty must be held in abeyance until we have sorted out the descriptive and the semantical uses of the word 'illusion'. Only when we have appreciated this difference in use, shall we have rendered ourselves immune from those frantic retreats and those sly probings which force philosophers to undertake these retreats. We shall see what certainty amounts to.

IV

The Argument from Illusion pretends to open up a space between our experiences and the world, a space into which may then be inserted a skeptical lever which prizes the entirety of experience off the face of the world, *externalizing* the world, as it were, from experience. This initial space, I am arguing, is a mythical replica of the space between language and the world, and it is then a space we may skeptically exploit only in so far as we are prepared to treat the content of experience as a language, as a system of semantical vehicles or of meanings. The world would then be that which confers semantical values upon these. But then, if my argument has been correct, the objects of experience, if taken as semantical vehicles, must be unintelligible, since we have no way of determining whether they bear the (+) semantical value: there is no way in which we can apply the rule which gives them their meaning. So in totally externalizing the world, we render the objects of experience unintelligible at the same time as we convert them into semantical vehicles. Skepticism, in forcing the breach, pays too heavy a price, for in then making the breach untraversable, it makes experience meaningless. Doubtless, in the crucial sense relevant here, the objects of experience *are* meaningless, but only because the objects of experience are not semantical vehicles, not because they are semantical vehicles we cannot apply! They are meaningless in the way in which the *world* is meaningless.

It is essential to skepticism that there be this space, and it is fatal to skepticism that there should be this space. The *reason* it is essential is this. The skeptic must allow everything to remain *just as it is,* only there be no way of telling whether it all is illusory or real. The whole of experience must be indifferent with regard to the latter distinction. Now we must make meaning indifferent as to variations in truth-value: a sentence means what it does whether it is true or false. The semantical indiscernibility of the objects of experience, which is insisted upon if not celebrated by those theories we have mentioned which *neutralize* the objects of experience, is a mythical replica of this semantical neutrality of semantical vehicles generally. The unedifying spectacle of the quests for certainty, which we have been anatomizing, consists first in an acquiescence in the status of the objects of experience as semantical vehicles, and then in the futile search for some internal mark of the $(+)$ semantical value: some differential vivacity or intensity which is to be the mark and guarantee of satisfaction of an external relation between 'experience' and the world. But experience could not *conceivably* display such a mark if it were not first semanticized and prized off the world.

By just this fact, however, *neither can we suppose the objects of experience to bear an internal mark of semantical failure.* But from this a crucial consideration follows. Such mistakes as *may* be discerned within experience are therefore irrelevant to the questions of skepticism. For the mistakes, if we may call them that, which the skeptic is exploiting, are as it were perpendicular to the surface of experience. They concern satisfaction of a relation external to the objects of experience, not relations within experience itself. The skeptic so phrases his questions that they cannot be answered *within* experience, and then flaunts us with our incapacity to go outside experience and to see whether, on the other side, there is a relationship satisfied or not. Accordingly, the mistakes which I *can* detect within experience give no evidence for the skeptic's extravagant conclusion. The mistakes of interest to the skeptic cannot be detected. So at best, the mistakes we make and discover ourselves as making provide a skeptic with a sort of *proportion*: as a mistake *within* experience is to a correct taking, so a correct taking within experience is to a correct taking external to experience, i.e., of the world. But the latter correct taking is not ever one which I can discover myself as having achieved, if I cannot get beyond or outside my experience. So I never can tell whether or not a mistake of the relevant sort has been made. It is, indeed, not plain that I understand what sort of mistake I am allegedly liable to at every turn. That I might be always dreaming, that my experience might be just as it is but it all is illusory: these are skeptical possibilities which cannot be removed at the level of experience. The material he calls in question cannot exonerate itself, nor be used by us in its own exoneration, without begging just the question that the skeptic raises. So the sort of mistake *he* is concerned with is different, logically, from the sort of mistake we discover *through* experience. He has to call in question the *whole* of experience, including that to which we would ordinarily appeal in the removal of error.

It follows from this that whenever we discover ourselves as having made a mistake, whenever we realize that we have been in error, we *through just that fact* demonstrate ourselves as immune at that point to the skeptic. It is not only that the skeptic can draw no support from his position from the fact that we make mistakes, but that very fact counts against the skeptic's claims for the entire class of sentences (or semantical vehicles) in connection with which the mistake was made and discovered. Through discovering our mistakes we demonstrate ourselves as capable of crossing the gap between semantical vehicles and whatever confers semantical values on these. That gap then will be useless to the skeptic, who must create, in consequence, a gap we *cannot* cross. But then, in so far as we cannot cross it, the skeptical position collapses. For it then makes untenable what he must, as a skeptic, require, namely that the semantical vehicles mean what they mean, that understanding remain what it is, though semantical values may vary: that we may understand whatever we do understand and yet not have knowledge. If my argument has been sound, then, skepticism regarding the 'external world' is impossible. We cannot have the understanding he requires without the possibility of the knowledge he denies.

The Refutation of Skepticism

Since the mistakes we may discover are of no support to the skeptic, and the successes we may have are no defeat for him, since all of these are within experience, a certain urgency is drained from the enterprise of finding things regarding which we cannot make mistakes: the issue is not to discover incorrigibilia so much as to make certain that, when mistakes have been made, we can discover that they have been made.

It is at this point that the distinction between a *descriptive*, in contrast with a *semantical* use of a term becomes especially crucial. Consider, for example, the word 'real'. It has many familiar descriptive uses, contrasting with 'bogus', with 'artificial', and the like. Often a real *x* will differ from a non-real *x* only in terms of the causes, e.g., a real Rembrandt will have been caused by Rembrandt in a direct way. But a *semantical* use of 'real' cuts entirely across these distinctions. In the sense of 'real' which is *skeptically* relevant, *descriptively* real Rembrandts are no better off than their non-genuine counterparts. Ordinary language philosophers, notably Austin, have merely argued at cross-purposes to those of the skeptic by insisting upon one or another descriptive use of these terms, by pointing out that there are criteria for their application, and by pretending therefore not to understand what the skeptic might mean. But a skeptic ought always to have in mind a semantical use. He is not, therefore, defeated through the fact that there are descriptive uses. It has been a virtual disaster for philosophy that the same set of terms enjoy semantical and descriptive meaning; and that considerations pertinent to the one have carelessly been allowed to swamp the other. Philosophically, it is only the semantical uses which are important: *they* only concern the space between language and the world.

These distinctions apply, perhaps nowhere more importantly, to the problems which arise in connection with illusions. So long as we use the term 'is an illusion' descriptively, rather than semantically, it is not even plain that there is anything of deep epistemological interest in the phenomenon of illusion. We get into difficulties here only when we *confuse* the experience of illusions with the illusoriness of experience, which is a fatal philosophical mistake. What do we experience when we sustain illusion?

There is a current answer which has great appeal to realists, and which, so far as I know, derives from a thought of Ryle's, namely that when we have an illusion the fact is that we experience *nothing*,[1] so that the *right* answer to the question is *no* answer. For rather than experiencing something invariant to illusoriness and veridicality, the argument is that to sustain an illusion is to have no experience at all, but falsely to believe that there *is* an experience. This move, briskly attractive as it may seem, is perhaps finally as disastrous as the theory it means to reject. For it *seems* to be some sort of experience when I sustain an illusion, and there is no internal criterion for deciding whether I am having an experience or only *seeming* to have one. A step more and one will identify a neutral content invariant to the two cases, and then let the difference be determined by external grounds. And then one is precisely back to the position one began by repudiating. And after all, that there *is something* going on when we sustain an illusion, is a fact to be explained, not a fact to be explained *away*. It is not ever to the interest of philosophers to deny plain facts.

I should like to suggest the radically simple solution that the problem, which has exercised epistemologists from the beginning and from which, perhaps, the entire enterprise of theory of knowledge first took its rise, *is not really an epistemological problem at all*. In the typical case, what we experience when we sustain illusions is just what is correctly described as 'illusions'. It is an objective feature of the world that sticks look bent in water, that bent sticks in water look like what we would expect straight sticks to look there, that the moon appears the size of a penny, that ropes, under certain conditions, look like snakes. These are objective features of the world. No less than that snakes are viviparous and the moon is made of grains of dust. The sentence 'I perceive an illusion' is made true by an illusion, if I perceive one, and is made false by

---

[1] 'When (or in so far as) we suffer from sensory illusion, there is no object at all, physical or non-physical, which we are perceiving in any possible sense of the word "perceiving". There is simply the (completely) false belief that ordinary perceiving is taking place.' D. M. Armstrong, *Perception and the Physical World* (London; Routledge and Kegan Paul, 1961), p. 83. Again: 'When we suffer an illusion, we do not perceive although we *may think* we perceive.' *Ibid.* p. 98.

anything which is not an illusion. I maintain, then, that the world contains, as further items in its inventory, illusions of various sorts. And one learns to identify these as one learns to identify other things, with this difference: since an illusion *appears* to be something other than it is, one has first to be able to identify their non-illusory counterparts. Since their learning presupposes learning of another sort, it is easy to think of these as enjoying second-class ontological citizenship. But that is not the case. For in fact the expression 'is veridical' is itself a derivative predicate, which is to be learned only in contrast with 'is illusory'. To learn that something is 'veridical' in this sense is a secondary piece of learning without it following that the things to which the description applies are secondary from an ontological point of view. It is only that one cannot begin learning one's way about the world by first identifying illusions as such. This would have as its equivalent, one might think, learning language first with *false* sentences. But my contention is that 'is illusory' and 'is veridical' have descriptive and not merely semantical uses. And that they *do* have this descriptive use has contributed as much as anything to the philosophical obscurity of the problem of certainty. The descriptive uses belong to a different dimension of language than the semantical uses, and it is the latter which alone are relevant to skeptical doubts. And just as mistakes provide no inductive support for skepticism, neither do illusions provide any, for illusions, taken as features of the world, are in principle discoverable to be such. And whatever is in principle discoverable as such is of no support to the skeptic. The skeptic is rather concerned with whether the whole of our experience, including such distinctions as we may draw within it between illusion and reality is not *in toto* illusory. This cannot, of course, be discovered through experience. If the *whole* of experience is illusory, the term 'illusory' cannot be used to point a contrast within experience, and in fact is being used now semantically rather than descriptively. For now experience as a whole must contrast with reality which, by definition, is 'external' and confers upon experience either the (+) or the (−) semantical value, depending upon whether a semantical relationship is satisfied or not. Since, as the skeptic charges, we cannot tell this, experience is rendered meaningless *in a sense of* 'meaningless' which has application solely to semantical vehicles, and in this way the skeptic has done himself in. He has done so for we now cannot say even what reality means, or what it means for experience to be veridical. The questioning by the skeptic has involved a subtle transformation of the objects of experience into a language, and a correlative transformation of the concept of illusion from a descriptive to a semantical one. But when the latter occurs, the position of the skeptic is immediately exposed to the destructive force of our argument. Either way, it seems to me, there remains no essentially epistemological problem concerning illusions. The problems which remain belong not to philosophy at all, but to the empirical sciences, to the psychologist and the physicist and the optical physiologist.

An exactly parallel account can be given of hallucinations and delusions, where there is a content in experience which doesn't belong to the world. Of course, it must be said that there the question can always be raised whether what we take as hallucinations do not after all belong to the world as further, if exotic entities in its inventories: ghosts, disembodied spirits, vampires, and the like, impoverish the world by their absence from the inventory, or enrich it by their presence, and it is often a matter of faith which position we take. Yet it is an empirical question what the world contains, and decidable in principle whether, when *m* claims to have seen a ghost, he must be supposed hallucinated or merely privy to a rare bit of the world. So in effect, all cases of hallucination can be treated as questions of what there is, and to identify something finally as hallucination is to exclude it from the world's inventory, and since this is a purely empirical matter, the problem of hallucination dissolves into a problem of no immediate philosophical interest. This may be regarded as too brusque a way of dealing with the question. The cagier skeptic happens not to be concerned with what would be exotic entities if they existed, but what would be humdrum domestic entities if only we could prove to his satisfaction that they were not hallucinations, e.g., trees. The skeptic here asks whether ordinary experience might not be hallucinatory in the sense that the content of it would be just as it is, only there would be nothing there where we propose a tree. Imagine an experience putatively of a tree: one experiences the rugged bark, the soft stirring of the leaves, the woody odor and vegetal taste. But is this really a tree, he queries, and not a perfect hallucination? How are we to tell whether it is real?

It is not as though we would, were we to subtract everything from the real tree which it has in common with its hallucinatory counterpart, arrive, on the one side, at the residual property we sought and, on the other side, at a blank where the cherished property was lacking.[1] Reality, in this sense, is not a property and hence not a residual property, and any feature we might choose to identify as such could be bodily transferred by the skeptic to the hallucination, since he can tolerate no internal basis for distinguishing the two. Hence, if his query is meaningful, the distinction could only be made externally, and no decision at the level of descriptivity is to be tolerated by the rules of the game. But now, instead of real and hallucinatory trees, what we get is a content descriptively invariant and hence neutral as to the distinction, which must now be a matter, if of anything, then of external differentiation. And this is now to treat the distinction itself no longer as descriptive but as semantical, the 'real' tree being the same neutral content with a (+) semantical value, and since the latter cannot be determined through experiencing that content, the skeptic's query cannot be answered on its own terms. But neither ought we by this time so much as to try to answer it. For the issue has been transformed from a descriptive to a semantical basis, and to ask for an empirical solution to a semantical question is once again to mix the modes of discourse in an intolerable muddle which, once straightened out, leaves nothing of philosophical interest in the question of hallucination, or at least nothing of *epistemological* interest. And here the worn topic may finally be abandoned, and what is left of the interest it may still bear belongs to the empirical scientist: to the pathologist, the neurophysiologist, and the psychiatrist. Ontologists, or metaphysicians, will of course retain a measure of interest in the status of hallucinations, inasmuch as these belong to the same class of things (speaking noncommittally) as mental pictures and after images, and so fall within the purview of the mind–body problems. Concerning hallucinations, to be sure, there is always

[1] The recipe is Lewis's: 'Subtract, in what we say that we see, or hear, or otherwise learn from direct experience, all that can conceivably be mistaken: the remainder is the given content of experience inducing this belief.' C. I. Lewis, *An Analysis of Knowledge and Valuation* (Lasalle, Illinois; Open Court, 1946), p. 183.

the possibility of one or another sort of error: we may in deep hallucination suppose we are seeing things as they are, and I have no wish to deny that a large class of errors might always arise in connection with this class of phenomena. It would be tedious to enumerate these, and of no ultimate philosophical benefit, inasmuch as, after all, these errors are in principle capable of detection and, as such, are irrelevant to the skeptic whose problems require not an empirical but a conceptual dissolution. He may be right that at a moment it may be impossible by internal criteria to differentiate hallucinatory from real trees: but in so far as he regards it impossible to discover the difference within experience itself, he renders his position untenable by making this fatal shift from descriptive to semantical usage. But on the other hand, it is of no relevance whatever to the skeptic to attempt to find, *within* experience, descriptive uses for semantical terms either: to try to find experiential equivalents for 'exists' and 'is true' and the rest. But with this we must turn our attention more fully to the concept of experience as such.

9

EXPERIENCE AND EXISTENCE

I

The examples we use as paradigms of cognitive success are those in which we apply a sentence—or another semantical vehicle—which we understand, to the world which, as we experience it, satisfies conditions which confer the (+) semantical value on our vehicle. This involves, crudely speaking, a matching-up of sentence with reality, a feat the execution of which was once deemed unintelligible on the curious grounds that sentences can be compared only with other sentences.[1] It is difficult in the present stage of philosophy to recapture the spirit in which this principle was enjoined: it harks from the rabid anti-metaphysical heyday of the Logical Positivist movement, when references to reality seemed automatically to count as lapses into non-sense. This entailed the consequence that we could not talk about the application of language, though Moritz Schlick, whose heresy lay in talking about what was ruled out by these strictures, felt coolly un-moved by the suggestion that his words were meaningless: 'I refuse to sit in the seat of the metaphysicians', he wrote in mock self-defense: 'I have often compared propositions with facts, so I had no reason to say it couldn't be done.'[2] The argument against his achievement of what he regarded a simple feat was that 'If we analyze the process of verification...we shall find that it amounts to a comparison of proposi-tions.' But Schlick felt that at some point we must, and often do, make perpendicular turns from the surface of language. What could have motivated his *opponents*?

There is a comparable contention of Berkeley's to the effect that

---

[1] See C. G. Hempel, 'On the Logical Positivist's Theory of Truth', *Analysis*, II, 4, pp. 49–59 (1934–5), and 'Facts and Propositions', *loc. cit.* Also Moritz Schlick, 'The Foundations of Knowledge', in A. J. Ayer (ed.), *Logical Positivism* (Glencoe, Illinois; Free Press, 1959), especially pp. 214–19.

[2] Moritz Schlick, 'Facts and Propositions', *Analysis*, II, 5, pp. 65–70 (1934–5), reprinted in Margaret Macdonald (ed.), *Philosophy and Analysis* (Oxford; Blackwell's, 1954), pp. 232–7.

ideas cannot be compared to things, but only to other ideas.[1] And there is, after all, some justification in this, given the polemic context in which Berkeley was arguing. He was contesting Representationalism of the sort exemplified in Locke, according to which we arrive at knowledge through comparing ideas with reality. There are famous difficulties with this, largely in consequence of Locke's analysis of experience, according to which experience consists in just *having* ideas, so that by the time we got round to comparing an idea with reality, it will only be another idea we shall be comparing it with, since that is what our experience consists in. That we can only compare ideas with other ideas is hence merely a deductive consequence of Locke's theory of experience. So if an idea should derive a (+) semantical value from 'reality' we certainly could not know this without stepping off an empiricist basis.[2] Our only clue to the semantical value of an idea will be the degree and extent to which it 'coheres' with other ideas, and we might just as well *define* truth in that way. Berkeley in fact had arguments calculated to show that a reality external to our ideas is strictly unintelligible—we cannot succeed in having the idea of something not itself an idea[3]—and since reality must be identified with the system of ideas ('We eat and drink ideas and are clothed in ideas'),[4] it is not so much a coherence theory of truth as a coherence theory of *reality* to which Berkeley is committed.

Locke's ideas were, after all, semantical vehicles in disguise, and only incidentally pictures (hopefully) of reality. The relation of a picture to its subject is only one of a class of semantical relationships, and the comparison of effigies with their originals—Cardinal Montoya with the *Bust of Cardinal Montoya*—is only one way, and that a way idiosyncratic of effigies, of ascertaining semantical success. A sentence is but rarely an effigy of reality. The chief occasion on which it is one is when it is used to picture another sentence as the latter's quotation. As quotations,

---

[1] 'An idea can be like nothing but an idea; a colour or figure can be like nothing but another colour or figure. If we look never so little into our thoughts, we shall find it is impossible for us to conceive a likeness except only between our ideas.' George Berkeley, *Principles of Human Knowledge*, I, 8.

[2] *Ibid.* p. 20.

[3] *Viz.*, if one succeeds in comparing an idea with a supposed 'original', the latter must be perceived and hence, on Berkeley's account, an idea. But if not, then in what sense can originals be *like* ideas at all? *Ibid.* p. 8.   [4] *Ibid.* p. 38.

sentences replicate their originals, and they are successful replications when they show—without saying anything about—their originals. And while correctly showing may be taken as a case of semantical success, in the typical case sentences score semantical successes by saying something truly without *showing* that of which they truly speak. Comparison must not be taken here as something restricted to effigies. It is rather to be appreciated in the most general sense as a posture taken in connection with a semantical vehicle, to see whether it satisfies a semantical relationship with whatever confers upon it a (+) semantical value. And in this regard, *seeing whether a sentence is true* is a case of 'comparison'.

And Berkeley surely compares—in the sense of 'compares' which is pertinent here—*something* with ideas, namely descriptions of them, of which his books abound. And since ideas equal reality in Berkeley's system, this surely is comparing something with reality? One might counter this by suggesting that words—or descriptions—express ideas, so that in effect one is comparing only ideas with ideas after all. But since this merely describes in a somewhat different fashion exactly the relationship of comparing *descriptions of things*—ideas of ideas, if you wish—with things—ideas *tout court*—it hardly can be counted an objection against the possibility of our doing so. And since there is such a thing as a false description, reality, however characterized, must confer semantical values, since, as Berkeley uses 'idea' it is difficult to see that ideas *tout court* can be true or false. In any event, by pressing hard enough we find Berkeley's system perfectly compatible with the proposal that we know when we effect a comparison of the required sort with reality.

The Positivists had nothing so subtle, to my knowledge, in support of their claim that sentences (or propositions) could be compared only with other sentences. For in contrast with the Representationalist position, which in the end allows no such comparison, no intermediating theory of perception subverts the possibility that we can compare sentences with what we perceive; and, however we finally should characterize what we do perceive, nothing logically inhibits us from describing it, and hence of 'comparing' language and reality. Unlike in the Representationalist system, where we are prohibited from entering the space between ideas and reality, we actually *inhabit* the space between language and the world.

Perhaps Schlick's opponents were merely troubled by the word 'compares', which has, to be sure, a rather less than neutral overtone, suggesting, perhaps, the matching of a picture with whatever it represents, and hence demanding, for successful comparison, some isomorphism between language and reality. This would have been a very natural metaphor in a philosophical atmosphere framed upon the *Tractatus* of Wittgenstein, in which the paradigm semantical vehicle was the picture. Indeed, in the ideal language projected by the *Tractatus*, one could not *speak* of comparing language with reality. For exactly this relationship would be one of the things the ideal language could not describe: its ideality virtually derives from this order of incapacity. Concerning it, therefore, we are condemned to silence. So, if we have that in mind, Schlick's feat, charmingly described in English, is inexpressible in the ideal tractarian tongue, and hence is nonsense. Of course the *Tractatus* too is nonsense by that criterion, and so must be the criticisms of Schlick's opponents. Since Schlick's critics required precisely the sort of semantics which Schlick himself employed in order to impugn him, they must, in the denunciatory act, presuppose the meaningfulness of what they intended to stigmatize as nonsense. And so there is a nice irony in the contest. It is worth indicating, however, that the controversy is on the border of illegitimacy anyway. For Schlick is insisting upon a *descriptive* point against what must be interpreted as a *semantic* one, and the controversy, accordingly, is not genuine.

At any rate, nothing pictorial is required by my own account. I shall suggest later a notion of correspondence weak enough to forestall any such objections, but I must point out that I employed the word 'apply' rather than 'compare'. Like comparison, the concept of application has its own metaphorical overtones to be watchful against. But one ought not to let a Coherence theory of Truth be adopted by default, merely because one has some vague unease about connecting language, or whatever favored set of semantical vehicles one is working with, and reality. But concerning reality itself, a few words must be said.

It must be noted that even on an idealist account, reality does not present itself as coherent. Coherence has to be worked for, and while, on a coherence theory of *truth* we are able simply to jettison those stray sentences which fail to work together with the others in keeping the total system free of contradiction, it is less easy to jettison *things* which fail to cohere with other things. There are, thus, the vagrant ideas entertained (to keep to Berkeleian idiom) in delusions and dreams. No doubt we could make these cohere with the rest by employing sufficiently ingenious principles of physics augmented by whatever *ad hoc* assumptions would be convenient. But to insist upon this would be so subversive of science, would so reduce the predictive possibilities of the baroque 'laws' of such a system, that the sane rational course is to drum them out of the universe. We thus preserve a degree of rational coherence in the world by adopting the economizing expedient of relegating whatever does not fit to being 'in the mind'. But an idealist can hardly have recourse to this strategy inasmuch, putting it with perhaps excessive crudity, it is already his view that everything *is* ultimately 'in the mind'. Nevertheless, he is as obliged as anyone to draw some ontological distinction between what fits and what does not, and it is one of the precise offices of the word 'reality' to serve in effecting the distinction: what does not cohere is not 'real'. And to be real is to be without the mind in a sense precisely defined in opposition to being *within* the mind: what in this sense is within the mind is 'unreal'. This is a descriptive and not a semantical use of 'reality' and of 'unreal'.

But this distinction between reality and unreality is not a distinction I am concerned with when I speak of applying a semantical vehicle to whatever it is which confers semantical values. For I can easily apply a sentence to something wholly within the mind as to something 'real', and in speaking of the connection between sentences and reality, I employ 'reality' in a semantic sense, and so include in reality whatever is in as well as outside the mind. So I wish it to be plain that I am not speaking of applying something 'mental' (an idea, say) to something 'non-mental' (a chair, say) when I speak of the primordial connection between language and reality: I rather am speaking about applying a semantical vehicle to whatever confers semantical value, and the difference between mental and non-mental is indifferent to the distinction between semantical vehicles and reality. My concern is to break the identification, almost orthodox in philosophy, of mental contents with language, and hence I refuse the identification of the space between mind and world as the space between language and the world. Briefly, whatever distinctions there may be between what is 'in' and what is 'outside' the mind, these belong, relative to *my* distinction, equally to reality. In that respect, the descriptive contrasts between 'reality' and 'unreality' lie *within* reality when the latter is understood semantically. It is for that reason that I consider hallucinations as empirical, as part of what science rather than philosophy might be concerned with. And finally, that is why there is always an option between regarding the content of experience as hallucinatory or as of an exotic entity such as a ghost.

This has, I believe, a measure of philosophical importance. For when it becomes plain that the distinction belongs to reality, that it is a distinction within reality, there should be an immediate relaxation of the temptation, so taxing upon philosophers, to attempt reductions of the non-mental to the mental, or of one segment of reality to another. Mental and non-mental alike belong to the class of experienda, or belong alike to the world. What does *not* belong to the world is our experience of it. Experiencing the world, which is mediating between language and the world, is radically distinct from the world experienced, whatever distinctions within the world we might wish or need to make, and particularly with respect to the distinction between the mental and the non-mental. The space between the mental and the non-mental is a space within the world, not a space between the world and language which is *our* space.

II

These remarks are, perhaps, unduly cryptic, so I shall endeavor to clarify them piecemeal through considering some important philosophical theses to which they relate. In the course of the following polemical analyses, I shall incorporate the burden of my attack on Phenomenalism, at which I have already hinted, and in consequence of which I shall hope the realistic theses of this book will be vindicated.

(1) *Acquaintance and Description.* Bertrand Russell went as far, perhaps, as it is logically feasible to go in assimilating semantical to descriptive vocabulary without entirely obliterating the distinction. He

was concerned to purge the semantical vocabulary of every last descriptive overtone, leaving a pure semantical residue. Russell recognized that *any* word in the language will have some descriptive content. Even proper names, so called, are not purely referential, not purely, as Mill thought, possessed of denotation, with no connotation whatever.[1] We know that the name *Chaim*, for example, would be most appropriately used to name a male Jew: we would be surprised to find a woman answering to the name: and so the name has some connotative surplus in excess of the information that someone called by that name *is* so called. Again, Russell realized that any word may be used referentially, whatever its descriptive force. Plato did not hesitate to use predicates as names of the entities he is famous for having postulated. So any term has, or can be supposed to have, two dimensions of meaning, corresponding, in effect, to the *Sinn–Bedeutung* distinction of Frege, even though some words *in point of fact* may have no reference (*Bedeutung*) and others to have almost nothing *except* reference, though these, *in point of fact*, have *some* penumbra of meaning (*Sinn*). Or so it is in the natural languages. Russell had the curious notion of distributing this division of function between two non-overlapping vocabularies, one of which was to be purely referential, with no descriptive overtone whatever. And since in the natural languages no word is purely referential, almost everything except the bare referential function was swept up, by means of some ingenious analytical theories, to the descriptive surface of language. Thus even such a word as 'Socrates' would be taken as a predicate, and hence descriptive. Left over as the most likely candidates for the non-descriptive vocabularies would be the demonstratives, e.g., the English word 'this', the use of which is exhausted in its employment of indicating what is being talked about, without its saying anything about what it indicates. Since indication—or reference, speaking more generally—is never part of the descriptive meaning of sentences, sentences may be fully understood whether their terms indicate, or whether there is anything for them to indicate, at all. Russell put this somewhat obliquely by saying, in effect, that whatever a sentence might refer to (in case it should refer) is not *part* of the sentence, nor part of its meaning: 'The denotation', he

[1] John Stuart Mill, *A System of Logic*, chapter 1, section 5.

writes, 'I believe is not a constituent of the proposition except in the case of proper names, i.e., of words which do not assign a property to an object, but merely and solely name it.'[1] And one reason for this is, presumably, that we 'may know the proposition even when we are not acquainted with the denotation', whereas a name has no meaning other than what it does name, so we cannot understand (and *a fortiori* cannot know) the meaning of a name without being acquainted with what it denotes.

Russell was, during the period in which he was elaborating these views, much occupied with the question whether we can attain certainty, and of course, on his analysis of names, one cannot understand them without having, as it were, their denotation in one's pocket: there is, with names, no space between understanding and knowledge for discrepancies to arise nor for error to be possible: I have to know—be acquainted—with what a name names, or else the latter will just be a noise to me. Indeed, Russell went so far as to suggest that names admit only of one, and that the (+), semantical value: a non-referring name is a contradiction in terms. We may, meanwhile, be certain of a sentence only in the degree to which we are acquainted with its 'constituents'. This entails, or appears to entail, that the only sentences we finally could claim certainty for would be mere constellations of 'logically proper names', that is, pure demonstratives. This, however, would in its turn entail that we would always just be *indicating* what it is we were talking about without, unfortunately, our having the wherewithal to say something about whatever we indicated. This is almost the exact reverse of the quest for certainty. The latter attempts to sweep up into the descriptive part of language the whole referential apparatus, so that meaning will beget knowledge. Conversely, Russell attempts to force the whole of discourse down into the referential apparatus. And as the quest for certainty, in descriptivizing discourse, would find it could not *apply* it, Russell, in expunging descriptiveness in favor of the applicative words solely, would leave, in effect, no discourse to *apply*. In effect, Russell's program would eliminate language and world alike, in favor of the *connexion* between them. But when there is nothing

---

[1] Bertrand Russell, 'Knowledge by Acquaintance and Knowledge by Description', in his *Mysticism and Logic* (London; Allen and Unwin, 1917), p. 227.

any longer to connect, his 'perfect' language would only be a staccato of demonstratives. Followers of Russell hoped to differentiate[1] demonstratives, but this introduced descriptivity again. And again others sought to make the *shape* of the sentence—the 'sign design'—in some manner integrative: but then there would be an element of meaning we could not make into a demonstrative without its losing its function, and the logically perfect language must thence be unattainable. Critics of Russell have relished pointing out that the logical perfection of language would be the destruction of language.

Russell conceived of epistemological episodes as consisting in knowers being directly acquainted with whatever was named by a name which they understood through the act of naming, where acquaintance with the nominatum would be a precondition of understanding the name. My interest in this part of Russell's philosophy can best be made clear by drawing attention to a metaphysical thesis to which he was greatly attracted in this period: Neutral Monism. This is a view, deriving from William James (and to some degree from Mach) according to which the elements which we may suppose construct the universe are ultimately *neutral* with respect to any supposed distinction between mind and matter. What we do distinguish in fact as mental and as material are just the same neutral elements arranged into different sets of relationships, so that the identical element is 'mental' or 'material' depending not upon which other elements it may be related to—since these are neutral as well—but on the manner in which it is related to them. Russell coveted this theory, for it harmonized with his own principle of philosophical method, which was the principle of parsimony in ontology and constructivity everywhere else: one was to build the universe up out of the least number of distinct kinds of elements, even if at the price of increasing the irreducible number of arrangements into which they must enter. Nevertheless, he was unable, for a long period, to accept Neutral Monism, because of an objection which is philosophically inseparable from the theory of knowledge he held. Neutral Monism, he felt, could not give an adequate account of the difference between that *relation holding between a self and an experiendum*, on the one hand, and the *relationship holding amongst experienda* on the

---

[1] John Wisdom, 'Logical Constructions', *Mind*, vols. 40–2 (1931–3).

other. These latter relationships may indeed hold together, in different relationships, the same elements which would be mental or material depending upon the relationship. Still, the former relationship seemed to Russell to be 'in some way more immediate, more intimate, more intuitively evident'.[1] Now interestingly enough, it is just here that the logically proper names of his epistemology play a metaphysical role. For Russell thought Neutral Monism incapable of providing 'an account of "this", and "I" and "now"'[2]—these being the three primitive demonstratives he at the time thought were required. The incapacity does not mean that some Neutralist account of things, selves, and time could not be worked out, but the problem which he felt to be so intractable to Neutralism was not of that sort. Rather, as he wrote, 'it seems obvious that such "emphatic particulars" as "this" and "I" and "now" would be impossible without the selectiveness of mind'.[3] And, in another discussion, he added the suggestion that in a purely physical world (and his point goes through equally for a purely *neutral* world) there would be complete impartiality. All parts of time and regions of space would seem equally emphatic.[4] But the fact is that the rest of the universe shades off, as it were, in various directions from a center constituted by *I, now, here*; and *this*—which is the part of the world I (now, here) emphasize—seems to stand out solely in virtue of this relationship from whatever is not related to me in this manner, *however* it may be related to *this*. For this reason primarily—Russell had other arguments but these were less telling—he found it hard to suppose that Neutralism had gotten rid of consciousness. For to be conscious of *a* and to emphasize *a* amount to much the same thing. It is not that *a* is reconstituted ontologically through being emphasized by me: it remains unaltered in this process: but it is the *emphasis itself* which seems distinct from whatever might be emphasized (we have no choice over what does the emphasizing in our own case).

Russell apparently came less and less to feel the force of his objection, for he espoused Neutral Monism in his later writings without, so far

---

[1] Bertrand Russell, 'On the Nature of Acquaintance', in R. Marsh (ed.), *Logic and Knowledge* (London; Allen and Unwin, 1956), p. 158.
[2] *Ibid.* p. 169.   [3] *Ibid.*
[4] Bertrand Russell, 'The Philosophy of Logical Atomism', in *Logic and Knowledge* (London; Allen and Unwin, 1956), p. 222.

as I know, ever meeting his earlier argument. Yet his insight remains valid whatever analysis one might finally give of consciousness. I mean to say that one might be a Neutralist everywhere else, so that the elements of the world need have no characteristic which would ultimately tempt us to class them as either material or mental. Nonetheless, there remains a relationship distinct from all the relationships which may hold amongst the elements of the world, whatever may be the ultimate character of these, and distinct as well from such reflections of these relationships as may appear in language. This relationship will be neither in the world nor in language, since it is the relationship between the two, and it is constituted through an application of one to the other. I do not know how many relations of this order there are, e.g., whether it is necessary to suppose the application of a sentence or a term or a name or a picture are different or not; but if there are many, then as a class they stand in marked distinction to such other relationships as may be within the world or within language. The world may be irreducibly material, or mental, or both, or neither. But in so far as we think of naming, say, which is one form of application of language to the world, and of ourselves as making this application, then the act of application seems no more obviously mental than it does anything else. For the logically proper name—the 'emphatic particular'—may as readily denote a mental content as anything else: *this* pain; the feeling *I* have *now*; the image which is *here* (in relationship to another image). So the act of demonstration might be regarded as neutral to the distinction between mental and material; or for that matter, relative to this action, all other relationships and distinctions may be regarded as of a piece.

My task in this book is not to think out a metaphysics, but if I were committed to do so, I would think a characterization of the self correct which situated it between part of the world, taken as semantical vehicle (language), and part of the world taken as conferring semantical value on that, with the self an agent whose distinctive activity consisted in relating the two. The self then would be at right angles both to language and the world, and hence to whatever divisions might have to be distinguished within the world such as, for example, the mental and the material. As a self, which applies semantical vehicles to the world,

I am as distinct from whatever mental contents I apply these to as I am from any material content, supposing that distinction ultimate. It may well be that those parts of the world which are to be counted mental are constituted through the fact that one self at most can denote them, and hence they are related to that self in a unique and intimate fashion. Yet that relationship, however intimate it may be, does not render the contents so denoted more immediate than anything else the self may denote by means of a semantical vehicle: and it was the relationship between the self and experienda of *whatever* sort which Russell thought of as so singular. Even if the only things we experience *are* in some sense mental contents, we should have to distinguish the relations holding amongst them from the relationship between them and the self, which applies semantical vehicles to them; and *these* relationships are sufficiently distinct that it would be awkward to characterize *both* as mental. Philosophers, like everyone else, find it easiest to think in descriptive terms, and to define as much as possible in descriptive idiom. But the self's activities must be at least partially characterized in semantical terms. Hence there is a crucial and traditionally frustrating sense in which the self cannot be described. But this brings me to the next set of points I am concerned to explore.

(2) *Phenomenalism.* Russell, as noted, had an argument that a sentence cannot be a name, e.g., the name of a fact or the name of (as Frege thought) The True. His argument was that sentences are either true or false, but a noise which does not succeed in referring is not a name: sentences remain sentences even as semantical failures. but a name which is a semantical failure is a contradiction in terms.[1] The notion of semantical success is built into the notion of a name, as Russell

---

[1] 'There are two different relations...that a proposition may have to a fact: the one the relation of being true to the fact, and the other being false to the fact...whereas in the case of a name, there is only one relation it can have to what it names. A name can just name a particular, or, if it does not, it is not a name at all, it is a noise.' *Op. cit.* p. 187. If Russell had, as Frege, treated sentences as names, then he could not uphold his celebrated thesis that every meaningful sentence is either true or false: for a sentence which did not succeed in naming would be just a noise. On the other hand, there is little justification for this: sentences are syntactically defined, not semantically, and there is no special reason why a sentence need have a semantical value at all. Nor a name, for that matter: 'Buster' is a name in that it is and can be used to name: but I named no one with it just now, and it nevertheless remains true that it is a name, not just a noise. It is a name by the conventions of English nomenclature.

understood the matter. It follows that whoever succeeds in achieving an act of naming must, at the moment of success, be directly acquainted with whatever he names: otherwise he has merely made a noise. It follows moreover that one cannot name what does not exist, and this holds for logically proper names as well as for any. If, therefore, 'This' is a logically proper name—and not just a noise which may be *used* as a name—then 'This exists' is a curiously vacuous sentence. For if 'This' is being used correctly, it is being used to name. But since you cannot name what isn't, it goes without saying that whatever is named exists. So no information about *this* is being offered in the sentence 'This exists'. If the latter is meaningful, it is empty. I say nothing about what I name when I say that it exists. These considerations are reminiscent, perhaps, of the celebrated proof of his own existence provided by Descartes, which in fact trades on just the same apparatus. I cannot certainly name something which is not, so it follows that if I name myself with the pronoun designed for first-person reference, I exist: and I exist whenever I succeed in an action of self-reference. Hence I cannot coherently say 'I do not exist' since, after all, once the self-reference is made by the subject of the sentence, the *rest* of the sentence is invalidated. Yet the fact that it is invalidated is due to the fact that 'I exist' is empty. Descartes proved at best that he could not coherently say he did not exist, but he did this at the price of having to say that he was stating nothing informative about himself in the sentence 'I exist'. And so he naturally had next to puzzle out *what* he was—a vagarious query if 'I' had any meaning in excess of reference.

I mention these matters because they serve to underscore the treachery of the word 'exists' when we undertake to attach *it* to the world instead of using it to attach other words to the world. To use an example of Moore's, the sentence 'This growls' is informative in a way in which the grammatically indiscernible 'This exists' is not: the former attaches a predicate to whatever is demonstrated, but the latter merely demonstrates, perhaps adding only that the demonstration has been successful, which is unnecessary if Russell is correct in his claim that there are no unsuccessful demonstrations, nor names (in our idiom) with the $(-)$ semantical value. So 'This exists' reduces to 'This' when the latter is fleshed out with the circumstances of its *use* as the speech act consisting in demonstration. It is against the background of this that I should like to discuss Phenomenalism.

I realize that various policies and doctrines are comprehended under the label of Phenomenalism, but I shall characterize this whole family of teachings as follows: for every term *t* which has descriptive meaning, there is a rule of meaning for *t* which specifies a set of conditions [*k*] which, when satisfied, entail that *t* is instantiated, and such that [*k*] is satisfied only by experienda. To be sure, this may be regarded as a characterization of *Empiricism* in at least one of its varieties, and Phenomenalists might wish to place a certain limitation on, or give a certain characterization of experienda, e.g., that they must all be neutral or some such thing. But I think that Phenomenalism should be strictly neutral to the characterization of experienda, it being concerned only to make sure that nothing be regarded descriptively meaningful which is not exhaustively analyzable in experiential terms and, more radically, that nothing is to be regarded as meaningful which is not *descriptively* meaningful. Speaking crudely, the Phenomenalist is committed to the view that whatever we say, our meaning must be analyzed out in terms of actual or possible experiences. In its way, Phenomenalism is but one form of Descriptivism, in that all of meaningful discourse is held to be, by means of rules of meaning of various degrees of elaborateness, assimilable to the descriptive resources of language. It is not unexpected, therefore, that Phenomenalists are likely to be questers for certainty, and to make the comical effort of undertaking the final assimilation, which will bring to the descriptive surface of language and the experientiable surface of the world (and for the Phenomenalist the world just *is* the experientiable surface) the semantical predicates and applicative words. It will perhaps be useful to indicate that this is not to be effected, but that failure to effect it does not involve after all a defeat for Phenomenalism: it only makes Phenomenalism less interesting and important than it seemed to be in its own and in its enemies' eyes. There still will remain a question whether every *descriptive* term is reducible to the special subset of descriptive words which the Phenomenalist finds uniquely meaningful, but that contest is not of interest to us just now. Let us consider the Phenomenalists' encounter with the problem of existence instead.

Berkeley, who is the first parent of all Phenomenalists, claimed that he himself did not have any *idea* of existence. 'This I am sure,' he wrote in his notebook, 'I have no such idea of existence or annext to the word existence.'[1] On Berkeleyan principles, this entails that existence neither is an entity nor a property of entities, which may sound puzzling but is in fact rather crucial in Berkeley's final philosophy. Remember that *esse est percipi*. To exist is to be perceived, and nothing is perceived but an idea, hence only ideas exist. Therefore I am an idea or I do not exist. But Berkeley balked at considering himself to be an idea. Ideas (things) were inert and inactive. He was active: he was, as he put it, a spirit. A spirit *is* not an idea, but *has* ideas. *Ergo*, if only ideas, or what is perceived, exists, then I do not exist. But I do exist. Hence something exists which is not perceived, since there is something which is not an idea. Berkeley proposes that though he has no correct idea of himself, he has a 'notion'. Do I then have a 'notion' of existence? Presumably, if the word 'exists' is to do service on both sides of the line which divides ideas from spirits, it cannot be part of an idea nor an idea in its own right. And that is what I mean in suggesting that existence neither can be a thing nor a property of things in Berkeley's philosophy. Of course one need not subscribe to his view regarding spirits, which is internal, after all, to his philosophy. Nevertheless, there are problems with the seeming failure of 'existence' to present itself to me as an idea. And if it is *not* an idea, what exactly am I to offer in explanation of the fact that I understand the expression *esse est percipi*? If this sentence is true, yet not made true by an *idea*, we find that we have to waive, in order to state Berkeley's philosophy, some principles of meaning which it is the implicit purpose of that philosophy to establish. What is the status of *esse est percipi* if *esse est percipi* is true?

But disregarding this, we might at any rate ask what *esse* adds to *percipi*.[2] If I perceive *a*, it certainly follows that *a* exists in case I cannot

[1] George Berkeley, *Philosophical Commentaries*, p. 671. Cited by G. J. Warnock, *Berkeley* (London; Penguin Books, 1953), p. 198.

[2] Of course, Berkeley maintains that it adds *nothing*: let the reader, he challenges, 'try to separate in his own thoughts the being of a sensible thing from its being perceived'. *Principles of Human Knowledge*, Part First, p. 6. I interpret this as follows. We cannot separately perceive the being of a thing: so there is no idea of the being of a thing separate from the idea of the thing. Hence the idea of the being of *a* merely collapses into the idea of *a*.

perceive what is not (I can only *seem* to perceive what is not). But can I be said to perceive that *a* exists? Not really. For if *a* must exist in order to be perceived, there is no such thing as perceiving *a* as not existing, hence whatever I perceive exists, and the content of the two descriptions 'I perceive *a*' and 'I perceive *a* existing' cannot vary. Hence '*a* exists' collapses into *a*. This perhaps is why Berkeley supposed he could form no idea of existence: the idea of *a* and the idea of *a* *existing* would be indiscernible. Put another way, I cannot diminish the content of my perception by taking existence away from it, leaving, so to speak, *a* minus *a*'s existence. For *a* minus existence is just minus *a*. And with minus *a* there is no perception, for we cannot perceive what is not. So nothing remains over when I subtract existence from *a*. Since, when existence is taken away, the *thing* is taken away, and when existence is added, the thing is not in any way augmented, the existence of the thing is just the thing. So *esse* adds nothing to *percipi*. To ascribe *esse* to an experience is not to give a differential characterization of that experience, but only to announce the fact that it is an experience. So there is no special experience of existence. So, finally, the rule of descriptive meaning for '*a* exists' reduces to just the rule of descriptive meaning of '*a*'. Well, one can conclude that *esse* just is *percipi*, since the existence of *a* seems to collapse into *a simplicitur*. But this would be an ill-advised move. For while it plainly now guarantees that whatever is perceived exists, it achieves this through trivializing means, and amounts to nothing other than the uninteresting contention that whatever is perceived is perceived. This is too empty: *esse* has to have some meaning other than *percipi* for *esse est percipi* to be the startling thesis that Berkeley's seems to be. But then what *does* it mean? We cannot somehow get the existence of *a* to make a difference to *a*. But this, surely, is because existence is not an objective feature of the world, nor 'exists' a descriptive element of language. The reason we cannot, as Berkeley—who had almost perfect pitch in philosophy—recognized, form an idea of existence is because existence is not a trait of the world. Its use and meaning lie elsewhere.

Modern students of Berkeley have suggested as much. Warnock, for example, has a thesis we must consider.[1] First of all, he points out that

[1] G. J. Warnock, *Berkeley* (London; Penguin Books, 1953), pp. 236–46.

the falsity of '*x* exists' is compatible with the truth of any conjunction of sentences to the effect that '*m* seems to perceive *x*'. So, when I say I seem to see *x*, it of course is not required that I retract this sentence when it should turn out that *x* does not exist, but then neither can I hope to *define* '...exists' in terms of '...seems to perceive'. This, I believe, is correct. But there is nothing here which need have fazed Berkeley nor, for the matter, his Phenomenalistic scions. The question is how Warnock, who is astute, should have thought he had captured Berkeley's theory of perception with the idiom of *seeming to perceive*. Perhaps he felt that since Berkeley held that all we perceive are ideas, and because there is a common contrast between ideas and things, to perceive an idea is to seem to perceive a thing. But Berkeley does not countenance the contrast between things and ideas: things *are* ideas: 'We eat and drink and are clothed in ideas,' and no different senses are to be attached to '*m* perceives an idea' and '*m* perceives a thing'. To perceive an idea, briefly is not to seem to perceive a thing, but to perceive a thing—things just *being* ideas. So nothing like the 'seeming to perceive' idiom is true to the Berkeleyan theory. Of course, if *esse est percipi*, then it is not possible to be and not to be perceived. The moment we open up a space between *esse* and *percipi*, then not only might something exist unperceived but something perceived might not exist. But Berkeley did not tolerate the required space. And it is not clear that he even left space for seeming to perceive in contrast with perceiving.

Phenomenalists, who are constrained to abandon Berkeley's view that there are no unperceived existents, have, of course, opened up room between *esse* and *percipi*. Their characteristic manoeuver is to say that, though not in fact perceived, something which nevertheless exists *would* be perceived if such and such conditions held. And in this way they endeavor to absorb 'exists' into a descriptive, if subjunctive idiom. But then they, no more than Berkeley, employ an idiom of 'seem to perceive'. If they did, of course, then the falsity of '*x* exists' would, as Warnock points out, be compatible with any conjunction of sentences to the effect that '*m* seems to perceive *x*'. On the other hand, if they wish to maintain that '*x* exists' is entailed by '*m* perceives *x*', they, no more than Berkeley, can *define* 'exists' in terms of 'perceives' (or 'would be perceived'). What they require is that the existence of *x* is a necessary condition for the perception of *x*. But in saying this, trouble appears when one speaks of unperceived existents. To analyze this by saying that *m would* perceive *x* if certain conditions held would be circular, since the existence of *x* would be amongst these conditions. We would then get an infinite regression in trying to capture 'exists' phenomenalistically. Whatever the case, the Phenomenalist cannot, as Warnock suggests, characterize 'perceives *x*' as 'seems to perceive *x*'. For then one can easily imagine cases where one would seem to perceive *x* though *x* were not. And if one could seem to perceive *x* whether *x* existed or not, then Phenomenalism passes over into its rival theory, Representationalism, and 'perceives *x*' would become analyzed as 'seems to perceive *x* and *x* exists'—and 'exists' would remain still beyond the reach of Phenomenalistic language.

Warnock goes on to argue that the *force* of the word 'exists' is not to add some new description, but to commit the speaker in contrast with the non-committing (disclaiming) use of 'seems to be'. Thus I may say, without committing myself, that such and such seems to be the case. As his mentor Austin would have perhaps put it, when I say something *is* the case, I 'make a fresh plunge'. And so I do. But surely the whole meaning of *exists* is not exhausted through this performatory feature of its occasional use. Warnock is correct in the negative suggestion that 'exists' is not descriptive, which is why, after all, we are unable to 'form an idea of existence'. And he is right in suggesting that one takes a certain stand in asserting that something exists. But the latter is not the reason why the former is not descriptive. It is not descriptive because it is semantical. To say that '*x* exists' is to say that '*x*' is instantiated. And strict Phenomenalists are not exempt from this semantical employment. For if they mean to dissolve things down into appearances or seemings, then when they say they *seem* to perceive *x*, they must be taken *not* as expressing reservations about what they perceive but *emphatically* describing what they see as an *appearance*. To paraphrase a point of Chisholm's,[1] it is not that they seem to see an *x*, but they really see a seeming-*x*. And whether they are justified in their

---

[1] Roderick Chisholm, 'The Sense-Datum Fallacy', in his *Perceiving: a Philosophical Study* (Ithaca, New York; Cornell University Press, 1957), pp. 151–6.

claim that the world is made up of seemings, they are no less involved in a semantical employment of the word 'exists' when they say what they perceive, or what they would perceive.

To revert to the consideration that the rules of descriptive meaning for 'a' exists, is just the rule of descriptive meaning for 'a', we might now observe that this is half correct. In the expression 'a exists', 'a' is the component with descriptive meaning. So 'a exists' has no descriptive meaning in excess of that which attaches to 'a'. Yet that does not entail that 'a' and 'a exists' are synonymous. First of all, there would be a synonymy not with 'a' taken alone, but with 'a' used as in an act of *application*. So 'a' and 'a exists' under those conditions, would make the same sort of assertion. That assertion, however, is successful only if—a exists. And here 'a exists' seems not so much to express a commitment, but to express the fact that the commitment paid off as a semantical success. We shall see this ambiguity in semantical predicates once again, when we come to discuss truth, but here let us add one word more. If there is a rule of meaning r for 'a' such that r specifies a set [k] of conditions under which 'a' bears the (+) semantical value, then the meaning of 'a exists' is this: *the conditions [k] hold*. And that is why 'a exists' does not collapse finally into 'a'. For 'a exists' is a *semantically*, not descriptively augmented name. And the deep reason Berkeley could not form an idea of existence is because the word 'exists' is semantical, having application finally to the connection between descriptive words and what confers semantical values on them, without being a descriptive word in its own right. Warnock, an ordinary language philosopher, seeing that it is not descriptive, concludes that its meaning is its (ordinary) use—and finds we use it to make a commitment. But in making an exhaustive dichotomy of descriptive and performatory uses, he misses the entire semantical dimension.

Whether Phenomenalism will be successful in its program of (metaphysically) analyzing the world as made of seemings, or (linguistically) in analyzing the whole of the descriptive resources of language in experiential terms, is not affected by its failure in giving a phenomenalistically suitable rendering of 'exists'. It is only a failure of Phenomenalists to suppose this was a word or notion susceptible to their sort of analysis. Theirs is a theory restricted to the descriptive parts of language alone, and so belongs not to the theory of knowledge so much as to the philosophy of science. Whether we are obliged to suppose things to exist which we cannot experience as such is very much a matter of which theories are true, and this, I should think, is not a philosophical problem at all.

(3) *Two-language theories*: Occasionally the views of Phenomenalism are so stated that what the Phenomenalist is committed to is a theory of two languages, into one of which the sentences of the other are to be translated.[1] The receiving language is to draw its vocabulary exclusively from terms which have immediate application to experience. This translation, when completed, in case it should be completed or completable in principle, will have the effect of assimilating the total meaningful descriptive portions of language to a portion of itself, but a portion which has reference alone to that which may be experienced. Again, my concern is not with the question whether this can be effected for the descriptive portion of language, but with the program, often confused with this, of translating terms which purport to have reference to *reality* into terms which have no such purport. For the latter has the hallmark of the quest for certainty, without which, to be sure, the former would perhaps lose a measure of its attractiveness. Such a view, at any rate, was held by C. I. Lewis.

Lewis distinguished three types of empirical sentence[2]—or judgment, to use his slightly more psychological terminology—which are to stand in definite logical relations to one another. To begin with, there are what he termed non-terminating judgments, which are expressed in sentences which assert some fact about reality. They are called non-terminating because, according to Lewis, they admit of an infinite number of essentially inconclusive tests, and inasmuch as we are finite creatures, we are perforce 'less than theoretically certain', to use his own expression, of non-terminating judgments. It is not quite clear why Lewis should have thought sentences which assert some objective fact should be interminably testable: as I argued before, it cannot be because they are empirical, since in principle Lewis has stated the con-

---

[1] See especially A. J. Ayer, *The Foundations of Empirical Knowledge* (London; Macmillan, 1940).

[2] C. I. Lewis, *An Analysis of Knowledge and Valuation* (Lasalle, Illinois; Open Court, 1946), p. 182.

ditions under which certainty would attach to them, namely, through performing all the tests with positive outcomes. In *principle* it should be possible to arrive at certainty which is theoretical, whatever this might mean. In fact we cannot because we are finite. But this would be like arguing that a column of a billion billion billion digits has no determinate sum because *we* cannot complete the addition. Yet I am less concerned with this part of Lewis's account—which I think rather misguided—than I am with the connection between non-terminating judgments and the rest.

To begin with, non-terminating judgments are couched, as Lewis sees it, in a different *language* from that in which the other judgments are expressed. They are to be translated, as it were, from their own language into another, and the sentences of the language into which they are to be translated are their meaning. The sentences in the receiving language in fact express the (infinite number of) tests for the non-terminating judgments, and in principle, to understand a non-terminating judgment is to be master of a rule of translation which assigns to it an infinite set of sentences in the receiving language. This is, to be sure, an odd and special sense of 'translation'. Ordinarily, we say that *s'* in language *l'* is the translation of the sentence *s* in language *l* in case *s* and *s'* have the same meaning. We would not say that *s'* was *the* meaning of *s*, but only that it was the meaning of *s* in *l'*. But this presupposes that *s* has a meaning in *l*, and that its meaning in *l* is the same as its meaning in *l'*. Lewis, however, wants to say that unless *s*—a non-terminating judgment —is translatable into this other language, it is meaningless. And this is odd, because how are we to translate a sentence we do not understand? And that we do not understand them unless they are translated is surely Lewis's thesis. Ordinarily, I understand nothing said in Turkish until it is translated into a language I do understand: but a *translator* must understand both. But Lewis's view is that the meaning of non-terminating judgments is all in the language into which they are to be translated.

But then the rules of meaning for the receiving language must be different from those of the original language. The latter derive their meaning through rules of translation which carry them into the receiving language, so the latter must derive their meaning from another source. Whatever the case, the sentences in the receiving language are

terminating. And the claim finally is this, that non-terminating sentences derive their meaning from translation into an infinite conjunction
of sentences, these to be in a different language, and, moreover, each
of them is finitely testable.

The distinguishing mark of non-terminating judgments is that they
make some objective assertion: 'they assert objective reality, some state
of affairs as actual'.[1] If this is their distinguishing mark and, moreover,
if this is what makes them 'less than theoretically certain' and requiring
infinite test, then the sentences in the receiving language plainly cannot
'assert objective reality, some state of affairs as actually holding'. For
if they did that, then there would be some sentences, asserting objective
reality, of which we could be theoretically certain in a finite number of
tests, and we would be hard pressed to see why Lewis should have
thought that a sentence, which expressed objective reality, could not
finally be known. On the other hand, if they did not singly, they could
not severally, assert objective reality. And this then seriously raises the
question of how they could be thought *fully* to translate non-terminating
judgments. For suppose the sentence *s* 'asserts objective reality'. Then
some condition, having to do with objective reality, will figure amongst
its truth-conditions. Since no such factor can in principle figure
amongst the truth-conditions for the sentences in the *receiving* language
it is always possible that the infinite set of translations of such a sentence
should be true and it false. And how, if it is possible for *s* to be false
while *s'* is true, can *s'* seriously be regarded a translation of *s*? One
criterion of adequate translation is preservation of truth-value. If *s'* in
French is true while *s* in English is false, plainly *s'* and *s* are not translations of one another. So there is a dilemma here. Either the sentences
in the receiving language assert objective reality, in which case some
empirical sentences asserting objective reality can be known with
certainty, and part of Lewis's theory collapses. Or else they do not
make such an assertion, in which case the other part collapses—for how
are they supposed ever fully to translate non-terminating judgments?
What we see here, of course, is something to which our analysis must
already have sensitized us, which has nothing to do with reality, but
with the recalcitrance of semantical predicates to be absorbed into de-

[1] C. I. Lewis, *An Analysis of Knowledge and Valuation*, p. 184.

scriptive ones. Strictly, when *s* 'asserts objective reality' it acquires a semantical dimension. And any translation of it must preserve this semantical dimension. But if we translate it, then the semantical dimension is brought into the receiving language, and if our purpose was to have gotten rid of it, we might have spared ourselves the effort. But moreover, if the conjunction [*s*] of sentences in the receiving language is to be the translation of *s* in the original, [*s*] must not only bear the same semantical value as *s*, but *a fortiori* must bear *some* semantical value? And whence is this conferred? In the case of *s*, the (+) semantical value would be conferred, one would think, by the 'objective reality' it asserts. But what of [*s*]? To cope with this, we must discuss somewhat Lewis's conception of the 'expressive language', as he terms it: the philosophical tongue in which the sentences of [*s*] are cast.[1]

If *s* is a non-terminating judgment, its translation in expressive language will be an infinitely membered conjunction of what Lewis calls terminating judgments. These are implicative in form, stating what experiences will be forthcoming in the event of performing a certain action, e.g., 'If one bites into *x*, one will taste a sweetish savor'. This is a gesture towards a kind of operational reduction, and is what is distinctively pragmaticist in Lewis's analysis; and while it is perhaps the chief novelty of his account, I hasten past it to the problems which impress me as deeper. The terminating judgments take, as their antecedents and consequents, sentences which are of the third type which Lewis distinguishes, and these are formulations of *what is immediately given in experience*. They refer, or are made true or false by, that 'hard core of experience' to which we adverted in an earlier context in citing Lewis, which remains invariant to the difference between seeing a deer and having the experience of seeing a deer when there is none to see. In other words, these are sentences whose putative subject-matter is the same old, tirelessly rejuvenated data of Representationalist theory. Just a moment's reflection on his own formulation should have made Lewis realize, one would think, that if the content of experience will be the same invariantly as to whether what one experiences exists or not, the *existence* of that thing will not be an element of experience. Nor can it be described in expressive language, which neither asserts nor denies

[1] *Ibid.* p. 179 and *passim.*

'objective reality' of what is given. Hence if it were hoped by him to capture the notion of existence through an infinite array of sentences which are neutral with regard to the differences between existence and non-existence, the hope must have been in vain. But existence, we have argued, is not a property. So the language into which Lewis expresses the results of his unpacking will never have an entry for existence, however protracted the number of its entries. If, then, the entries in expressive language describe what is invariant as to whether it is 'there' or not, there will be no internal difference between sentences which describe what is 'there' and sentences which describe what 'seems to be there'. Since 'there' and 'seems to be there' do not describe differential features of experience, a description of what is there and a description of what seems to be there should be indiscernible. This extends to language what Lewis acknowledges for 'sense contents'.

Let us bear these matters in mind as we turn to examine the difficulties Lewis felt were presented by 'expressive' language. For they suggest that the main difference between 'expressive' and 'objective' language lies not in the terms of which they are composed but in the *use* to which they are put.

Imagine being presented with a deer, and told to perform the following task: to describe one's experiences of the deer without describing the deer. I submit that this cannot be done: one would have to think very hard, and then ultimately in vain, for some terms which apply to one's experience but do not apply to the deer. Doubtless one can describe what it is like to describe a deer. But what belongs to the description of the *describing* does not belong to what the *latter* describes! And similarly, in describing an *experiencing* of a deer, I must be careful to separate this from what I *am* experiencing. Lewis had the singularly vagrant notion that the expressive language must not only describe what we experience, but the *having* of experiences—which is like wanting descriptions which describe the fact that they are descriptions while also describing things. And he concluded that there is 'no language in which [the formulations of what is immediately given in experience] can easily be expressed without ambiguity'. Even if language were forthcoming with the verbal resources he demanded of it, it is extremely unlikely that the meaning of such sentences as 'There is a deer' should be expressed by predicates which would be false of deer were they applied to them. Consider Lewis's own essay at such a description: here he is concerned to describe his experience of walking down the staircase of Emerson Hall without describing the staircase of Emerson Hall:

There is a certain visual pattern presented to me, a feeling of pressure on the soles of my feet, and certain muscle sensations and feelings of balance and motion. And these items are fused together with others in one moving whole of presentation, within which they can be elicited but in which they do not exist as separate. Much of this presented content I should find it difficult to put into words.[1]

Well, no doubt I should have some difficulty in giving a certain kind of description of the experience of walking down a staircase, inasmuch as we are seldom called upon to give such descriptions. But I would have no slighter difficulty in describing a staircase, e.g., the worn staircase at Emerson Hall. I do not have the color-vocabulary, for instance, to register all those fine gradations of buffs and greys: I should have to wait for the shadows, which belong not to the staircase, to move so that I could get the colors which they covered, and so on. But what would be the point in any of this? I can make my descriptions as rich and as exact as may be required, whether of staircases or of walking down them. And perhaps there is no experience distinctive of walking down the staircase at Emerson Hall which does not reduce to whatever it is which is distinctive of the staircase at Emerson Hall. But all of this is irrelevant, I should think, to Lewis's problem.

There should, if he were right, be a hard kernel of experience invariant as to whether what is experienced takes place or not. So there should be a hard core of experience invariant as to whether I *really am* walking down the staircase at Emerson Hall or not. What I cannot, by the ground-rules Lewis has laid down, give a description of is the difference which presumably does not enter into experience, between *really and only seeming* to be walking down the staircase at Emerson Hall. And much the same considerations apply to describing the staircase at Emerson Hall and describing what only seems to be exactly the staircase at Emerson Hall but is not. If the difference between existing and

[1] C. I. Lewis, *An Analysis of Knowledge and Valuation*, pp. 172–3.

not-existing is indifferent to the content of my experience, is it not obvious that whatever description I give of what I experience will be neutral as to the difference?

Here Lewis might have taken a cue from the Phenomenologists. These philosophers are bent upon giving descriptions of the world indifferently as to any considerations of what really is there or not. They achieve this by putting brackets about their experiences, attempting to disengage themselves from any commitment as to the difference between reality and unreality thereby. This is a useful mechanism, but of course the brackets cannot be counted part of what the Phenomenologist describes. Their presence or absence is never part of the content of experience. Or if they were, new brackets should have to be put round them. So there is nothing, finally, in the Phenomenologist's *description* which corresponds to the brackets. Suppose, then, that the Phenomenologist sets out to describe a deer. He may give a hair-by-hair description of the haunches, or he may give a hue-by-hue description of the antlers, or whatever: it depends, in the end, upon how he is appeared to by the deer. But then, if he wishes this to be a description not of what appears but of what *is*, it is not as though his description would be different in the two cases: the difference, rather, would consist in withdrawing the brackets in the latter case, which amounts to asserting the description. The difference between descriptive language and 'expressive language' need not be a difference in vocabulary but a difference in *use*: the 'non-terminating' judgment is just a judgment *asserted*. The set of terminating judgments then is just another description of the same thing—a deer, say—in rather more detail. But to assert this would commit one as much to the world, to 'objective reality' as the rather more concise sentence which is its correspondent non-terminating judgment.

Further than this it would not be useful to pursue Lewis's analysis. One or two words might be said, however, by way of drawing a moral. It is, to begin with, a common criticism of sense-datum theory that the language purportedly about sense-data is parasitic upon language purportedly about physical objects, so that the philosophically favored receiving language (the 'empirical language', the 'phenomenalistic language', Lewis's 'expressive language') could not be mastered unless one mastered the language it was meant to replace.[1] But now we are in a position to see that the two languages need differ in no respect save the use which is made of them. In describing my experience of a deer, I am describing, after all, a deer. But I can assert that description and expose my description to the world, or I can withhold it, saying something uncommitting like 'It seems to be that...' There is room here for a great deal of Misplaced Slyness having to do with the limitations of our descriptive powers. Austin wrote that 'the original sin (Berkeley's apple, the tree in the quad) by which the philosopher cast himself out of the world we live in...is the view that, at least and only in a certain favored type of case, I can "say what I see" (or otherwise sense) almost quite literally'.[2] And philosophers, inhospitable to sense-datum theories and their near-of-kin, have raised gleeful counter-instances to the alleged excellence of purchase which some ill-advised Phenomenalist might have supposed his language had on his experience. Here Lewis's case is instructive in that he gave himself no credit for being able infallibly to put into words what he experienced,[3] though he perhaps committed to austinian eyes a deeper offense in supposing that it did not matter, that I am certain what I am experiencing whether I could formulate it or not.[4] But all of this is Misplaced Slyness: we have exactly the same difficulties in describing things as we have in describing experiences of things, which is hardly to be unexpected, given that what we experience are things. The differences between those who are committed to Phenomenalism and those who are not need not arise in the descriptive reaches of language, but only in the semantical or applicative portions.

Returning now to Lewis, we find that we do not after all require different languages in any philosophically interesting sense; and although there may be wanted a different set of words for the *having* of an ex-

---

[1] See, for a criticism of this objection, A. J. Ayer, *The Problem of Knowledge* (London: Macmillan, 1956), pp. 111–13.

[2] J. L. Austin, *Philosophical Papers* (Oxford; Clarendon Press, 1961), p. 58.

[3] 'Formulations of what is presently given in experience...are also difficult or—it might plausibly be said—impossible to state in ordinary language, which, as usually understood, carries implications of something more and further verifiable which *ipso facto* is not given.' C. I. Lewis, *An Analysis of Knowledge and Valuation*, p. 182.

[4] 'This difficulty of formulating precisely and only a given content of experience, is a relatively inessential consideration for the analysis of knowledge.' *Ibid.*

perience than would be used for describing what we have these experiences *of*, still, what I cannot hope to get into a description of reality is the fact that it *is* a description of reality. Or, if you wish: the difference between expressive and objective language cannot be expressed either in expressive or in objective language: the distinction does not belong to the descriptive resources of either language, and to look for it there, as Lewis and others have done, is but to misread semantical for descriptive vocabulary. So the difference between the languages is external to the languages. And then—since the difference sought to begin with is external to the two languages—why need we countenance two languages at all? There is just the one language. What Lewis has taken for expressive language is only a portion of 'objective language', minus the referential or semantical apparatus, which does not belong to descriptive language to begin with. Objective reality is not something asserted over and above what one says about the world: it is only what one says being *true*. Its being true is not *part* of what it says. Now consider just the portion of language Lewis picks out as expressive. Sentences in this also are used to assert objective reality. It is only that they will have different referenda. But there is no less a space between this language and the world than elsewhere. And so there are always risks of being wrong. So there is no hope of avoiding risks by retreating to this vocabulary. There *may* be advantages of some other sort, but it is hard to see what they might be; and when we desist from misreading the difference between the *mind* and the world, as the distance between *language* and the world, there should be as little temptation to translate the whole of meaningful discourse into terms referring to minds as into terms referring to (say) vegetables!

10

LANGUAGE AND THE WORLD

I

I speak of the world as that which confers semantical values upon whatever units of meaning, or descriptive meaning, there may be. Between these units and the world there is always a space, and hence there is a crucial respect in which we must, for the sake of philosophical understanding, regard semantical vehicles as not part of the world we propose to describe by their means. This was recognized by Austin, who wrote, in a manner curiously at odds with the performative stress of his discussion of language, and strangely in incongruity with the anti-descriptivist attitudes he is celebrated for holding, that 'There must be something other than the words, which the words are to be used to communicate about: this may be called the world. There is no reason why the world should not include the words, in every sense except the sense of the actual statement itself which on any particular occasion is being made about the world.'[1] This essential separation of language (to use the most conspicuous type of semantical vehicle) from the world has, I have argued, created the structure of philosophical skepticism. Philosophers, in one mythopoeic guise or another, have sought to combat skepticism by closing off this gap: by some mystical identification with what lies on the other side, by fusing language and world in some manner impeding their ever being detached again, or by adhering to the hither side of the gap in the hope of finding certitude without having to traverse these treacherous logical wastes. But my argument has been that knowledge—and hence certainty of the only sort which matters—logically depends upon the existence of this gap, for without it there would only be words without application and things which told us nothing: emptiness and darkness.

Language is, of course, part of the world: a natural process amongst

[1] J. L. Austin, 'Truth', in *Philosophical Papers* (Oxford; Clarendon Press, 1961), p. 89.

natural processes, as naturalists would wish to say.[1] As such, it is a phenomenon for linguists, a subject-matter for a science. It is a subject-matter for philosophy only in so far as it is *not* in the world, only to the extent to which there exists, between language and the world, the sort of space we have been describing. To treat of language exclusively as a natural process, and hence in the manner of a linguist, entails the attitude that there are no philosophical problems left. There are only the descriptive problems and the explanatory problems: how languages are caused, what laws they exhibit, how people in fact use them. Philosophy is concerned with none of this. It must acknowledge that in every sense required for the scientific treatment of language, language is in the world, a process amongst processes; with what connections it may have with the rest. The crucial connection is not *within* the world but between the world and language. In contrast with the other connections, this one is 'unnatural'. Philosophy, whose habitat is this interspace, is hence not one of the natural sciences. Epistemology, which is concerned with this space as the object of its inquiry, is not a natural science, e.g., a branch of psychology. Psychology describes us as we are in the world. Epistemology describes us only in so far as we are *not* in the world, but in the space between language and the world. Epistemology describes no *facts*.

Let us at this point project two extreme philosophies of language, which we may distinguish as Externalist and Internalist, depending upon whether language is taken as external to the world or as internal to the world. The philosophies in question divide on what the proponents of each regard as the paradigmatic analysis of the meaning of a sentence. Externalists will take as paradigmatic one or another variant of what I have designated here as *descriptive meaning*. To understand a sentence *s* descriptively is to know under what conditions *s* will be true. The *extremest* version of Externalism flatly identifies meaning with descriptive meaning in so strict a manner that, unless a sentence can sensibly be supposed true or false, it is nonsense. Such, for example was the program of analytical reduction pursued by Russell, and which his theory of definite descriptions paradigmatically exemplifies. The

[1] J. H. Randall, Jr., 'Art of Language and the Linguistic Situation: a Naturalistic Analysis', *Journal of Philosophy*, LX, 2 (1963), 29.

Verificationism of recent philosophical history comes close to this extreme view as well, and we all are familiar with the tensions it introduces in such theoretic concerns as meta-ethics, to take a conspicuous example. A sentence which makes an essential use of a moral predicate must, if it is not to be meaningless, be either true or false. And if the latter, then a metaphysical and an epistemological problem arises as to what are the truth-conditions for sentences of this sort, and how we shall know whether these truth-conditions hold.

Internalists regard the meaning of a sentence as its *use*. Here the questions regarding sentences which employ moral predicates will not be either metaphysical nor epistemological: the problem only is to determine what *use* we in fact make of the language of morals, and this is an empirical, not a philosophical question at all. Thus to say that it is the use of moral predicates to express an attitude towards, or to commend the things to which we apply them, is to make a factual statement regarding the actual use of moral language. Internalists see language primarily as a set of instruments for the facilitation of social existence and, in the extreme version, questions of truth-and-falsity collapse completely into empirical questions of use. Thus it may be the use of 'The cat is on the mat' to give (for example) information, which it may do successfully or not. And one may say, in this regard, that we after all very seldom do *say* such a sentence unless we mean to alert someone, or inform someone, or console someone, or whatever.

The early Wittgenstein was an Externalist. The *Tractatus* took description as the paradigmatic office of language. The later Wittgenstein was an Internalist, for whom the *use* theory of meaning was paradigmatic. As a matter of historical accuracy, it may be remarked that in neither of his phases was Wittgenstein an extremist, though he plainly fathered extremists on both sides. It is interesting to note that, in the ideal language of the *Tractatus*, skepticism could not be expressed, since skepticism would have to do with a *connection* between language and the world. And again, on a purely Instrumentalist account, when questions of truth-and-falsity are collapsed exclusively into questions of use, skepticism cannot arise either. Skepticism can arise only when the world is put at a distance by language, but on the extreme Internalist view, language is too integrally interconnected with the world for there to be the distance required for skepticism to insert itself. Skepticism is possible only when the Externalist view can be stated, and it is no accident that Descartes, who was the Externalist *par excellence*, should have permitted all the problems of philosophy to develop through the matrix of skeptical doubts. Nor is it an accident that Wittgenstein, whose anti-cartesianism bordered upon paranoia, should have found respite from the skeptic by adopting an Internalist view of language. Of course, he was in this an unwitting latecomer to this tactic, for the American Realists, no less than such radical Pragmatists as John Dewey, had long since insisted upon an extreme instrumentalism of language and thought, and a concomitant shrugging to one side of the useless torments of traditional epistemology.

Internalists, of course, commit themselves to a special view of man, not as a *res cogitans*, concerned to describe the world correctly, but as a *res agens*, concerned to modify a world in which he is perforce located, or into which (as the Existentialists say) he is *thrown*. And there is an accompanying resolution of *knowing that*, as the paradigm of knowledge, to *knowing how*: it is not that there is a contrast between changing the world and understanding it, as Marx said in a famous thesis on Feuerbach, but rather that the *way* to know—or understand—the world is *exactly* to change it. So Internalists regard language as a force in the world, a causal energy, interacting with the world and so changing the world in consequence. On this view, then, it is natural to think of the world as essentially plastic and indeterminate relative to language, to see theories as biting into the world, interpenetrating and so re-creating the world in their image. For how can language at once be a causal, shaping force *and* the world have a structure indifferent to our descriptions of it? The *latter* view, of course, is the Externalist one. It sees the world as fixed, as having a structure antecedent to and unmodified by our descriptions, since language and the world are external to one another. And it sees the task of man finally as Descartes saw it: to get clear and distinct ideas of how the world is.

Finally, one will get a very different view of philosophy itself depending upon which of these positions one takes. Much of philosophy, which is traditionally Externalist, will sound obvious nonsense to the pure Internalist. And most of Internalism will sound irrelevant and indeed unphilosophical, to the Externalist. As between these counter-charges of nonsense and irrelevance, it is difficult to find a neutral basis for deciding which philosophy is correct. Or it would be so were it not plain that there is not a single fact insisted upon by either school that the other need deny. And when that is seen, it should be seen that most of the controversies in twentieth-century philosophy are not genuine controversies at all, because the contest between Externalism and Internalism is not a genuine conflict. It is not genuine because they are complementary positions.

II

When he was an Externalist, Wittgenstein held the interesting thesis that language is ideally composed of pictures of the world, so that, between the world and language, there is a parity of structure. If, however, language were as he says, what he says could not be said. The relation between language and the world cannot be stated in a language which only *shows* the world and does not (because it cannot) show the relation of showing itself. The picturing relationship is at right angles to language, and it is at right angles to the world. Externalism, being a philosophical theory, and philosophical theories being generally about the space between language and the world, could not be stated in language if language were wholly the way Externalism says it is. For what we have to do is to make statements *about* language and *about* the world if we are to express the Externalist position. Externalism, in the *Tractatus*, was an attempt to destroy philosophy by making it unstatable. If it were successful, the *Tractatus* would destroy itself. Hence *it* can be stated only in so far as it is not a complete statement regarding language.

Internalism, too, is an attempt to destroy philosophy, and in a way it, too, is self-destructive. For if what it says is true, it itself cannot be stated. In order to make a statement about itself, and about language, it must take a stand outside of language and outside the world with which it says language always interacts. It requires, for its own statement, a relation between itself and what it is about which is exactly the sort of relation it means to deny. Even on the most radical Instrumentalism, which insists upon the utter plasticity of the world *vis-à-vis* language, which is to give it shape and form, there must be at least one fixed, invariant state of affairs, namely, that language is a causal force in the world and that Instrumentalism is accordingly true in a way it would wish to avoid by speaking of truth as a matter of mere effectiveness in shaping the world. Both extreme Externalism, and extreme Instrumentalism thus require suspension of their views in order to get themselves stated. The reasons, however, are somewhat different for Externalism is a philosophical theory and Internalism, for better or worse, an empirical theory. And the conflict between them *cannot* then be genuine. Let us now consider why.

Externalism, by definition, cannot get into the language, which it insists is external to the world, that external relation between the world and language. Hence it leaves no place for *itself* in that language. And, indeed, how could it do so, since it is concerned with the relation between language and the world, and this is not an *internal* matter either of language or the world? Internalism, to its own frustration, is little better off, leaving no room for *itself* in the world within which it describes language as located. Internalists wish to say that language interacts causally with the world as *one part* of the world: it is a part of the world interacting with the other parts. And much evidence can be brought forward to show how words cause things to happen. But suppose that language modified the world each time it were used, leaving the world different than it was before? *This* statement cannot leave the world different from what it was before: it means to state a general fact regarding language and the relation between it and the rest of the world. But in so far as it does, it *withdraws* from the world to talk about it, and so stands to the world in just that relation insisted upon by Externalists. *About* the world, Internalism says: language is a causal force. This would be a statement much like this: sex is a causal force, electricity is a causal force. And theories can be built up which show the way in which language, and sex, and electricity, change the face of the world. Now these are empirical theories, as Internalism really is. But an empirical theory does not talk about its own relation to the world! It talks (directly) about the world. Internalism, in so far as an empirical theory, is made true by the facts. But the statement 'Internalism is made true by the facts' is *not* an Internalist statement: it is a statement *about* Internalism, and about the world. It is an Externalist statement. The relationship between Internalism and the world is not a relation within the world, even if all the relations talked of by Internalism are relations within the world. *This* relation is *between* the world and Internalism.

Suppose Internalism true. Then language is a causal force in the world, and the relations between language and the rest of the world are relations within the world. These relations, if ultimate, would be shown in that language which has no place for Externalism: the language which shows or says what is. So no fact brought forward in support of itself by Internalism need be denied by the Externalist—or, at least, need be denied on any different grounds than those upon which an Externalist would base a denial of *any* empirical claim. Internalism is of a piece with the other descriptive sciences. But once this is seen, Internalism need deny nothing insisted upon by Externalism. It cannot deny any *facts* asserted by Externalism, for Externalism asserts no fact: it asserts only a connection between sentences and facts, a connection which is not a *further* fact. Internalism has the mad, characteristic philosophical desire to flatten connections between sentences and facts into further facts in the world, or into further features of language. But when it succeeds in this, it must withdraw from the presumably enriched world to claim a victory: and in claiming this victory the relationship tirelessly insisted upon by Externalism opens up again. Internalism is a descriptive theory, and has a suicidal desire to treat semantical predicates descriptively. And in this mistake it betrays itself for what it is: another quest for certainty. It says, regarding the problem of crossing the gap between language and the world, that there is no problem since the gap is in the world already, and hence that there is no gap. But here we repeat Austin's words: language is in the world in every respect except the one crucial respect. And the respects in which it is in the world are irrelevant to the respect in which it is one term in a relationship whose other term is the world.

III

Any theory of language must be compatible with the *semantical in-difference* of linguistic units, which is to say that the rules, in conformity with which sentences are formed, must make it as easy to generate true as false sentences. That a sentence should be true or false is not internally determined as a grammatical feature of sentences. Hence it follows that semantical differences are extra-linguistic: it must be in principle possible to understand a language completely, without know-ing whether anything one understands is true or false. From an In-strumental point of view, understanding a sentence is just knowing how to use it. So in a sense, Instrumentalism (which we may as well use as a model for Internalism in the way in which we use the Picture theory of the *Tractatus* as a model for Externalism) then trivially satis-fies a criterion of semantical indifference rather handily. All it has to do is then give a natural explanation of semantical *differences*. And if we think of sentences as instruments, we have perhaps an appropriate idiom for this. Thus we speak of a saw as not cutting *true*: and we have the verb 'to true' which covers orthogonal activities in general—straightening, lining up, adhering to an established vertical, bringing into a position, and the like. A saw may then be regarded as semantically neutral, indifferent as to whether it is *used* to cut true: there is nothing internal to the saw which determines that it cut true, any more than there is in the flute that which is logically prophylactic of false notes.

But notice, when we have said this, that we are withdrawing in-sidiously away from a completely *natural* account of language, i.e., as a force in nature. For truth and falsity, even when we take these as characterizing performances with instruments, are relative to some set of norms alien to nature: miscarriages are no less natural than births, diagonals no less natural than straight lines, and the laws of nature are indifferently applicable to a saw which goes along a line *we* want it to, or which tears obliquely through a piece of wood. You can work out perhaps a naturalistic theory of falsehood. But then you first have to have some system of human norms and aims relative to which some-thing is false or true. So falsity and truth are not just ordinary natural qualities. Without the norms, without the *withdrawal* from nature, there would be neither. So some distance has to be opened up between ourselves and nature before we can get a naturalistic theory of falsehoods And there is so far, then, some logical support for the Externalist.

Suppose that we now let 'success' and 'failure' go Instrumentalist proxy for 'truth' and 'falsehood'. Dewey might have preferred this idiom. It is not plain that this makes our new semantical predicates altogether naturalistic, for while an explanation can be given, in causal terms, why something succeeds or fails, it does not follow yet that success and failure are purely natural predicates. At any rate, a sentence is true if it is used 'correctly' in a natural situation, and if it succeeds in fulfilling its use. A sentence is false if it fails, or if he who uses it fails. Sentences then are semantically neutral relative to their successes or failures. This is, perhaps, much in the Internalist spirit. *But it will not do.* It will not because we have to preserve, in this translation, a connection with the ordinary concept of truth and falsity, and making a true statement is to achieve a *special kind of a success*. Language may be used and abused in so *many* ways, sentences may fail or succeed in so many ways, but only *one* sort of failure corresponds to the semantical failure we register with the predicate 'false'.

A Naturalist such as John Herman Randall emphasizes the multi-fariousness of linguistic usage. 'Language', he writes, 'is in fact a verit-able toolbox of varied specific tools: sentences, statements, ejaculations, prayers, wishes, promises, questions, and the rest.'[1] In this there is an echo of a Wittgensteinian point,[2] and an echo of the polemic Austin had in mind with the 'Descriptivist Fallacy'.[3] For Randall adds: 'Traditionally, far too great an emphasis has been placed on 'statements' as the normative tools of language.'[4] And so there may have been. If philosophers had been concerned to describe language, just as language, they would have been radically biased in taking the descriptive function as exclusive or even as dominant. Unfortunately, it is only with the descriptive offices of language that the problems traditional to philosophy take their rise. For these problems have not to do with

---

[1] J. H. Randall, Jr., 'Art of Language and the Linguistic Situation: a Naturalistic Analysis', *Journal of Philosophy*, LX, 2 (1963), 42.
[2] Ludwig Wittgenstein, *Philosophical Investigations* (New York; Macmillan, 1953), p. 61.
[3] J. L. Austin, 'Truth', *Philosophical Papers* (Oxford; Clarendon Press, 1961), p. 99.
[4] J. H. Randall, Jr., *op. cit.*

the way language, as a natural process amongst natural processes, is to be described, but rather with the way in which language, however described, relates semantically to the world. And the one specific relation to the world which is crucial is the relation philosophers have thought of as: describing the world *truly*. So though there are other uses, these are irrelevant to the questions of philosophy of language, in so far as we take the philosophy of language to be concerned with the questions which animate the difference between Internalism and Externalism.

IV

There is a rather neanderthal metaphysical urge to which philosophers are quaintly susceptible. It is the urge to suppose that there can be a description of the world only if there is some structural feature in common between language and the world. Hence the natural impetus to suppose that language might ideally consist of pictures of facts, in case the world may be interpreted as the set of facts ('not things'). For in that case, the world and language have in common a structure, invariant to picture and depicted. Galileo supposed the world must be, in essence, mathematical. For how otherwise should we succeed in describing it mathematically, as plainly we are able to do with such impressive predictive results? Other philosophers, his contemporaries many of them, supposed the world to be made up essentially of primary qualities, those qualities which, as it happens, corresponded to the basic vocabulary of mechanics. In all these cases, the ontology one adopts is but a projection of one's language on to the surface of reality, which is then reeled back and set up as a discovery of how the world must be if we are to speak of it as we do. The shadow cast by language is taken for the ultimate substance of the screen upon which it is cast. I believe we can explain this primitivism as follows. If language may be conceived of as at once within the world, and without the world, the world will be differently thought of depending upon whether we think of it as containing language within its inventory, or as external to language, conferring upon units of language this or that semantical value. When we think of the world as the general relatum of semantical vehicles with the (+) semantical value, we are inevitably going to parcel the world up into units which correspond with the types of semantical vehicles we employ: into *things* for words to refer to, into *facts* to make sentences true, into *classes of things* to constitute extensions of general terms, and the like. Philosophers, asked what the world is made of, may answer: of things, qualities, relations, facts, classes: and they will bicker savagely as to whether facts are certain sorts of things, whether classes of things are things in their own right, and so on. Such contests and such claims must seem insane to scientists, who see the world as made of atoms and stars and fields and fish—the sorts of things we read of in encyclopedias of the world. When we think of language as *within* the world, it is hard not to fall into this stance: language is one of the sorts of things there are, and the ontologies of philosophers, those catalogues of facts and things and classes, must seem lists of *fantastic monsters.* They are seen this way, and philosophers themselves talk this way themselves, when they think there are facts and things in the way in which there are molecules and enzymes. Facts and things belong to the world only when the world is considered as external to language. The primitivism I speak of is due to a confusion of these relationships, as though 'facts' were amongst the world's items when we think of the world as a subject for sciences. When we bring language back *into* the world, facts and things and qualities and classes disappear. They disappear for they are but articulations of the surface of the world which exactly reflect the articulation of language into the types of semantical vehicles. Ontology is nothing but the itemization of these types of articulation. It is not another or a super science.

Internalism is not immune to this primitivism. How inevitably, after all, must the suggestion sound that the world is essentially plastic and capable of attaining this or that shape, once one decides that language is a certain sort of shaping instrument! Thus Randall writes: 'Nature displays certain "passive powers" or potentialities of being shaped into linguistic form'—otherwise, 'Language and communication would be left hanging, suspended above nature, as an incomprehensible addition to its processes.'[1] And here we must see, dramatically, the difficulty philosophers have had in keeping clear the way in which language is

[1] J. H. Randall, Jr., 'Art of Language and the Linguistic Situation: a Naturalistic Analysis', *Journal of Philosophy*, LX, 2 (1963), 50.

both internal and external to nature: how communication must be impossible or at least unnatural unless in every sense language is internal to nature. But then, in internalizing it, nature has to be made after all distinct from language, must be after all external, must be passive if language is active, must be made plastic if language is shaping. And what does this in the end come to except to make that curiously primitive plunge which here consists in regarding nature as *already linguistic* in a certain way? For 'nothing could be applied to any material if it were really of a different order than the material, that is, if it were not a manipulation of something originally "abstracted" or "isolated" from it.'[1] So nature is frozen language, as language is liquid world.

What the world contains we must leave it to science to say: the questions of ontology arise only when we ask how the world must be in order that language may get a purchase upon it. The world, as it were, flattens out in order to receive language: it falls into the shape of things, of facts, of qualities and of classes, depending upon the semantical vehicle applied. The facets of the receiving surface of the world are determined completely by the structure of semantical vehicles, so that language and world reflect one another faithfully *when* (and *only when*) we conceive of the world as external to language. This explains why since pre-socratic days, philosophers have spoken *as though the world were made out of language*.

It is conceivable that if our language were composed of different semantical units, the world would articulate itself in a different way than it does. Yet invariant to any such transformation of world *cum* language is the relationship between language and the world. This is an absolute. Whatever the vehicle and whatever facet of the world confers the appropriate (+) semantical value, the relationship whose terms are language *and* the world, will be invariant. When the semantical vehicle in question is the *sentence*, the relationship is truth and the (+) semantical value is called 'true'. I turn accordingly to this topic, entering thus the space between language and the world which Internalists have sought to collapse.

[1] J. H. Randall, Jr., 'Art of Language and the Linguistic Situation: a Naturalistic Analysis', *Journal of Philosophy*, LX, 2 (1963), 49.

11

TRUTH

I

Theories of truth have enjoyed scant popularity in recent philosophical discussion. Much as theories of knowledge have tended to yield place to descriptive analyses of the actual use of cognitive terms, so have theories of truth given way to analyses, in the same genre, of the words 'true' and 'false', as well as of expressions in which these characteristically occur. Philosophical sobriety, as Austin put it jocularly, enjoins us to shun preoccupation with *veritas* and concentrate upon *verum*.[1] And with luck, of course, a skilful analysis of 'true' might altogether obviate the need for a theory of *truth*. For it might plausibly turn out that we are not required to suppose that there is anything answering to the concept of truth, or better, that we are not even required to suppose there is such a concept, in case the *use* of such expressions as 'That's true'—in actual speech—should prove quite different from what linguistically obfuscated philosophers have supposed. Then the ancient question 'What is truth?' would not demand an answer but a dissolution. Such, at least, was the hope.

Concerning 'true'—and let us restrict ourselves just to this for the moment—there have been two main types of account. According to one of them, we use this word to ascribe a property to a sentence, so that the meta-sentential phrase '*s* is true' employs 'is true' as a predicate which ascribes some property to the sentence named by '*s*'. Advocates of this theory are less anxious to characterize the property ascribed than they are to insist upon the predicative status of 'is true'. This status will be unaltered by, and indeed is compatible with, any theory of truth, i.e., any theoretical account of the property ascribed. The second type of account denies the predicative status of 'is true'. Rather, its

---

[1] J. L. Austin, 'Truth', *Proceedings of the Aristotelian Society*, XXIV (suppl.), 1950. Pagination from George Pitcher (ed.), *Truth* (Englewood Cliffs, New Jersey; Prentice-Hall, 1964), p. 18. Pitcher's anthology conveniently collects a number of papers to be referred to in this chapter.

meaning is exhausted through its use, and its use lies not in ascribing a property to a sentence, but in expressing some attitude towards a sentence: an attitude of agreement or concord. Briefly, we are not *saying* anything so much as we are *doing* something when we use the expression. And an examination of actual usage will reveal that this is how we *do* use the expression. Accordingly, whatever it may be that advocates of the first type of theory may believe themselves to be clarifying, it is *not* the words as used by speakers of the vernacular. So the relevance of the first type of theory to *our* (*sic*) concept of truth is questionable: at best it is relevant to some quite technical use of 'true', but since all the problems of truth arise in connection with *our* use, the technical use is philosophically irrelevant.

It must be noticed that at this point, the positions just sketched display an array already familiar from our discussion of theories of knowledge. Thus, just as there is a performatist, or non-descriptivist account of 'I know', so is there one of 'is true'. Descriptively, again, there is little doubt that 'is true' could be used to ascribe an absolute property, or a relation in terms of which a subject is redescribed, *viz.*, *s* is redescribed as true in virtue of satisfying some relationship or other, just as an event *e* is redescribed as a cause in virtue of satisfying some relationship. Then again, this relationship might be internalist or externalist in the sense specified in chapter 10. Internalistically, the relation would be a natural one, or at least reducible to a natural one or set of natural ones. In this case we should have a naturalistic theory of truth. In view of the structure of positions possible, and its parity of form with the structure of positions held in regard to 'know', it would seem *prima facie* inconsistent to give a quite different sort of analysis of 'is true' than we have given of 'know' or, for that matter, of 'exists'—which also is susceptible to much the same sort of array, and much the same sort of metalinguistic polemic.

If we allow ourselves to be swayed by these structural considerations, we are virtually obliged to give, or at least to find uniquely acceptable, a cognitivist account of 'true' and hence to acquiesce in the predicative characterization of 'is true'. And at any rate, we are more or less obliged to hold this in view of what has been the guiding logical principle throughout our inquiry, namely that if *m* knows that *s*, then *s* must be true. If '*s* is true' is entailed by '*m* knows that *s*', then 'is true' must be predicative, for otherwise '*s* is true' is not logically capable of being *entailed*. Of course, as may be expected, a performatist argument is available which yields something reasonably close to the incompatibility of '*s* is not true' with '*m* knows that *s*'. Thus a man cannot sensibly *say* 'I know that *s* but *s* is false'. This is an inconsistent performance, in which *s* is at once asserted and denied. But this then makes 'I know that *s* and *s* is true' redundant. As a redundancy at the performative level, however, it must consist in the gratuitous execution of what amounts to the same performance twice over, *viz.*, in the present instance, make two assertions of *s*. Nor is this implausible, for it is recognized in the literature that, to embed a sentence *s* in the context '. . .is true' amounts to the assertion of *s*, while it has been a thesis of this book that 'I know that. . .' has the force of asserting the sentence therein embedded.

The difficulty with this as a reconstruction of our entailment, however, is this. According to it, '*s* is true' would be entailed by 'I know that *s*' (or by '*m* knows that *s*' for that matter, since to be in position to assert the latter is in effect to be in position to assert *s*) only in the way in which '*m* knows that *s*' is entailed by itself. The two expressions, in brief, would be completely synonymous, as they are at the performative level: different forms of words for attaining the same end, namely, asserting a sentence. But this is not what we have in mind with the entailment of '. . .is true' from '*m* knows that. . .'. For the former is at best *only part* of the analysis of the latter. Otherwise, indeed, the theory of truth, like the theory of knowledge, would become just the theory of assertion, and no special problem of truth would remain over, once we had a theory of knowledge. All that would remain, perhaps, would be the question, of negligible philosophical interest, of why we should use one form of words rather than the other.

For these reasons, then, I am more or less committed to a cognitivist account of 'true'. Since, however, the avant-garde stance, for some decades now, has been anti-cognitivist, I must deal, if only briefly, with the arguments my opponents have found apparently so persuasive. Then I may turn to the matter of which, amongst the types of cognitivist theories, seems most likely to be an adequate philosophical theory of truth.

II

The most radical view of the matter was advanced in a highly condensed and influential paragraph of the brilliant Frank Ramsay, who held there that, in saying that *s* is true, I am not saying anything not already said when I just say *s*.[1] For Ramsay proposed that '*s* is true' just *means* what *s* means. Since there is no increment of meaning attaching to '*s* is true' in excess of what already attaches to *s*, no *loss* of meaning is incurred by subtracting this curiously inert fragment which, since it contributes no meaning to anything to which it may be attached, hardly can be supposed to have any meaning of its own. This leaves only the question of why we should have used '*s* is true' rather than just *s*. As it happens, this is not mere prolixity: Ramsay suggested that the words 'is true' serve to *emphasize* whatever they are appended to, or that they serve as stylistic embellishments (like 'indeed' or 'to be sure').[2] To emphasize *s* is not, then, to augment the meaning of *s* but to underscore that meaning, whatever it is. Ramsay's theory then collapses into a proto-performative analysis of the force of the words 'is true'. It is perhaps worth an historical footnote to point out how much this theory resembles the emotivist theory of *moral* language. That, too, allegedly, has no descriptive meaning, but is *used* to express an attitude or feeling. Indeed, the traditional triumvirate of Truth, Goodness, and Beauty have been rather fiercely replaced with emotivist theories of 'true!'—meaning 'I agree!'; 'good!'—meaning 'I commend!'; and 'beautiful!' —meaning 'I like!' Be this as it may, '*s* is true' does not mean, after all, just what *s* does: it means perhaps what *s*! does: but it may nevertheless plausibly be argued that the descriptive meaning of the latter is entirely borne by *s*, even if the meaning of *s*! is not exhausted by its descriptive content.

Later performatists have concurred with Ramsay to the extent of isolating the meaning of *s* from whatever meaning, or kind of meaning may belong to the action performed by using the word 'true' in connection with *s*. Disagreements have been only over the sort of action

---

[1] Frank Ramsay, 'Facts and Propositions', *Proceedings of the Aristotelian Society*, VII (suppl.), 1927. Pagination in Pitcher, pp. 16–17.

[2] 'They are phrases which we sometimes use for emphasis, or for stylistic reasons...', *ibid.* p. 16.

it is. For Ayer, thus, to say that *s* is true is to assert *s*.[1] And for Strawson, to say that *s* is true is to express agreement with anyone who may have asserted *s*: it is to echo his assertion.[2] These may be regarded improvements upon Ramsay's theory in that they more exactly specify the *sort* of emphasis involved, e.g., we might emphasize *s* by saying something like '*s*, by God!'. There are all manner of ways of emphasizing, and these later philosophers have explained why *this* sort of emphasizing expression rather than another.

It is often urged as an argument in support of the so-called 'assertive redundancy' theory that I cannot seriously both make a statement and in the same breath, as it were, deny that it is true.[3] Hence, if I make a statement I am *committed* to say that it is true if I say anything about it at all. This, of course, does not prove that in saying that *s* is true I am in fact merely making the statement that *s*. But more important, it cannot establish Ramsay's thesis at all. It at best establishes that saying that *s* is true has the same force with making a statement with *s*. And this throws the emphasis from the sentence itself on to the *speech act* which consists in using the sentence to make a statement. So *s* is true does not actually mean the same as *s*. It would mean the same as ⊢*s*. In which case, subtracting *s*, we have some sort of equivalence between '...is true' and ⊢..., as contexts. But then the remaining question would be why use the one context rather than the other? Why *say* that *s* is true rather than (just) assert *s*?

There is, however, a more telling difficulty. Suppose the whole force of '*s* is true' is exactly equivalent to the force of making an assertion that *s*. Then the context in both cases is that of making an assertion. And making an assertion is an *action*. But since the assertion of *s* is then

---

[1] A. J. Ayer, *Language, Truth and Logic* (London; Gollancz, 1950), pp. 88–9.

[2] P. F. Strawson, 'Truth', *Analysis*, IX, no. 6 (1949), reprinted in Margaret Macdonald (ed.), *Philosophy and Analysis* (Oxford; Blackwell's, 1954), pp. 260–78; and 'Truth', *Proceedings of the Aristotelian Society*, XXIV (suppl.), 1950, reprinted in Pitcher, pp. 32–53. Strawson's view is described by Austin as follows: 'That "is true" is not used in talking about (or that "truth is not a property of") *anything*...he thinks that to say that ST *is* to *do* something more than just to assert that S—it is namely to *confirm* or to *grant* (or something of the kind) the assertion, made or taken as made already, that S.' Pitcher, pp. 30–1.

[3] 'To make a statement and deny it is true or vice versa is an old-fashioned, unvarnished contradiction.' Gertrude Ezorsky, 'Truth in Context', *Journal of Philosophy*, LX, 5 (1963), 114.

an *action*, not a sentence, so '*s* is true' is an action, not a sentence. It would be a triumph of depth-grammatical analysis to demonstrate that what by surface-grammatical criteria is a sentence is in fact not a sentence at all but only the assertion of one. There are immense advantages to such a view, not the least of which is this. Only sentences can be asserted. So, if '*s* is true' is not (really) a sentence, *it* cannot be asserted. Accordingly, 'It is true that *s* is true' would not be a sentence. So we could not generate even the first step in a regression of the sort slyly envisioned by those who want to know whether it is true that *s* is true, and true that it is true that it is true, etc. These questions cannot intelligibly be asked.[1] On the other hand, if '*s* is true' is not really a sentence, neither does it admit of truth-conditions, since nothing not a sentence sensibly can be taken as having truth-conditions. Since *s* is a sentence, and does have truth-conditions, its meaning being specified with respect to these, we are further than ever from Ramsay's view that the meaning of '*s* is true' is one with the meaning of *s*. They are not even commensurable, differing as much as an arm differs from a salute. But then to re-establish Ramsay's thesis would require us to treat '*s* is true' as a sentence. When we do this, however, fresh and perhaps deeper difficulties appear.

If it is a sentence, '*s* is true' will surely have different truth-conditions and accordingly a different descriptive meaning from *s*. Let *s* have what meaning it will, e.g., let *s* be some sentence about the moon, e.g., saying that the moon is granular. Then *s* is made true (speaking crudely for the moment) by some feature of the moon. But '*s* is true' is not about the moon: it is about the sentence *s*, and will (again speaking crudely) apparently be made true by some feature of *s*. How then can they mean the same? Again, *s* changes its function depending upon whether it appears in the context '...is true' or outside any such content. In context, the mark *s* becomes a name, designating the sentence *s*. But if

---

[1] Bernard Bolzano believed there is an infinite set of true sentences if there are any. For if *p* is true, it is also true that *p* is true, and true that it is true that *p* is true... *Paradoxien der Unendlichen* (Hamburg; Felix Meinder, 1955), section 13. Friedrich Waisman comments on this curious argument in *The Principles of Linguistic Philosophy* (London; Macmillan, 1965), p. 32. But he is ramsaian with a vengeance, contending that each of these infinite number of sentences 'does no more than state the proposition *p* in a more and more complicated way'.

s (the sentence) is taken as a name it does not name itself but something else: perhaps, as Frege thought, the True. The difficulty in recognizing these differences is due to the fact that the same inscriptional design is exhibited both by the sentence and by the *name* of the sentence. But this is easily avoided by giving *s* a name distinct in shape from it, e.g., let us name it ESS. Then 'ESS is true' will be patently about *s*, while *s* itself will be about whatever—say the moon. Here there is not the slightest temptation to suppose that *s* names itself, and thus distinguishing *s* from its name, we thwart those paradoxes which arise through self-reference. This insight was, of course, Tarski's.[1] Tarski's so-called Semantical theory of Truth is essentially the view that '*s* is true' assigns a property—truth—to the sentence named by '*s*'. That the same sign-design should be used for name and nominatum is accidental. We could refer to *s* by some other expression, e.g., say 'The sentence uttered by the first scientist on the moon'. Being about a sentence, '*s* is true' may be regarded as a metasentence, an element in a language used to talk about a language.

Either way, then, there are difficulties in the Ramsay theory. But on the other hand, there are difficulties with the difficulties. If '*s* is true' assigns the property of being true to the sentence named by *s*, the fact remains that it is a peculiar property. It cannot, to begin with, be a property of the sort ascribed to *s* by the sentence '*s* contains four words'. Here it is obvious that 'ESS contains four words' would be false if ESS were simply what the sentence is about, since ESS has no words at all, or at best the one nonce-word, which it is. But if ESS names the sentence 'The moon is granular' one can, by inspection of the latter, see that 'ESS contains four words' is true. The point to be made is not this. 'The moon is granular' would not be the sentence it is if it contained less or more than four words. It would be another sentence altogether. But by parity of reasoning, 'The moon is granular' would not be the sentence it is if it were not true, assuming 'is true' ascribes the sort of property that 'contains four words' does. But this would make it a structural impossibility for the same sentence, retaining its

[1] Alfred Tarski, 'The Semantical Conception of Truth', *Philosophy and Phenomenological Research*, IV (1944); reprinted in H. Feigl and W. Sellars (eds.), *Readings in Analytical Philosophy* (New York; Appleton, Century, Crofts, 1949), pp. 52–79.

integrity, to be (as the case may be) *either* true *or* false. The same sentence cannot contain both four words and less (or more) than four words. But it is usually supposed that the same sentence can be either true or false. Indeed, if its truth were one of its structural or internal features, the Quest for Certainty which we have been so anxious to repudiate would be rehabilitated. It is a commonplace, however, that without change in internal structure, sentences may undergo transformations in semantical value, so 'is true' cannot assign a property to whatever sentence it is applied to in case that latter is regarded an internal property of that sentence. Again, the property in question cannot be the sort of property which grammaticality, for example, is. For let *s* be an ungrammatical sentence in a language *l*. Then a master of language will be able to specify precisely what changes in syntax, person, tense, inflection, mood, or whatever, will transform *s* into its grammatical equivalent. But to be grammatically equivalent means, *inter alia*, to have the same truth-value as the ungrammatical original. Now let *s* be a false sentence. No master of the language in which it is a sentence can suggest any set of changes which, leaving truth-value unaffected, will make *s* true! Moreover, mere mastery of a language will not suffice to tell what sentences in it are true or false, inasmuch as a sentence may satisfy any criterion of grammaticality and have either of the standard truth-values. Indeed, *no* change in *s* is required in order for *s* to go from true to false. All that is required is a transformation in the world. It is because the world can be transformed without this being registered on the surface of language that a skeptic is able to leaving meaning intact and raise questions about truth.

'Questions of truth' take us ahead of our story: the issue remains as to whether there *are* questions of truth apart from questions of 'true'; and because there are certain difficulties in thinking of truth as a property of sentences, performatists have insisted, no doubt precipitously, that it cannot be the role of '...is true' to ascribe a property to sentences.[1] Rather, these words are used to express agreement, to concede, and other like performances. Such is the view of Strawson, advanced in a celebrated paper on the subject and later defended in an equally cele-

---

[1] 'Truth is not a property of symbols; for it is not a property.' P. F. Strawson in *Philosophy and Analysis* (Oxford; Blackwell's, 1954), p. 262.

brated debate with Austin who upheld, rather strangely in view of his performatist account of 'I know', a cognitivist account of 'is true; and, indeed, a version of the so-called Correspondence theory of truth. A few words on this debate might be in order. Austin proposed that a Correspondence theory supposes that 'a rather boring yet satisfactory relationship between words and world...does genuinely occur' and that our words 'is true' should be 'our way of describing it'.[1] Strawson showed, correctly I think, that the force of these words is not to describe a relationship. Rather savagely, he contended that the 'correspondence' theory requires not purification but elimination'.[2] On the other hand, only a few pages after this liquidating scare, he says 'for *B*'s statement to be true, it is *of course* necessary that the words used by *A* in making the statement should stand in a certain conventional (semantical) relationship with the world'.[3] Since to accept such a relationship as having to be satisfied in order that a man's words be true is exactly to accept the Correspondence theory of truth, it is difficult to see how it has been eliminated if, as he insists, it must hold as a precondition for someone's correct use of the words 'is true'. It turns out, then, that the quarrel is over the use of the words 'is true'.[4] We must, as Strawson says, distinguish between the semantical conditions which must be satisfied 'for the statement that a certain statement is true to be itself true' and 'what is asserted when a certain statement is stated to be true'.[5] Since—as I shall propose—it is the former with which a theory of truth should be concerned, the latter can then have but sociological interest and, more important, we cannot hope through finer descriptions of the latter, to obviate the need for theories of truth. Inasmuch as it is commonly held that Strawson won this debate, it ought perhaps to be emphasized that the essential victory was conceded by the putative victor, and the contest thus shifted to philosophically irrelevant grounds.

Since Strawson's seminal papers, his discussions and ripostes to critics have had the form of progressive refinements on the matter of the exact

---

[1] J. L. Austin, in Pitcher, p. 31.   [2] Strawson, in Pitcher, p. 32.
[3] *Ibid.* p. 43.
[4] The issue is diagnosed as confused by Strawson, who attributes the source to our 'Asking the question "When do we use the word 'true'"?' instead of the question "How do we use the word 'true'?"' *Ibid.* p. 44.
[5] *Ibid.* p. 43.

force of the words 'is true'. In their own terms, such philosophical descriptions have a point, and one point thought telling by those who conduct them is by way of demolition of Tarski. As a piece of technical work in formal semantical theory, it is argued, Tarski's work may be considered impressive and perhaps correct. But Tarski claimed more for his work than just this: he claimed to have captured ordinary usage. Since he failed in this (it is charged),[1] his work, whatever interest it might have, cannot be accepted as an analysis of the words 'is true'. Since it is the occurrence of these in ordinary language which it is the task of philosophers to clarify, it is far from clear that Tarski's 'is true' comes even close to this.

I cannot, however, accept this. First of all, we cannot lose sight of the crucial fact that the words 'is true' are attached to expressions which are structurally distinct from the sentences to which they refer, e.g., 'The third sentence of Plato's *Republic*', 'What the witness said', 'The sentence I just uttered', etc. Often I can in fact repeat the sentence in question, but sometimes I cannot. Sometimes I do not even know what sentence it is to which I refer, but nevertheless will say it is true on general grounds, e.g., the witness is a man of utter probity so that whatever he said must be true if he says anything at all. This is 'blind assertion'. Performatists are inclined to regard this as a deviant case,[2] which accordingly cannot make Tarski's point. But of course it is not deviant at all. Briefly, 'The first sentence uttered by Plato' and such other expressions as may figure in blind assertion, refer to sentences just as ESS does. The 'blindness' does not affect this. It has relevance only to quite extra-logical considerations of whether I *know* to which sentence reference is made. The distinction between blind assertion and knowing assertion simply does not touch Tarski's point. Tarski's theory is that in the context formed by '...is true' only the names of sentences may be inserted,[3] and the possibility of blind assertion only underscores

[1] 'It thus appears that Tarski's definition of truth is very far removed from "the common sense usage", since the predicate "true" so defined could have hardly any (if any) application to language as ordinarily employed.' G. J. Warnock, '*Truth*', in *Encyclopedia Britannica* (1965), XXII, 524.

[2] See Gertrude Ezorsky, 'Truth in Context', *Journal of Philosophy*, LX, 5 (1963), 117; and Warnock, *loc. cit.* p. 525.

[3] Alfred Tarski, in H. Feigl and W. Sellars (eds.), *Readings in Analytical Philosophy* (New York; Appleton, Century, Crofts, 1949), pp. 54-5. That it is a name is due to

that it is typical that the name of the sentence appears there, even when a sentence's physical self is used as its own name. But *names* are not asserted! Sentences are. And it would seem obvious to me that sentences in which the subject is the name of a sentence are used to report something of that sentence, and that it would be the non-predicative, concessive use of 'is true' which would be deviant.

Tarski's results are too profound to be dismissed, and the evidence is at least as strong that, in saying that *s* is true, we are saying something about *s*, as it is for any of the performatist rivals to this theory. And performatists might after all have pondered: why use *these* words to express agreement, why not say just 'I agree that...'? Clever things have been suggested, e.g., that I do not so much use these words to express agreement with someone else as to use them when a certain doubt has been dissolved. Then '*s* is true' might be a crow of self-congratulation.[1] But again why not just *say* what we mean? Why use the words 'is true'? Whatever expressive equivalent we find, we must ask why we use *these* words. Might we not more plausibly suppose that agreement and excitement and emphasis and the rest are the peripheral uses, and that there is the obvious standard use in accordance with which, to say that *s* is true is to say something about *s*? Surely it does not seem inapposite to speak of certain of Newton's hypotheses as true long after the doubts they dissolved *were* dissolved.

But what sort of thing would we be saying? And what kind of property would we be ascribing to a sentence? Well, once we make up our minds to give an answer to this question, it ought not to be impossible to find the right answer. But this would be to provide a theory of truth. So let us begin the long voyage back from *verum* to *veritas*. The promised land of ordinary linguistic usage has only been a parenthesis in an old and still unsuccessful investigation.

the fact that the subject of a sentence grammatically has to be a noun or noun expression, and that, in order to say something about a given thing, we must refer to it by its name and not by itself. Of course, if '*s* is true' is not (really) a sentence, but an act, these considerations become inapplicable.

[1] Gertrude Ezorsky, 'Truth in Context', *op. cit.* For Professor Ezorsky, to say that *s* is true is (*a*) to execute a performance but also (*b*) to express that *s* is verified: and the announcement of this is the performance. This preserves the dignity of 'true' and retains what the author patently regards as the manifest advantages of the performatist account.

III

Let me begin with a pronouncement: to say that s is true is one with saying that the truth-conditions for s are satisfied. Now, in saying either thing we are not, after all, really contributing anything to the *meaning* of s. It is not part of the meaning of a sentence that its truth-conditions should be satisfied, when the meaning itself just is the truth-conditions. Were it otherwise, then we would not have the same sentence, with just the same meaning, invariantly as to its semantical value. So there is that much to Ramsay's thesis that the meaning of 's is true' is one with the meaning of s: the former does not augment the meaning of s any more than 'a exists' augments the meaning of 'a'. That the truth-conditions for s should be satisfied doubtless gives us a reason for asserting s, but to say that the truth-conditions are satisfied is not tantamount to the assertion of s. Comparably, to say that o is *good* is to give a reason for choosing or preferring o without necessarily being tantamount to the act of choice itself. A man might not wish to assert, or be in a position to choose, these being social acts, and governed in a measure by rules and conventions not wholly germane to questions of truth or goodness. Since the question of whether or not the truth-conditions of a sentence are satisfied is independent of the meaning of a sentence, nothing which is relevant to the determination of a sentence's meaning can determine which truth-value in fact is borne by it; and inasmuch as any such determination must be external to the entire set of such factors, there is that much to be said already for a Correspondence theory of truth, according to which it is in virtue of satisfying some *relationship* with something external to itself that a sentence is true. A relational property remains a property.

Once again, let r be a rule of descriptive meaning for s, assigning a set $[k]$ of conditions which must be satisfied if s is to be true. To understand s is to understand what it would be for s to be true and, indeed, in so far as we have no understanding, or insufficient understanding of what it would be for s to be true, we in so far lack understanding, or sufficient understanding of s. But nothing is contributed to our understanding of s by the further information that s is true. Briefly, one's understanding of s may attain whatever degree of perfection is demanded without one's ever attaining to knowledge that *s* is true. Now a man may understand the world better when he comes to know that *s* is true. I am saying only that he does not understand *s* better. For the meaning of *s* is invariant to truth as understanding is invariant to knowledge.

I have argued that it has in principle to be possible to know that *s* if one understands *s*, but I shall not consider the skeptical issues any further. Rather, I shall concentrate instead upon clarifying the notions of correspondence and of *satisfaction*. The latter is the most immediately vexing, for, if *s* may have the same truth-conditions [*k*] invariantly as to whether or not these are satisfied, satisfaction seems just to be one further semantical relationship, and I have only shifted the entire problem from the truth of *s* to the satisfaction of [*k*]. To this I must merely confess guilt. Satisfaction *is* but one of the disguises of truth itself. I have now to justify employing this disguise.

We speak of *relations* as satisfied, e.g., by their terms; and in this respect, to speak of the truth-conditions of *s* as satisfied is to conceive of the latter as relationships. They are of a curious kind, however, and of central philosophical importance, for they straddle the space between language—the system of semantical vehicles—and the world. Their terms lie on either side of this gap when the relationships are satisfied, and to *describe* these as satisfied is to describe this space as traversed. It is not to describe the world, nor to describe language, but rather their successful conjunction. Even when a sentence should be about language, so that either term of the relation, when the former is true, is a bit of language, still, the bit of language which makes it true lies on the other side of the gap from the sentence it makes true, and so belongs to the world. Language thus may lie on either side of the gap, but only in radically different capacities. And this is inevitable, given that language, as we have too often said, is at once within and without the world. For the *world* is the other side of the gap when this side is constituted of language used descriptively.

Correspondence is a relation, itself straddling the gap. It is satisfied whenever the truth-conditions for a sentence are satisfied: but these latter are no less semantical relations than it. There is no way to transform these into *descriptive* relations, and while it is possible to give a non-circular definition of 'is true', this only will be because other semantical terms appear in the *definiens*. 'Satisfaction', at any rate, here concerns semantical relations, and correspondence thus holds between sentences and their correspondents—bits of the world even when, untypically, also bits of language.

It is for these reasons that, if '*m* knows that *s*' is to entail that *s* is true, *m* must be able to traverse the space which the semantical relations straddle. For only so can he tell that the relations are satisfied. He must be able, in brief, to connect up bits of the world with semantical vehicles, as well as connect the latter with one another (as a reasoner) and connect bits of the world with bits of the world (as an agent or doer). So I have argued that if skepticism were correct, and he could not cross the gap, then his language would be unintelligible to him: that he would not have a language. But in fact the gap in question is our habitat. It is not a hopeless sink whose nether shore we are hopelessly stranded upon. Experience *must* contain this space, and not have, as its content, one of the boundaries of a space we then must despair of crossing by experiential means.

We have, I should hope, penetrated to the structure of thought which makes such theories of experience so compelling and so hopeless. As I have argued at length, the 'ideas' of an earlier epistemology are but semantical vehicles in disguise, so that the relation between any given idea and its alleged correspondent is a semantical relationship. Being such, it *naturally* follows that one cannot tell, from the fact that one has and understands an idea, whether the relation in question is satisfied, since the satisfaction of a semantical relationship is always external to semantical vehicles as such. So, if all we knew were our own ideas, the so-called Problem of the External World would be hopelessly insoluble. Let us nevertheless acquiesce in the theory for a moment, in order to bring out a useful sort of point.

Suppose that *m* has an idea *i* which is taken as evidence by him for an external correspondent, e.g., suppose he subscribes to a causal theory of experience, or holds, as some contemporary epistemologists do, that the existence of an external correspondent is the *best explanation* of the fact that we have the ideas which we do have. So, *i* is evidence for the existence of its correspondent *a* in case *a* causes, or serves to explain, *i*.

If, however, all we have access to are our own ideas and never their alleged external causes, the status of this set of causal laws, which we must invoke in order to use our ideas as evidence, is something which calls for a considerable degree of philosophical suspicion. Certainly none of our ideas can be used as evidence for these laws, since it is only in virtue of the laws that our ideas are to be counted as evidence to begin with. So the laws in question can derive not an increment of evidential support from our experience.

Suppose that these curious laws should be accorded the status of *rules*, in the sense in which we introduced this notion earlier. So that we can go from *i* to *a* because there is a rule according to which *i* just *means* that *a* exists. This would be, I think, a very bad move indeed. It leaves, for one thing, a very difficult question of *false* ideas. For now *every* idea (or *no* idea—since we could not make an internal differentiation) would have to be taken as adequate evidence for its correspondent. But secondly, we will be treating ideas in such a manner that just to have an idea entails knowledge, for it follows from the fact that we have an idea that its correspondent exists: hence every inference to the external world must be underwritten by an ontological argument. It is an ontological argument for, in fact, the correspondent of an idea *instantiates* the idea: it is what it is an idea *of*. And what we would in effect be doing is treating ideas not as evidence for other ideas, but rather as evidence for their own instantiation: which is like using a sentence, not as expressing evidence for another sentence, but as evidence for its own *truth*.

Thus the celebrated expression 'the testimony of the senses' is corrupt. It is so because it conflates, and so confuses, two distinct notions of evidence, one of which is unexceptionable and the other of which is unacceptable; and it uses the unexceptionable sense as providing insidious support for the unacceptable one. The unexceptionable sense is that in which our sense of smell is to tell us that there is, say, fish in the neighborhood, the characteristic smell of fish being good evidence for the presence of fish. The unacceptable one is that in which our sense of smell is supposed to tell us that there really is a smell, and to be evidence for *that*. And this is exactly to confuse *Sinn* with *Bedeutung*, to confuse descriptive and semantical notions, *both* of which get built into the notion of causality which the causal theory of experience invokes. For our smells—our *ideas* of smells, to use the favored idiom—are supposedly caused by real smells in just the way in which the latter are caused by fish. And it supposes that the same principles of causality by means of which we find our way about in the world may carry us to the world to begin with. Which is like arguing that the same principles of meaning which carry us from sentence to sentence may be used to carry us from sentence to the *world*. But I should wish to say that we require no principle to carry us from our experience to the world, for the world is what we experience. What we do not experience are ideas of the world which are (hopefully) adequate evidence for the external existence of the world. The senses provide us with evidence which carries us from part to part of the world. But we do not go from our senses to the world. What we sense is in the world, and to suppose us to be *outside* the world is exactly to treat the content of our senses as semantical vehicles. For what is outside the world in *that* respect is only language. And it is surreptitiously as *language* that the great misleading tradition in epistemology has treated the objects of experience.

IV

A sentence *s* is true when, and only when, a relation of *correspondence* is satisfied, with *s* corresponding to whatever satisfies the truth-conditions of *s*. Otherwise *s* is false. Failure of correspondence, of course, does not automatically confer falsehood upon a sentence, inasmuch as a criterion for bearing any semantical value is that a sentence have *descriptive* meaning, and not every sentence need have this. In case *s* has descriptive meaning, then and only then is *s* false in case correspondence fails, *viz.*, for lack of a correspondent. In view of this, the answer is 'None' to the question 'What property is being ascribed to *s* in predicating "is true" of *s*?' At least we ascribe no simple, absolute property here, no property the presence or absence of which may be ascertained through an examination, however exhaustive, of *s* itself and in isolation. Rather, it is *redescription* of *s* in virtue of successful correspondence. Comparably, no examination of an event, just as such, will entitle us to identify it as a *cause*. Rather 'is a cause' is a redescription of an event in the light of its success in bringing about another event. So 'is true' is a contextual redescription of a sentence when, to speak in vulgarly pragmatist terms, the sentence 'pays off'.

It may be asked what sort of relation 'correspondence' is. To begin with, of course, it is not a relationship exemplified in the world, inasmuch as it takes the world as one of its terms. So it would be different from such relations as 'next to', for example, which is a relation both of whose terms are typically in the world. On the other hand, it is but one of a large and rather familiar class of relations which take, as it happens, the world as one term and some type of semantical vehicle as the other, e.g., such relations as those which hold between names and their bearers, concepts and their instances, terms and their extensions, pictures and their occasions and, if we are philosophically unreconstructed by the earlier arguments of this book, between our ideas and the external world. Since correspondence is but *one* of this quite crucial class of relations, that is perhaps as far as we need go in saying what *kind* of relation it is. It is perhaps feasible that, by subtle analysis, we could effect a reduction within this class of relations, e.g., we could regard all of them as cases of correspondence, the differences being between the types of semantical vehicle, on the one hand, and with their appropriate correspondents, on the other. I shall suggest a direction for such a program below.

Let me, however, speculate a moment on the Externalist position with which this account of truth seems to go. I am fairly convinced that, for a child, the first semantical vehicles he masters function for him as *inductive signs* for what we could call their correspondents. It is, moreover, a spontaneous exercise of parental care to re-enforce this fundamentally sound extension of inductive instincts. There is no inherent reason why 'Dinner' should not be as much taken as an inductive sign of dinner as, say, the welcome clatter of dinnerware. And in a group of persons living in total congruence with nature, such semantical vehicles as they might have would be inductive signs, i.e., *signals*, on the basis of which one might go as securely to what they signal as one would go on the basis of any natural sign. Inductive expectations could, of course, be abused, and thwarted, when whatever was signalled failed to forthcome, but perhaps no more so than is consonant with the vagariousness of inductive expectancies in general. So for the child in any group, and for the members of a sufficiently primitive group, what we would speak of as semantical vehicles would only be part of the world, connected via induction to other parts of the world.

There is, of course, a difference. For what would be an inductive sign to all members of the group would not be an inductive sign for the signaller himself. When the hostess says 'Dinner is served', thus, she provides her guests with a signal which releases gustatory expectations: but she is not signalling to *herself.* And it is through this asymmetry, I should think, that there occurs, finally, that immense and radical transformation from a signal system to a semantical one. One learns to use language idly and deviously, to mislead, for example, by linguistic feints. A child, thus, achieves a kind of practical joke in emitting a signal in full knowledge of the absence of whatever it would be inductively taken as a signal *of,* and we may proceed from this infantile wit through a series of nuanced steps to the higher offices of literary expression, where language is, by a set of conventions, put inductively out of play. We thus create between language and the world a *space* when we disengage language from its primordial inductive functions. This, to speak pompously, is the space in which civilization must arise.

When language is used purely as a set of signals, there is no institution of *assertion.* There is no need of a convention of assertion until there is the institution of the idle, non-signalizing uses of erstwhile signals. Once sufficient distance from the world has been achieved, conventions have to be introduced to mark the difference. Thus crossed fingers, quotation-marks, the contexts of play and pretence, as well as special tones and cadences and accompanying gestures and expressions, serve to make plain that one is not using language assertively. No special mark of sincere assertion is afterwards commonly required, it being assumed that this is the *normal* mode of linguistic employment. One might surmise that such words as 'is true' and the like are special signals, not of features of the world, but rather that words are being used in a signalistic way, that one is engaging descriptively with the world. To say that *s* is true is, then, in effect to say that *s* is an assertion, or to be taken as such. And it might take its informative role from the fact that in the context it might not be plain whether language were being used idly and in some secondary capacity, or in its primary mode of vouchsafing information.

In its inductive phase, we have a natural use for 'is true'. A sentence is true when what it inductively signals is present where expected, and false otherwise. It is in this perspective that the semantical predicates connect with such descriptive uses as 'false leads' or 'false alarms'. And indeed, we might retain this entire inductivist account of truth and falsehood providing we are willing to sacrifice certain features of inductive procedures as commonly characterized. Thus if we learned to use all of our sentences in association with whatever they inductively signalize, our stock of signals would be laughably small; and smaller still if we built up inductive habits with language by repeated association in the manner famously described by Hume. There is little doubt that the sentences men use are, as a class, very reliable inductive signs for whatever they may signal. Men, as Hume himself remarked, by and large typically tell the truth, this being essential to the institutions of society. But while we have an impressively large class of cases where sentences prove true, it is perhaps hardly ever the case that any *specific* sentence has been observed true on a large number of occasions. The feature of language most generally under investigation in recent times has been its *generativeness*, which means that speakers and hearers are respectively capable of producing and understanding infinitely many distinct sentences, including sentences neither has either spoken or heard before. And this means that if we persist in regarding sentences as true when they are successful signals, we must recognize that we have an ability in that case to take sentences as inductive signs in the absence of a history of successful pairing of individual sentences and the states of affairs we optimistically assume them to signalize. In view of these factors, we must in all likelihood commit ourselves to a rather more complicated theory of learning than anything built upon purely Humean lines. And we cannot, in the end, separate the learning of language from learning how the *world* is. For to understand a sentence when it has descriptive meaning is to understand how the world must be in case that sentence is true.

Since there is no way of understanding the descriptive parts of language without also, andthrough that very fact, understanding the described parts of the world, there is a very natural philosophical tendency to suppose that there has therefore to be a common structure between language and the world: a common logical form, as Wittgenstein suggested. So they may have. But this would explain how we understand language and how we understand the world, and would thus pertain to questions of meaning rather than of truth. Thus *s*, when true, may in fact share some logical form with whatever makes *s* true. But truth does not depend upon this parity of form, and correspondence is not a matter of the matching-up of a sentence with what corresponds to it in the manner in which a picture matches a face. That is a picture theory, not of meaning but of *truth*, and nothing of this sort is entailed by my account. All that is required is that we be able to *associate* sentences and the world. And the terms of an association need resemble one another no more than any signal need resemble what it signalizes. Correspondence is a weak and an external relation, even though Correspondentialists in the past have often supposed truth to consist in the *isomorphism* between sentence and fact. Once *that* demand has been extruded, there are no immediate obstacles, I should think, to a Correspondence theory of Truth worked out along the lines suggested in this chapter.

Now I have used, with rather studied casualness, the word 'correspondent', as designating the bit of the world which will confer on a sentence the (+) semantical value appropriate to sentences. To provide some more responsible characterization of correspondents is an obligation. Philosophers in the early modern period—Moore, Russell, and of course Wittgenstein in the *Tractatus*—made a great deal of the notion of *facts* as that which makes sentences true or false, there being as many orders of facts as there are orders of propositions which one wanted to think of as sensibly admitting truth-values. Elimination of a given order of propositions by reduction to another then amounted to an ontological economization; and in a ruthless Constructionist like Russell, the lowest number of orders of facts he could honestly manage to attain would be the maximal ontology he would be obliged to countenance. In his great logical atomism lectures of 1918, he held as mutually irreducible, atomic facts, negative facts, general facts, and then facts of a peculiar order, described (in our own idiom) by a sentence which uses a sentential predicate. Since those days, critics have bridled at the idea that facts should count as part of the furniture of the world, and have inverted Wittgenstein's bright slogan that the world is the sum total of facts, not things, by saying instead that the world is the sum total of things, not facts.[1] As Strawson put it, 'Of course statements and facts fit. They were made for each other. If you prize the statements off the world, you prize the facts off it too; but the world would be none the poorer.'[2] One could retort, of course, that if the facts leave with the statements, the things leave with the names, and again the world would be none the poorer. For names and things again were made for each other. But such a retort would be ill-advised. Whatever ontology we choose, we must be able to attach language to the world, and the naming relation is perhaps the least compromising lien. An individual will be anything which bears a single name, and the difficulty with facts has commonly been that the relation between them and (true) statements has been taken as but an instance of the naming relation—which automatically converts facts into things, *viz.*, the things named by sentences. But not every semantical relation need be an instance of the naming relation all over again.

That 'fact' is a semantical concept can certainly be seen from the free interchangeability of 'It is a fact that...' with 'It is true that...' in ordinary discourse; and it would be as little enlightening to say that *facts* are what make statements true as to say that *truths* are what make them true. It would be generally preferable if we could simply suppose that things are what make sentences true, and it ought not to be insuperably difficult to work this welcome suggestion out in detail. Consider, thus, the singular statement 'Jones is F'. I shall say that the individual Jones is the correspondent of this statement, and so makes this statement true if, and only if (i) 'Jones' refers to Jones and (ii) Jones instantiates F. So here a concrete thing is *at once* a referendum for a name and a correspondent for a sentence. We are able, for at least this class of statements, to resolve the semantical relation of *truth* into a *pair* of semantical relations, *reference* and *instantiation*. Instead, then, of requiring *things and facts*, we need get on only with things; and we may

---

[1] P. F. Strawson, in Pitcher, p. 42.   [2] *Ibid.* p. 39.

regard the thesis that, in addition to things there are facts, as due to an overwhelming philosophical propensity to project on to the surface of the world the connections between language and the world.

We may radically simplify our ontology at the price only of complicating the structure of the space between language and the world. And to do this requires a full-scale theory of reference, which I do not propose to undertake in the present work. Quite plainly, the 'general facts' of Russell's theory will have to yield to a theory of reference for general propositions, and 'negative facts' will perhaps yield to a theory of reference for negative terms. But until this shall have been elaborated, it is difficult to say whether there are negative things or not. Sartre would deny that there are any, and Sartre may be exactly reconstructed (again, unfortunately, not here) by showing that what *he* calls the *Néant* is but the space between language and the world of things. These fascinating matters I postpone for another work.

v

A theory of truth is like a theory of knowledge. We add nothing to the knowledge we have by a theory of knowledge. We would know everything we otherwise know, whether we have such a theory or not. All the theory does is enable us to know what knowledge we have, without adding anything to the knowledge. We add nothing, similarly, to the body of truths by having a theory of truth. All we are able to do is to describe them as the truths they are. Philosophical theories are in general like that, adding nothing. In this they are, perhaps, like the phenomenon of consciousness. Consciousness of the world adds nothing to the world. By bringing it to consciousness, we contribute nothing to it, and consciousness is surely not a further item in the world *of* which it is conscious. An animal is conscious of the world, but it is not conscious of that consciousness. Consciousness can only redeem from darkness a world which would exist without it and without which it could not exist. For were there no world, there would be no consciousness either. Philosophy is in this way redemptive too. In redeeming from unself-consciousness something which could exist without it, and without which it could not exist, it makes the only contribution of which it is capable. In one respect, everything would be the same without it. In another sense this is not so. To bring things to consciousness is painful and peculiarly useless, but without it we would not know what we are. Philosophy is the consciousness of consciousness. The philosophy of knowledge is knowledge about knowledge. Such knowledge, too, is painfully attained and useless. But without it we would not know that we know, nor, fundamentally, what we are. For the space between language and the world is a space within ourselves, since we are within and without the world, and the gap which lies at the core of our being is what defines our essence.

INDEX

Acceptability of hypotheses, 129–30, 139
Acquaintance and description, 24 n., 208–14
Action and knowledge, the analogy between, 53–4, 66–71, 131–2, 133–4. *See also* Basic actions
Adequate evidence, 26–7, 48, 63, 73–4, chapter 5 *passim*
  and acceptance rules, 129
  as analogous to adequate explanations, 123–5
  criterion of, 122–32
Albritton, Rogers, 133 n.
Al Ghazali, 92
American Realists, 234
Analytical sentences, 178–81
Anscombe, G. E. M., 58, 182
Anselm, St, 164–7, 178
Applicative words, 176–8, 210, 216
Aquinas, Thomas, 65 n.
Argument from Illusion, 191–202
Aristotle, 14, 33
Armstrong, D. M., 198 n.
Ascriptions of knowledge, 4, 13
Assertion
  and knowledge claims, 3, 9, 10, 18–19, 26, 39, 47–8, 96
  as social acts, 18–19, 26, 50, 260
Austin, J. L., 5 n., 7, 8, 29 n., 32 n., 77, 114–21, 197, 220, 229 n., 231, 237, 243, 247 n., 251
Ayer, A. J., 39, 77, 129 n., 137 n., 247

Basic actions, 66–8, 147
Basic sentences, 28–9, 31, 43, 47, 48–9, 57, 58, 64, 144–5, 188
Being, 156–8
Belief, 72, chapter 4 *passim*
  as representational, 93
  as sentential state of persons, 86–96
  ethics of, 153
  whether its grammar is same as for knowledge, 75
  whether part of knowledge, 73–5, 121, 153–5.

see also Knowledge and belief
Bergson, Henri, 57, 59 n
Berkeley, George, 17, 36, 45 n., 160 n., 171, 192, 203–5, 217–19, 221
'Blind assertion', 252
Bolzano, Bernard, 248 n.

'Can', 55–7, 57 n.
Cardinal number of a set, Frege–Russell definition of, 25
Carnap, Rudolph, 126 n.
Carroll, Lewis, 30–1, 134
Cartesian program for epistemology, 51–4, 62
Categorical grammar, 94–5
Causal skepticism, 135–7, 143–4
Cause, 30, 134, 262
Champawat, Narayan, 73 n.
Checking procedures, 110–12
Chisholm, Roderick, 39, 73 n., 102, 129 n., 145 n., 220
Chuang Tzu, 25 n.
Church, Alonzo, 163 n.
Clark, Michael, 73 n.
Cogito, 4, 5
Coherency, as a semantical criterion, 171, 192, 204, 206–7
Comparing semantical vehicles with the world, 203–8
Compatibilist theories of knowledge and belief, 74–5, 77, 121
Concepts, as semantical vehicles, 160, 161
Consciousness, 155–8
Conservation of distinctions, the principle of, 95
Contents of experience, the alleged neutrality of, 169, 171, 173, 189–90, 191–3, 201, 225, 228
Contingency of events and of sentences compared, 127–8
Correlatives, simultaneous and non-simultaneous, 14–15, 17–18, 33
Correspondence, 48, 49, 140, 144–5, 147, 171, 181, 206, 258–9
Demonstratives, 175, 209–10, 212–14, 215

Index

Index